LIFE IS LIKE A GLASS OF TEA

LIFE IS LIKE
A GLASS OF TEA

Studies of Classic Jewish Jokes

by
RICHARD RASKIN

Second Edition

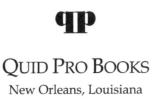

QUID PRO BOOKS

New Orleans, Louisiana

Previously published in 1992, in the First Edition, by Aarhus University Press, Aarhus, Denmark (© 1992 Aarhus University Press); and by the Jewish Publication Society, Philadelphia, Pennsylvania. The research was supported by grants from the Danish Research Council for the Humanities and the Aarhus University Research Foundation.

Published in 2015 by Quid Pro Books, in the Second Edition, as part of the *Classics of the Social Sciences* Series.

ISBN 978-1-61027-320-6 (pbk.)
ISBN 978-1-61027-321-3 (ebk.)

Front cover: *Abraham Arguing with God*, by Richard Raskin.

QUID PRO BOOKS
Quid Pro, LLC
5860 Citrus Blvd., Suite D-101
New Orleans, Louisiana 70123 USA
www.quidprobooks.com

For Marilyn, Adina and Melanie

Table of Contents

Foreword, 2015, by Marc Galanter 1
Preface, 2015, by the author   5

Introduction
A New Approach to the Study of Jewish Jokes 7

Chapter 1
Rabbinic Judgment
Interpretive Properties of the Classic Jewish Joke 13

    The History and Variants of the Joke 14
    Three Interpretations of the Joke 17
    Interpretive Properties of the Classic Jewish Joke 23
    Publication History 33

Chapter 2
Man versus God in a Classic Jewish Joke 45

    The History and Variants of the Joke 46
    Competing Jewish Conceptions of Man's Relationship to God 50
    Two Interpretations of the Joke 56
    Publication History 61

Chapter 3
The Ten Commandments Joke and the Issue of Ethnic
Self-Disparagement 71

    The History and Variants of the Joke 72
    The Issue of Ethnic Self-Disparagement 77
    The Parodistic Triad 88
    Publication History 95

Chapter 4
The Ultimate Jewish Mother Joke 101

    The History and Variants of the Joke 102
    Interpretive Options 108
    A Final Note   112
    Publication History 114

Chapter 5
The Original Function of Groucho Marx's Resignation Joke 121

Introduction 122
Annie Hall 123
The Friar's Club Incident 125
Quotation Record 130

Chapter 6
The Meaning of Life 131

The History and Variants of the Joke 132
Interpreting the Dying Rabbi Variant 149
Publication History 155

Chapter 7
On the Evolution of Jewish Jokes 167

From Non-Jewish to Jewish Joke 167
Improving the Joke 173
The Development of Parallel Variants 176

Conclusion 181

Supplementary Publication Histories 185
1. Another Doctor 186
2. Cardplayer 189
3. Dachshund 190
4. Dead Shames 201
5. Dying Merchant 203
6. Funny, You Don't Look Jewish 213
7. Job Announcement 217
8. Left-Handed Teacup 222
9. Live Under Water 230
10 Mother's Manoeuvre 233
11. Who's Counting? 235
12. Umbrella 238

Bibliography 241

Additional Chapters to the Second Edition 257

Dilemma Resolution in the Hen-and-Rooster Joke 259
Far From Where? A Classic Jewish Refugee Joke 269

Name Index 275
Acknowledgments 278

Foreword to the Second Edition

Jews and Jokes

Marc Galanter

Humor is no small matter for Jews and those who study them. Responding to a 2013 Pew survey of American Jews, four out of ten said "having a good sense of humor" was "an essential part of what being Jewish means to them." Humor was outranked by several items like "remembering the Holocaust" and "leading an ethical life," but attracted more than twice as many responses as "observing Jewish law."[1] Enthusiasts have sometimes projected the well documented association of Ashkenazic Jews with jokes in post-Emancipation Europe as representative of an intrinsic and emblematic Jewish trait. Many sorts of humor may indeed be found in the Jewish Bible and in the Talmud, although the joke genre is not conspicuously present.[2]

Jews have not always enjoyed a reputation as the "people of the joke."[3] Indeed, until recent times, Jews were widely regarded as deficient in humor. In 1893 the Chief Rabbi of the British Empire gave a lecture intended to refute the assertions of historians Thomas Carlyle (1795-1881) and Ernest Renan (1823-1892) that Jewish history

---

[1] Pew Research Center, *A Portrait of Jewish Americans: Findings from a Pew Research Center Survey of U.S. Jews* 55 (Oct 1, 2013). http://www.pewforum.org/2013/10/01/jewish-american-beliefs-attitudes-culture-survey/.

[2] Yehuda T. Radday and Athalya Brenner, eds., *On Humour and the Comic in the Hebrew Bible* (Sheffield: Almond Press, 1990); J. William Whedbee, *The Bible and the Comic Vision* (Minneapolis: Fortress Press, 1992); Hershey H. Friedman, "Humor in the Hebrew Bible," *Humor: International Journal of Humor Research* 13: 258-285 (2000).

[3] Elliott Oring, "The People of the Joke: On the Conceptualization of a Jewish Humor," *Western Folklore* 42(4): 261-271 (Oct. 1983). Reprinted in Oring, *Jokes and Their Relations* (Lexington: University Press of Kentucky, 1992).

revealed no trace of humor.[4] As late as the mid-twentieth century the trope of Jewish humorlessness surfaced in the conversations of Alfred North Whitehead, who failed to find any humor in the Bible and regarded the Jews as "singularly deficient in humour ... till they lived among the Europeans."[5]

Notwithstanding these nay-sayers, humor became intimately connected with Jews — at least with Ashkenazic Jews — in the course of the past two centuries. Their flourishing in the joke genre is reflected in the judgment of a leading authority on the comparative study of humor, who announced "the triumph of the Jews as the world's greatest joke tellers."[6]

Jewish jokes are the most written about and the most intensely studied, if not the most widely told, of all jokes. Measuring joke activity is daunting. Half a century ago a New York psychiatrist conducted an admittedly unsystematic study of the number and subject of jokes told in New York City.[7] Jokes were collected by some 92 rapporteurs over a five year period ending in 1961. Jews were the subject of some six percent of all the jokes told and those made up just two percent of all the different jokes collected. (No distinction was made between jokes told by Jews and jokes told about Jews.) New York was America's most Jewish city and the network of a psychiatrist seems unlikely to have undersampled Jews. A more current but no less dodgy estimate of the Jewish connection to jokes confirms the middling magnitude of the Jewish presence. In late July 2015, I googled "Jewish joke," "senior joke," "blond joke," and so forth. "Jewish joke" got some 227,000 hits — a little more than half of "Irish jokes" (457,000) and just a tenth of "blonde jokes" (2,190,000) or "sex jokes" (2,520,000). If these results are even roughly indicative of the relative volume of jokes in circulation, it seems that the modest presence of Jews in the joke corpus is paired with an outsized presence in the literature about jokes.

Richard Raskin's *Life is Like a Glass of Tea* is an important addition to this literature. It is distinctive among books about Jewish jokes — or jokes generally for that matter. Collections of jokes are frequently labelled boastfully as complete, giant, canonical, or mammoth, as

---

[4] Hermann Adler, "Jewish Wit and Humor," *The Nineteenth Century* 33: 457-469 (1893).

[5] *Dialogues of Alfred North Whitehead*, Lucien Price, ed. (Boston: Little Brown & Co., 1954) pp. 93. Compare pp. 163, 199.

[6] Christie Davies, *The Mirth of Nations* (New Brunswick: Transaction Books, 2002) p. 74.

[7] Charles Winick, "A Content Analysis of Orally Communicated Jokes," *The American Imago* 20: 271-291 (1963).

encyclopedias, libraries, treasuries or treasure chests, barrels, carloads or even "an endless repast." Raskin's wonderful book doesn't aspire to such total "all you can eat" buffet coverage. Instead it focuses on a limited set of jokes.

But on another dimension, this little volume is far more comprehensive than most collections or studies of jokes. For each of the jokes that it takes up, it doesn't present or analyze a single favorite or "best" text. Instead it treats each joke as an array of possible versions, branching and changing through time. It presents multiple versions of each joke — from a dozen to thirty specimens — taken from published sources in the original Yiddish, English, French, German, Danish, Italian, and Spanish — spanning the period from the late nineteenth to the late twentieth centuries. It traces the unfolding career of each joke, the way it has been altered, rearranged, polished and (sometimes) fortunately perfected over the course of its career.

Raskin is concerned with the development of these jokes and with their interpretive properties, so far as these are manifested in their written versions. His concern is not which version is the funniest or the most successful in eliciting laughter, which he regards not as an attribute of the text, but as dependent on the setting, the skill of the teller, and the susceptibilities of the hearers. His focus is on the joke text as aesthetic object, on what makes a joke a lovely piece of work. He is concerned not only with what makes jokes funny but with what makes some of them profound. His imaginative response to this puzzle makes this little book a distinctive and engaging contribution to the literature on Jewish jokes and on jokes generally.

MARC GALANTER
John and Rylla Bosshard Professor Emeritus
of Law and South Asian Studies,
University of Wisconsin–Madison

Madison, Wisconsin
August, 2015

Preface to the Second Edition

Richard Raskin

What a delight that after a long period of unavailability, this book has been given a new life for the benefit of current generations of readers and researchers, and is once again in print, now with two new chapters.

Life is Like a Glass of Tea is still unique in that it contains sustained and comprehensive analyses of individual jokes, followed by publication histories that enable readers to see how each joke evolved over time and in different languages and cultural settings. The distinction it draws between the hopeless task of trying to explain what makes jokes funny, and the more fruitful process of looking closely at any given joke's interpretive properties, is still relevant, as is the conceptual model it proposes for studying those interpretive properties.

I am greatly indebted to Professor Marc Galanter, whose own book — *Lowering the Bar: Lawyer Jokes and Legal Culture* (2005) — is a modern classic and who generously conceived the idea that *Life is Like a Glass of Tea* deserved to be republished. And I am deeply grateful to Professor Alan Childress, founder of Quid Pro Books, for bringing Marc Galanter's idea to fruition and for his exceptional graciousness throughout the process of producing this new edition.

My thanks also go to Claes Hvidbak, Carsten Fenger-Grøndahl, and Søren Mogensen Larsen at Aarhus University Press for kindly authorizing the republication of this book and to Tønnes Bekker-Nielsen for publishing the book in 1992. One of the new chapters originally appeared as an article entitled "Far from Where? On the

History and Meanings of a Classic Jewish Refugee Joke," in *American Jewish History*, Vol. 85, No. 2 (June 1997), pp. 143-150. An earlier form of the other new chapter appeared in Danish as an article entitled "Dilemma-løsning i en klassisk jødisk vittighed" ("Dilemma Resolution in a Classic Jewish Joke") in *Udsyn – Tidsskrift om jødisk liv, Israel og Mellemøsten*, Vol. 25, No. 1 (June 2010), pp. 12-14. For these permissions I wish to thank the editors, Dr. Diane Ashton and Merete Næsbye Christensen, respectively.

Each of the eight jokes singled out for close study in this book is a little storytelling masterpiece in its own right, and my hope is that the reader will draw pleasure and nourishment from each of them as I have over the years.

RICHARD RASKIN

Aarhus, Denmark
August, 2015

Introduction

A New Approach to the Study of Jewish Jokes

The present book differs from previous research on Jewish humor in three major respects: 1) for the first time, individual jokes will be singled out for sustained and comprehensive study; 2) the history of each joke will be traced through successive stages in its evolution; and 3) the ways in which the meaning of each joke can be understood, will be clarified with the help of an interpretive model developed for that purpose.

Six classic jokes have been chosen for close study, with an entire chapter devoted to each of them. This is a departure from a standard procedure in the literature on Jewish humor: that of citing numerous jokes in rapid succession, as illustrative material in support of an argument or a theoretical model. This practice, initiated by Freud in his pioneering book on *Jokes and Their Relation to the Unconscious* (1905), has the advantage of building on a broad corpus of stories; it also ensures a fast and entertaining pace. Its major drawback is that any one joke receives very little attention – generally no more than a few sentences – and when a joke is treated in such a cursory manner, opportunities are missed to look into interpretive issues and to compare different forms the joke has taken. I have deliberately gone to the opposite extreme, lingering over each joke and reluctantly letting go of it when its history and meanings have been described as exhaustively as possible.

The research for this study was carried out in specialized libraries in New York, San Francisco, London, Paris, Copenhagen, Jerusalem and Tel Aviv, as well as at my "home base" at the Danish State and University Library in Aarhus. While working at these facilities, I sifted through hundreds of anthologies of Jewish jokes, written in English, German, French, transliterated Yiddish, Italian, Spanish and Danish, from the early 19th century to the present. As far as I know, no other attempt has ever been made to trace the evolution of individual jokes.

Each chapter will begin with a discussion of the history and variants of the joke in question. Both during and after this presentation of the joke's development, interpretive questions will be taken up, focusing on different ways we might understand – and different attitudes we might hold toward – the comically deviant behavior enacted in the punchline. In this context, we will be disengaging the implicit value system of each joke, examining its distribution of positive and negative values to behaviors designated as normal and deviant. As the reader will soon see, this approach will lead us from the very start to an awareness of interpretive properties that are specific to classic Jewish jokes, and which have not previously been described in the literature.

At the end of each of the first six chapters, the reader will find a "publication history," providing all of the samples I have been able to collect of the joke in question. (Publication histories of a number of other jokes mentioned for comparative purposes, will be gathered in a special section near the end of the book.) Although each chapter deals with one major joke, and in that respect is an independent study in its own right, concepts will nevertheless be introduced in such a way that successive chapters build on the previous ones. For this reason, the reader will find it advantageous to read the chapters in the order in which they are presented, beginning with the first one, in which the groundwork will be laid for all the subsequent studies.

A seventh chapter, on ways in which classic Jewish jokes evolve, will be based primarily on observations made in the course of the six foregoing analyses, but the history of other jokes will also be drawn upon. In a concluding chapter, I will summarize what I believe to be the four major properties specific to classic Jewish jokes. Supplementary publication histories will then follow, after which a comprehensive bibliography will be provided.

Now that the reader knows what to expect in this book, I should say a word or two about things the book will not include. For example, at no point will I try to explain why we laugh at any given joke.

Many theories of humor have, of course, been proposed by philosophers and psychologists, according to whom laughter may be triggered by a sudden perception of incongruity (Schopenhauer); or "some eminency in ourselves by comparison with the inferiority of others" (Hobbes); or the sudden transformation of a strained expectation into nothing" (Kant); or an abrupt transfer of attention from great things to small (Spencer); or the guiltless enjoyment of another person's misfortune (Nietzsche); an inoffensive defect or ugliness of a physical or moral nature (Aristotle); a degradation of the living to the status of the mechanical (Bergson); a gain of otherwise prohibited pleasure, combined with the saving of psychic energy (Freud).

Each of these views refers to structural or thematic properties often found in various types of humor. The trouble is that a joke fitting any of the above categories can be funny *or unfunny*, and we are back where we started.

It is because they distinguish between good and bad jokes that professional comedians have always been skeptical about theories of humor formulated by people whose livelihood does not depend on making people laugh, and who generally overlook this crucial distinction. Groucho Marx's reaction to a theory Max Eastman brought to him is a case in point. Looking back on their discussion, Eastman wrote:[1]

Groucho Marx told me that if with my analysis of humor I could provide a test by which a good joke could be distinguished from a bad one without trying them out on the public, I would soon be the richest man in Hollywood. He also confided that he thought I would probably die poor.

Equally instructive is an incident concerning the Marx Brothers' film, *A Day at the Races* (1937). Before the filming began, the Marx Brothers played scenes from the script on a five-week tour before live audiences. Whenever a gag failed to get a laugh, it would either be dropped or changed by scriptwriters Pirosh and Seaton, and tried out in its new form at the following show. Groucho deliberately held back on wiggling his eyebrows and leering as he delivered his lines, because it was the joke's own funniness that was to be gauged on the basis of audience response. Of all the changes that were made in the script during this pre-filming tour, the following one is the most interesting:[2]

A line that went "That's the most obnoxious proposal I've ever had" was not getting the laughs it seemed to deserve, and so it became a "revolting" proposal, a "disgusting" proposal, and "offensive" proposal, a "repulsive" proposal. Still not funny enough. It became "disagreeable" and "distasteful," and it bombed altogether. When it was a "nauseating" proposal, it was hilarious.

---

[1] Max Eastman, *Enjoyment of Laughter* (New York: Simon & Schuster, 1936), p. 279.

[2] Joe Adamson, *Groucho, Harpo, Chico and Sometimes Zeppo. A Celebration of the Marx Brothers* (London and New York: W. H. Allen, 1973), p. 313. It was in the unforgettable "tutti frutti" ice cream scene that the line was used. When Tony (Chico) says: "One dollar, and you remember me all your life," Dr. Hackenbush (Groucho) replies: "That's the most nauseating proposal I ever had."

What examples of this kind show, at least to my satisfaction, is that nobody really knows why some things strike us as funny and others don't. Consequently, I will make no further mention of theories of laughter in this book, and will refrain from proposing any new explanation.

I have also chosen not to review systematically the enormous literature on Jewish humor, except with respect to the issue of ethnic self-disparagement. In that context, and whenever else it seems appropriate, references will be made to Freud's book, as well as to the contributions of such researchers as Bergler (1956), Grotjahn (1961), Reik (1962), Memmi (1966), Katz and Katz (1971), Ben-Amos (1973), Goldstein (1976), Ziv (1986), Davies (1986) and Dundes (1987). This literature is extremely rich and varied, containing many articles and books which have helped to clarify important concepts and to bring significant patterns to light.

Among the objections that might be raised to various aspects of this study, three are worth mentioning at this point.

The first concerns my reliance on printed sources alone for describing the history of each joke. Folklorists in particular might find it strange that I have not attempted to monitor the oral circulation of these stories in the present and recent past. To that I would reply that research teams with the resources for doing just that, systematically and in a number of countries, could build upon and supplement the work done in this book, and that their contribution would be another valuable step in the right direction.

Similarly, it could also be argued that my coverage of the jokes is incomplete since anthologies written in such languages as Hebrew and Russian, are not included in the study. Again I would encourage researchers able to read those and other languages that lie outside of my own range of competence, to help complete the work begun in this book.

A third objection is of a different nature. It could be argued that it is better to cite jokes, rather than attempting to study them in depth, because of the danger E. B. White warned about when he wrote, "Humor can be dissected, as a frog can, but the thing dies in the process..." Anyone who has ever tried to "explain" a joke knows from first-hand experience that White's warning should be taken to heart. But a crucial distinction can still be drawn between: a) trying to explain what makes a joke funny, on the basis of one or another theory of humor; and b) looking closely at the various meanings a joke can have. In avoiding the *explanatory* and opting for the *interpretive* approach, I have acknowledged that what makes us laugh should be regarded as the inner secret of the story, lying outside the range of analysis. Since the jokes studied here have been respected in this way, they have a far better chance of surviving the ordeal than they might otherwise have had.

This book is intended for anyone who is interested in a deeper understanding of classic Jewish jokes, and who believes that individual jokes – as expressions of a people's relationship to itself and to its world – can be masterpieces of folklore, and deserve the same thorough study that is routinely accorded to works of High Culture.

Aarhus, Denmark
March, 1991

וויטצען און שפיטצען

אדער

אַנעקדאָטען

דאָס זינד וויצינע און שפּיצינע עָרצייהלונגען וואָס
קומען צו ניק אין אויסמאַנג אין דער וועלט מיט מענטשין
וויא קלײנע נאָלט אין דער מאָשע אום רעסטע צוא
נעבין בייא יעדער בעשטע נעלענענהייט

מאת אמ'ד

ווילנא
בדפוס האלמנה והאחים ראם
שנת תרל"ד לפ"ק

ВИТЦЕНЪ УНДЪ ЩПИЦЕНЪ.
т. е.
Анекдоты.
А. М. Дика.

ВИЛЬНА
Въ типографіи Вдовы и братьевъ Роммъ.
На жмудскомъ переулкѣ въ домахъ
подъ № 327. и 328.
1873.

The title page of an early collection of Jewish jokes: Isaac Meir Dick's
Witzen un Spitzen oder Anecdoten, published in Wilna in 1873.

Chapter 1

Rabbinic Judgment

Interpretive Properties of the Classic Jewish Joke

Two Jews have come to a rabbi to settle a legal dispute. Two dignified Jews with beard and earlocks, just as required. As usual, the rabbi's wife is also seated in the room. The rabbi says to one of the Jews: "So, what's your complaint?" He answers that the story is such and such, and he has to pay and he has to do this and he has to do that; in short, he gives such a fine account and argues his case so clearly that the rabbi has to say: "You're right." The rabbi then addresses the second Jew: "And what do you have to say?" The second Jew is nobody's fool either, and he also has a mouth to defend himself with; he argues his case so clearly that there is nothing left to be said, and that he owes nothing – not one cent. The rabbi says to him: "You're right." The rabbi's wife has never heard the likes of this and says to her husband: "You should live and be well! How can both of them be right? When one wins, the other has to lose." The rabbi says to his wife: "You're right, too."

Immanuel Olsvanger, *Rosinkess mit Mandlen* (Zurich: Die Arche, 1965; originally published in 1920), p. 138; subsequently reprinted in *Röyte Pomerantsen* (New York: Schocken, 1965; orig. pub. 1935), p. 168. My translation from the Yiddish.

The History and Variants of the Joke

The Earliest Form

When this story first appeared in an anthology of Jewish humor, published in Budapest in 1879, its central character was a judge, not a rabbi; and the quarreling parties were not identified in ethnic terms:[1]

EVERYONE IS RIGHT

Two men involved in a dispute, went to a judge. When the plaintiff had presented his case, the judge said: You are right; when the defendant had argued his case, the judge told him that he too was right. When a fellow magistrate asked the young judge: How can you award the case to both parties? He answered him: You're right too!

While nothing in this version of the joke explicitly tells us how to view the judge's curious behavior, the word "young" can function as a cue suggesting that inexperience may be the explanation.[2]

This early form of the joke can in turn be traced back to an incident that reportedly occurred in Milan sometime in the first half of the 19th century. The Italian novelist, Alessandro Manzoni, wrote in a non-fictional work originally published between 1851 and 1855:[3]

A friend of mine, whose memory I honor and hold dear, told of a curious scene which he himself had personally witnessed, at the home of a justice of the peace in Milan many years ago. He had found the judge between two litigants, one of whom was heatedly arguing his case; when he finished, the judge said to him: "You are right." "But your honor," said the other one immediately, "you must also hear me out before you reach a decision." "That is perfectly reasonable," answered the judge: "speak your case and I will listen attentively." This second litigant then put such passion into arguing his case and succeeded so well that the judge said to him: "You are also right." Also present was his child of seven or eight who played quietly with some toy or other, while attentively following the dispute; and who at this point, looked up stupefied and exclaimed with some authority: "But Daddy, they can't

---

[1] Julius Dessauer, *Der jüdische Humorist* (Budapest: Selbstverlag, n.d.), p. 122; my translation. In the card catalogue of the Jerusalem University Library, "1879 (?)" is given as the year of publication. The German text is provided on p. 33 below.

[2] A similar distribution of roles – though without even a hint as to why the judge deviates from the prescribed behavior – is found in Alexander Moszkowski's even more rudimentary version, published in Germany in 1908, and provided on p. 33 below.

[3] Alessandro Manzoni, *Del Romanzo Storico* (1851-1855) in *Opere*, ed. Riccardo Bacchelli. (Milan/Naples: Riccardo Ricciardi, 1953), vol. 53 of *La Letteratura Italiana*, p.1059; my translation. The Italian text is provided on p. 33 below.

both be right!" "You're right too," said the judge. How the story ended, either my friend never related, or it has slipped my memory...[4]

We have no particular grounds for suspecting that Manzoni's friend was pulling the writer's leg by telling a joke as though it were a factual account; or for assuming that a story Manzoni remembered as an actual event, had been told to him as a joke. In the absence of any indication to the contrary, Manzoni's word, and that of his trusted friend, should be taken at face value.

What this suggests is that a story that would subsequently become one of the most perfect examples of Jewish humor, was inspired by an event that had apparently occurred outside the Jewish community, and that was totally devoid of any reference to Jewishness. This could help explain the ethnically neutral role-distribution and setting found in the earliest form of the joke when it was first included in Jewish anthologies.

The Bribed Rabbi Variant

The earliest version of the story in which the central figure is a rabbi, was published in Berlin in 1910. The other characters in the story are also Jewish: the rabbi's wife, and the two litigants, whose names (*Gelenkwasser* = the water which accumulates at joints, and *Aschtopf* = ashpot, i.e. an inversion of potash) are presumably parodies of Jewish-sounding names.[5]

One day, Elkan Gelenkwasser came to [the rabbi] and recounted his dispute with Markus Aschtopf, for the rabbi to make a decision. He brought along a fat goose.

The rabbi said: "Elkan Gelenkwasser, there can be no doubt. You are right!"

Then Markus Aschtopf slipped into the house. He brought two geese along, and the rabbi said:

"Markus Aschtopf, there can be no doubt. Now you are right."

The rabbi's wife, who had overheard these bogus judgments, shouted to him indignantly:

"You crook, you shame to the rabbinic profession, how could you say first to Elkan Gelenkwasser and then to Markus Aschtopf: 'You are right'?...When only one of them can be right?"

---

[4] I am grateful to my colleague, Leonardo Cecchini, for locating this passage, which is referred to and partially cited – but with no source given – first by Olsvanger in *Rozinkess mit Mandlen* (op. cit.) and subsequently by Löwit in *Jüdische Schwänke* (Vienna: R: Löwit, 1928), p. 148.

[5] Manuel Nuél [Manuel Schnitzer], *Rabbi Lach und seine Geschichten* (Berlin: Hesperus, 1910), pp. 58-59. The story is also included in Manuel Schnitzer's *Rabbi Lach. Ein Kulturdokument in Anekdoten* (Hamburg: Verlag W. Gente, 1921), p. 80.

To which the rabbi said:
"Now you are right!"

When the joke is told in this manner, we are left in no doubt whatsoever as to how we are expected to understand the rabbi's behavior, or what attitude we are invited to hold toward him.

The Standard Litigation Variant

From about 1920 to 1948, virtually all published retellings of this joke in Europe and the United States, involve the same constellation of characters: a rabbi, his wife, and two male litigants who are identified as being Jewish. Unlike the earlier version involving bribery, this standard variant does not include an explanation as to why the rabbi deviates from common-sense logic in dealing with the situation at hand.

The best example of this variant happens to be the earliest one, included for the first time in Immanuel Olsvanger's *Rosinkess mit Mandlen* (1920), and subsequently reprinted in his *Röyte Pomerantsen* (1935). I have already cited Olsvanger's Yiddish version at the very start of this chapter, and hope that the flavor of his verbal embellishments has been captured at least to some degree by the translation.

The Standard Divorce Variant

In 1948, a new American variant begins to appear, substituting the marital complaints of a husband and wife for the law suit between two businessmen:[6]

There was once a rabbi who was so open-minded that he could see every side of a question. One day a man came to him to request that he grant him a divorce.
"What do you hold against your wife?" asked the rabbi gravely.
The man went into a lengthy recital of his complaints.
"You are right," he agreed when the man finished.
Then the rabbi turned to the woman.
"Now let us hear your story," he urged.
And the woman in her turn began to tell of the cruel mistreatment she had suffered at her husband's hands.

---

[6] Nathan Ausubel, *Treasury of Jewish Folklore* (New York: Crown, 1948), p. 22. This American variant would subsequently appear in Rywell (1960), Rokeach (1960), Rosten (1970), Berman (1975), Pollack (1979), and Triverton (1981).

The rabbi listened with obvious distress.

"You are right," he said with conviction when she finished.

At this, the rabbi's wife, who was present, exclaimed, "How can this be? Surely, both of them couldn't be right!"

The rabbi knitted his brows and reflected.

"You're right, too!" he agreed.

As to why the joke eventually evolved as it did on American soil, a part of the answer may be that in the U.S., in contrast to Czarist Russia, for example, disputes involving business dealings between two Jews would normally be settled by the regular judicial institutions. Another factor favoring the substitution of marital problems for a financial dispute in the newer American variant, is a higher incidence of divorce in the New World than in the more tradition-bound communities of Eastern and Central Europe. While each of the two standard variants has its charm, my personal preference is for the divorce variant, because of its more symmetrical constellation of roles, including as it does – in its classical form – two sets of husbands and wives.[7] On the other hand, no retelling of the joke has ever matched the flavor of Olsvanger's litigation variant.

Three Interpretations of the Joke

As the joke – in either of its two standard forms – progresses, the rabbi's successive judgments involve a compounding of logical contradictions. If we ask ourselves how, according to the premises of the joke, we are implicitly invited to understand the rabbi's deviation from the behavior expected of him, three very different explanations may come to mind.

---

[7] Occasionally, however, a judge and clerk or lawyer take the place of the rabbi and his wife (Adams 1952, Hershfield 1959), or the rabbi's wife is replaced by a student (Hakel 1965, Rosten 1970, Berman 1975, Pollack 1979, Triverton 1981).

Role-Fiasco

The rabbi can be viewed as a bungling incompetent, with no real understanding of the situation in which he finds himself or the behavior prescribed by his role.

When the first visitor has told his side of the story, the rabbi doesn't know enough to refrain from expressing any judgment whatsoever until he has heard the other side. He is incapable of realizing that each of his visitors may deliberately distort the truth in order to place him/herself in a more positive light, and that facts which may emerge when the second one has spoken, might change the rabbi's view of the case that was made by the first one.

A second and more serious sign of incompetence is that in telling the second as well as the first visitor that he/she is right, the rabbi doesn't even realize that he is embroiling himself in a logical contradiction, while failing to solve the problem that has been brought to his attention – his verdict being of no help whatsoever to his visitors.

And his wife's objection, embodying the common sense the rabbi lacks, doesn't get through to him either. Instead of yielding to reason, the rabbi makes an even bigger mess of the situation by further violating the rules of logic.

Among those anthologists who apparently favored this interpretation of the joke, viewing the rabbi's performance as simply incompetent, are Neches (1938) who presented the rabbi as forgetful and preoccupied, Schnur (1945) for whom the rabbi was so willing to see the other fellow's point of view that he was unqualified as a judge, and Learsi (1941 and 1961), who had the rabbi hail from Chelem (or Chelm), the capital of lunatic logic in Jewish folklore.

To whatever degree we understand the rabbi's behavior in this manner, we feel invited to laugh at, dissociate ourselves from and feel superior to the rabbi, whose deviance from common sense is interpreted as an utterly incompetent management of his own role.

Tactical Manoeuvre

The rabbi can also be seen as a very shrewd tactician who knows exactly what he is doing and why.

Seen in this perspective, his strategy consists in agreeing with whoever tries to convince him of anything, because in expressing agreement, the rabbi accords what is wanted by that person and makes further discussion unnecessary. Furthermore, the act of agreeing is a relatively easy move to make, requiring no argumentation. And it minimizes the risk of offending anyone, while bringing a potentially troublesome situation to as quick and painless a conclusion as possible. Of course it doesn't solve the problem of the two visitors; but it simplifies matters considerably for the rabbi.

And the best part of it all is that even when the rabbi is caught in a flagrant inconsistency, as he is by his wife, he can use the very same tactic against her. In doing just that, the rabbi has the added pleasure of appearing to give in to her while outrageously compounding the very offence she has charged him with. There is simply no way he can lose.

This is somewhat reminiscent of another well-known joke:[8]

– "Why is it you Jews always answer a question with another question?"
– "And why shouldn't we answer a question with another question?"

Here again, the fact of being questioned and implicitly criticized is turned into an occasion for committing the offence one more time as a response to the critic. But what makes the "Rabbinic Judgment" story more elegant than the question joke in a purely tactical respect, is that the rabbi manages to turn the situation around to his advantage, and to get away with the offence one more time, by telling his critic that she is right! Or to look at the situation from another angle: she is allowed to win the momentary dispute with her husband in such a way that she loses it. The question joke does not have this exquisite twist.

When "Rabbinic Judgment" is seen in this light, our relationship to the rabbi can best be described as a pleasurable sense of complicity with a shrewd operator whose deviance from the norm is a strategy for gaining his own objectives in what is essentially a game-situation.

---

8 Early variants of this joke can be found in T. L. Hirsh, *Jüdisches Witzbuch* (Berlin: Reform-Verlagshaus, 1913), p. 37, and H. Itler, *Jüdische Witze* (Dresden: Rudolph'sche Verlagsbuchhandlung, [1928]), p. 33.

He is not corrupt, as in the earlier variant in which favorable judgments were sold for a bribe, and the rabbi was crude and grotesque in our eyes. Here, his goals are more elevated and the game he is playing is considerably more refined than in the bribery variant. However, his behavior is in no way seen as a model to emulate, and is even cited as a kind of show-case example by Rokeach at the beginning of *The Open and Closed Mind* (1960). Here, the rabbi is presented as embodying a "closed system of belief," and as having as his underlying motive "to preserve somehow the illusion of infallibility."

Exemplary Deviance

It is also possible to view this joke in a philosophical perspective, in which case the rabbi's deviation from a common-sense norm takes on a positive value in our eyes, while the norm he violates becomes the negative pole within the joke's implicit value system.

We can begin by looking more closely at the norm embodied by the rabbi's wife, who believes that two people holding opposite views of the same situation, cannot both be right. "Rightness" for her is a finite quantity, so that however much of it is granted to one party in a dispute, an equal amount of it must necessarily be withheld from the other. She also believes that anyone who makes two logically incompatible statements must be in error. According to her way of thinking, reality is consistent with itself in a straightforward and simple manner, and the truth is therefore subject to the elementary rules of logic.

The rabbi embodies a very different principle: that opposite views of the same situation can both be right, which means that "rightness" for him is in unlimited supply. He is also perfectly willing to make two logically incompatible statements when each seems correct to him – and to compound the original violation of logic by telling his wife that she is right *too* (the "too" signifying that he maintains the incompatible judgments for which he is being criticized, while expressing his sincere opinion that his critic is also right).

For the rabbi, reality is multi-facetted and internally contradictory in its very fabric – an outlook which a Marxist or Hegelian might call "dialectical". In contrast to this view of reality which allows for the interplay of opposites, the common-sense outlook of the rabbi's wife now seems unsuited for dealing with the complexities to which the rabbi's more supple and more open mind is well attuned. The rabbi's view that truth supersedes logic and is not subject to its rules, is presented by the joke (when "Rabbinic Judgment" is understood in this manner) as a higher and more enlightened conception of the truth, while the normal conception embodied by the rabbi's wife now comes across as simplistic and reductive.

The work of three Jewish thinkers might be cited briefly in this connection.

One is Martin Buber, who suggested that when Adam and Eve ate of the forbidden fruit, their eyes were opened to the contradictions inherent in all things–the "knowledge of good and evil" referring to an awareness of the opposites teeming within all creation, rather than to specifically moral categories.[9] This awareness of the contradictory nature of reality is a painful one from which God had benevolently sought to protect mankind. And once that irreversible awareness came, God expelled Adam and Eve from the Garden of Eden, lest they eat from the Tree of Life and be condemned to live on for all eternity in the face of contradiction.

Morris R. Cohen's "principle of polarity" is equally relevant here. In Cohen's own words,[10] this principle

asserts that in all determination there are opposing elements or categories, such as unity and plurality, identity and difference, activity and passivity.

The obvious value of the principle of polarity is in enabling us to avoid one-sided and interminable (because indeterminate) issues, and in making us more hospitable to the complexity of seemingly paradoxical facts [...] All this is of the utmost importance in metaphysics or general philosophy where we are subject to two great temptations: (1) to hasty generalization about objects like the universe which are not as determinate as is commonly supposed, and (2) to deny the vision of others who see things from a different point of view.

For Cohen, two contradictory statements can both be true, and this state of affairs requires – not the abdication of understanding (a danger inherent in the Hegelian dialectic[11]) – but rather a special effort to discern in what respect each of the two statements is true.

More recently, Henri Atlan – a French physician and biologist – wrote a ponderous book intended to show that "there are different

[9] Martin Buber, *Good and Evil* (New York: Scribners, 1952), pp. 67-80.

[10] Morris R. Cohen, *Studies in Philosophy and Science* (New York: Holt, 1949), pp. 12-13.

[11] Morris R. Cohen, *Reason and Nature. An Essay on the Meaning of Scientific Method* (Glencoe: The Free Press, 1953; originally published in 1931), p. 166.

modes of rational thought, different ways of being 'right', legitimate though different, when accounting for the evidence of our senses."[12] Broadly speaking, Atlan seeks to reconcile scientific and mythic ways of thinking, and in the opening paragraph of his book, the story he cites to illustrate his basic thesis is the joke we are studying here– which, as Atlan understands it, implicitly proposes the rabbi's behavior to us, as embodying a higher synthesis of apparently conflicting approaches to reality.

When our joke is understood in this philosophical perspective, we can look up to the rabbi for his ability to understand that both of the parties to the dispute are right, each in his/her own way. (Perhaps it was to preclude our suspecting either of the litigants in the Olsvanger version of being a fraud that the text insisted on their being dignified or distinguished-looking Jews – *sheyne yidn*[13] –, with beard and earlocks, as required by custom; in other words, honest people worthy of respect.)

In declaring both of them right, the rabbi has overcome the difficulty evoked in the Yiddish proverb: "*Az beyde baaley-dinim zaynen gerekt–iz shlekt,*" rendered by one translator as: "When both litigants are right, justice makes a sorry sight."[14] Not bound by the usual rules of adjudication, the rabbi – seen in this context – embodies a way to avoid being unjust in a situation with which judicial institutions are unequipped to deal fairly. In this respect, the story stands as a reply to the proverb, or as a model for resolving the problem it depicts.

---

[12] Henri Atlan, *A tort et à raison. Intercritique de la science et du mythe* (Paris: Seuil, 1990), p. 6; my translation.

[13] In a footnote to another joke, Olsvanger explained that "a sheyne (or schejne) id" is an esteemed and learned man ("angesehener, gelehrter Mann"), though the expression can also mean literally a beautiful Jew (p. 25). Supplementary information can be found in Mark Zborowski and Elizabeth Herzog's *Life is with People. The Jewish Little-Town in Eastern Europe* (New York: International Universities Press, 1952): "Perhaps the most generally used term for the upper social register is the sheyne yidn, the fine – or literally, the beautiful Jews... This use of the word beautiful to connote other than physical qualities is characteristic of a people for whom intangibles have a concrete reality. One speaks of a beautiful deed or a beautiful event. To call a house 'sheyn' means, not that its aspect is pleasing, but that the household is orderly, dignified, harmonious" (p. 73).

[14] Hanan Ayalti, *Yiddish Proverbs* (New York: Schocken, 1971; orig. pub. 1949), pp. 32-33.

Interpretive Properties of the Classic Jewish Joke

The Basic Triad

As shown above, the rabbi's deviance from the behavior prescribed for his role in the given situation, can be understood in three very different ways, which I have called role-fiasco, tactical manoeuvre and exemplary deviance. As it turns out, the same three interpretive frameworks can be useful for understanding many classic Jewish jokes, a number of which are susceptible to interpretation in two of the three perspectives. ("Rabbinic Judgment" is the only joke I know of to which all three frameworks are fully and equally applicable, which is why that joke was chosen as the first one to be studied in this book.)

Returning now to the three perspectives, I will try to describe each of them in terms which are sufficiently general that their applicability will not be limited by the thematic content specific to any given joke.

ROLE-FIASCO

Here a comic deviance is perceived as a display of a character's outrageous incompetence in: a) performing or sustaining a given role; b) assessing what behavior or attitude a given situation calls for; or c) thinking logically and realistically.

To whatever degree a joke lends itself to this reading, it is conservative in the sense that it appeals to our identification with an established norm and to our readiness to perceive a violation of that norm as ridiculous. When we laugh at a joke understood in this way, our laughter signifies our dissociation from and feelings of superiority toward a comic figure who is seen as failing to manage his performance in accordance with the appropriate social or logical code.

TACTICAL MANOEUVRE

Seen within this framework, the comic figure in the joke is essentially a player who is out to get away with something, to pull something off, to evade a responsibility, to get more than his share of something he wants, to get the better of, or turn the tables on, someone else, to get around a prohibition, etc.

In this context, social interaction is a game, behaviors can be seen as moves, and every event can be expressed in terms of someone's winning or losing.

Our attitude toward the comic figure is generally one of complicity, and we can often derive a measure of wish-fulfillment from the joke by vicariously participating in the victory enacted in the punchline. When the joke is viewed in this way, our attitude toward the norms involved and toward their violation, is essentially permissive.

EXEMPLARY DEVIANCE

Within this third interpretive framework, the comic behavior on display in the punchline is seen as a positive model we are implicitly invited to admire and emulate, even though it marks a break with conventional codes.

Here we identify with the deviance and adopt a critical stance with respect to the violated norm. In other words, we approve of the violation, and are invited to see the norm as a needless limitation of human possibilities.

In this respect, the third perspective is radical in nature, and through it, the joke may offer fresh insight and encourage us to rise above established conceptual or behavioral patterns which in one way or another involve the sacrifice of something vital.

The following table may help the reader to visualize the ways in which the three frameworks in this basic repertory of interpretive options, differ from and complement one another.

THE BASIC TRIAD[15]

	ROLE-FIASCO	TACTICAL MANOEUVRE	EXEMPLARY DEVIANCE
comic behavior exemplifies:	incompetent performance, inappropriate conduct, defective reasoning	goal-directed strategy for getting away with something or winning	a transcendence of a limiting conceptual or behavioral prescription
our relation to the comic figure:	dissociation from	complicity with	identification with
status of violated norm:	positive	neutral	negative
status of the violation:	negative	acceptable	positive
our gain includes:	sense of superiority	wish-fulfillment	insight
basic orientation:	conservative	permissive	radical

Virtually any Jewish joke involving more than wordplay, will be susceptible to interpretation in at least one of the above frameworks. Those which can be understood in two (or three) of the perspectives, constitute a special group of Jewish jokes which are the very best of the classics, and whose richness derives in part from their openness to alternate interpretive options.

A concept borrowed from the psychology of visual perception, will now help to concretize the importance of that property.

---

[15] Chapter 3 will introduce an additional set of interpretive frameworks, called the "parodistic triad." For the time being, I will confine our discussion to the "basic triad"- a term that will become useful at a later point, when we will be working with two sets of perspectives.

Reversible Perspective

Psychologists of visual perception have long been interested in a class of optical figures which embody a property called "reversibility," defined as follows:[16]

REVERSIBILITY; REVERSIBLE FIGURES. A class of figures for which there is more than one perceptual interpretation. In these circumstances, rather than all interpretations being seen simultaneously, a single interpretation is seen which abruptly gives way to some other. These changes in interpretation are called reversals.

One of the first to describe this phenomenon was a Swiss mineralogist named Necker, who reported in 1832 that while examining drawings made of certain crystalline forms, he often experienced "a sudden and involuntary change in the apparent position" of the structure. What Necker noticed was that a rhomboid – now known as a "Necker cube"– can alternately assume first one and then another of two different configurations when looked at steadily and repeatedly.[17]

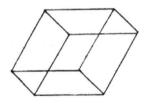

Necker cube

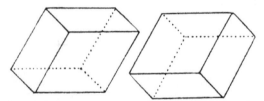

Alternate configurations of the Necker cube

"Rubin's Figure"[18] is undoubtedly the best-known illustration of reversibility – in this case involving either facing black profiles or a white vase. Rubin, a Danish psychologist, pioneered the figure / ground concept which was to play a major role in gestalt psychology.

---

[16] C. D. Frith in *Encyclopedia of Psychology*, edited by Eysenck, Arnold and Meili (Bungay: Fontana/Collins, 1975), vol. 2, p. 940.

[17] L. A. Necker, "Observations of some remarkable optical phenomena," *The London and Edinburgh Philosophical Magazine and Journal of Science* 1, 5 (November 1832), pp. 335-337.

[18] Edgar Rubin, *Synsoplevede Figurer* (Copenhagen: Gyldendal, 1915), opposite p. 32.

Other types of reversible figures include "Schröder's Staircase"[19] and a so-called "puzzle picture"[20] in which we may alternately see an old and a young woman.

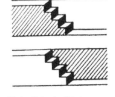

| Rubin's Figure | Schröder's Staircase | Puzzle Picture |

Returning now to "Rabbinic Judgment," I would suggest that each of the three interpretations outlined above may successively occur to us, like the alternate configurations of a Necker Cube or the profiles-and-vase reversals of Rubin's Figure. A mental image of the rabbi as a bungling incompetent may suddenly give way to a picture of him as a shrewd tactician, which might in turn be replaced by view of the rabbi as an embodiment of a higher sense of truth. This ongoing process of interpretive reversals as we continue to consider the meaning of "Rabbinic Judgment," might be represented schematically as follows:

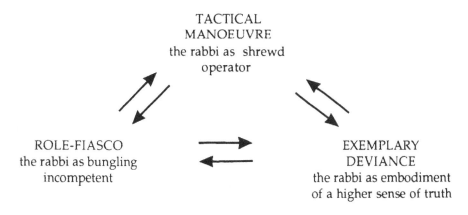

TACTICAL
MANOEUVRE
the rabbi as shrewd
operator

ROLE-FIASCO
the rabbi as bungling
incompetent

EXEMPLARY
DEVIANCE
the rabbi as embodiment
of a higher sense of truth

[19] H. Schröder, "Über eine optische Inversion bei Betrachtung verkehrter, durch optische Vorrichtung entworfener, physischer Bilder," *Annalen der Physik und Chemie* 181 (1858), pp. 298-311.

[20] Edwin G. Boring, "A new ambiguous figure," *American Journal of Psychology* 42 (1930), p. 444.

Reversibility as an interpretive property, involves different ways of understanding and of relating to the comically deviant behavior enacted in the punchline. This property of reversible perspective should not be confused with a mechanism found in jokes in which an unexpected *turnabout* occurs in the situation depicted. A turnabout of that kind can be seen in the following well-known joke:[21]

Cohen, on his death bed:
- Are you there, my darling Rebecca?
- Yes, my dear husband.
- And you, Moses, my dear son?
- Yes, Papa.
- And you, my little Abraham?
- I'm here, Papa.
- And you, Solomon, my faithful cashier?
- Yes, Mr. Cohen.
- Then who the hell is minding the store?

When a turnabout is involved, a shift takes place as the story-line crosses over from its initial frame of reference to a new one found in the punchline. No competent listener or reader can fail to register this shift *within* the story, and upon which the whole point of the joke hinges. Turnabouts of this kind are common to the jokes of many ethnic groups, and have been exhaustively studied in the literature on humor.[22] The same is true of "double entendre," where the very point

---

[21] This early specimen of the joke appeared with Arthur Szyk's illustration in *Le juif qui rit* (Paris: Albin Michel, 1926), p. 109; my translation. The publication history of this joke will be found on pp. 203-213 below.

[22] See, for example, Victor Raskin's *Semantic Mechanisms of Humor* (Dordrecht /Boston/- Lancaster: D. Reidel, 1984). Raskin designates as "script overlap" the co-presence in the joke

of a joke depends on our grasp of a verbal ambiguity or play on words.

Reversible perspective – which is specific to a limited group of classic Jewish jokes and has never been discussed in the literature on Jewish humor – is in play if *after* having heard the punchline of a joke, we are left oscillating between two or more interpretive options.

This is in sharp contrast to most jokes, both Jewish and otherwise, which are "closed" in the sense that they unequivocally settle the questions they raise, leaving no doubt in our minds as to what we are expected to make of the comically deviant behavior. The following joke, for example, can be understood in only one way – in this case, in terms of tactical manoeuvre:[23]

A rich man was enjoying the company of the celebrated wit, Herschel Ostropolier.

"Herschel," he said, "if you can tell me a really spontaneous lie – without thinking – I'll give you a ruble."

Herschel's answer was instantaneous. "What do you mean, one ruble – you just said *two!*"

With those Jewish jokes characterized by reversible perspective, when the punchline is sprung, we immediately register the humor of the comic event and know perfectly well that the story has come full-circle and is complete; but at the same time, we experience it as being open-ended. We feel a need to replay the comic event in our minds because the most basic question on which the joke hinges has not been cleared up, and could be settled in more than one way. Consequently, we are unsure as to what attitude we are expected to hold toward the comically deviant behavior enacted in the punchline. As we continue to consider the story, competing interpretations may succeed one another in our minds, with the result that our perception of the underlying meaning of the joke may alternate between two or three possible readings. Needless to say, we never feel finished with a joke of this type, which should be told – as Olsvanger told the "Rabbinic Judgment" story – in a way which favors the free interplay of alternate interpretive options, rather than hinting at one or another of them.

---

of two opposite frames of reference, the passage from one to the other constituting what I have called a turnabout.

[23] Henry D. Spalding, *The Encyclopedia of Jewish Humor* (New York: Jonathan David, 1969), p. 69. This joke appeared in Loewe (1920, p. 38), Richman (1952, p. 397), Rywell (1960, p. 114) and Novak and Waldoks (1981, p. 30).

Not everyone enjoys this open-endedness or reversibility. But for those who do, these jokes have an inexhaustible richness of a kind that makes stories of the more conventional variety seem flat in comparison. While closed jokes quickly lose whatever charm they have with successive retellings, classics of the reversible type retain all of their magic.

A possible objection should be dealt with at this point.

It could be argued that if the "Rabbinic Judgment" joke had the qualities of openness and reversibility just described, then why hasn't anyone noticed that before? And if those qualities have gone unnoticed, then how is it possible to claim that the joke functions like a reversible figure?

To that challenge, I would reply that in one way or another, we have to account for the radically different uses made of essentially the same joke at the start of Rokeach's *The Open and Closed Mind* (1960) and Atlan's *A tort et à raison* (1986). As already indicated, Rokeach sees the joke as exemplifying what amounts to a tactical manoeuvre in the context of a closed (and therefore suspect) belief system, while for Atlan, the rabbi's deviation from the norm is exemplary and points the way toward an ideal of intellectual pluralism.

No one would say about Rokeach and Atlan: "They can't both be right." Clearly, each of them sees in the joke a meaning that the story is perfectly capable of expressing. What each of them doesn't see, however, is that the joke can be understood in other terms as well.

While I cannot argue that anyone has in the past experienced the "Rabbinic Judgment" joke as a reversible figure, I have demonstrated that one property of this story is a susceptibility to being interpreted in more than one way. This, in itself, is the basis for what I am calling reversibility, and I would suggest that anyone who has been confronted with alternate ways of understanding this story – as you have while reading the present chapter – is likely to experience it from that point on as a reversible figure.

Impossible Figures

In many Jewish jokes – including "Rabbinic Judgment"– the punchline crystallizes a construct which makes no sense at all, but in so logically compelling a manner that we are both disoriented and fascinated by the exploit. A similar impression is created by "impossible figures," which are actually visual jokes:

Penrose Triangle[24]   Two-prongued trident or
                                            three-stick clevis[25]

Impossible figures induce cognitive confusion, by defying their own logic in so rational a way that we cannot conceptually grasp how they fit together. As a result, no one interpretation can account for more than a portion of such a figure, and the two interpretations required by its incompatible parts, are themselves mutually incompatible.

The following is probably the best example that can be found of a Jewish joke constructed in this way:[26]

> Two sages of Chelm went out for a walk. One carried an umbrella, the other didn't. Suddenly, it began to rain.
> "Open your umbrella, quick!" suggested the one without an umbrella.
> "It won't help," answered the other.
> "What do you mean, it won't help? It will protect us from the rain."
> "It's no use, the umbrella is as full of holes as a sieve."
> "Then why did you take it along in the first place?"
> "I didn't think it would rain."

Similarly, the punchline of "Rabbinic Judgment" completes a construct which fits together in the same manner as a "Penrose triangle" or "two-pronged trident."

When either reversibility or an impossible figure is found in a Jewish joke, that property is the basis for much of what we perceive as the story's Jewish flavor. And when both are present – as in

---

[24] L. S. and R. Penrose, "Impossible objects: a special type of visual illusion," *British Journal of Psychology* 49 (1958), p. 31.

[25] D. H. Schuster, "A new ambiguous figure: a three-stick clevis," *American Journal of Psychology* 77 (1964), p. 673.

[26] Ausubel (1948), op. cit., p. 338. Curiously, there is no impossible figure in the precurser on which this joke was probably based. The publication history of this joke will be found on pp. 238-240 below.

"Rabbinic Judgment" – the properties interact to produce the purest essence of that special flavor.

PUBLICATION HISTORY

Alessandro Manzoni, DEL ROMANZO STORICO (1851-1855) in OPERE, ed. Riccardo Bacchelli. Milan/Naples: Riccardo Ricciardi, 1953), vol. 53 of LA LETTERATURA ITALIANA, p.1059.

Un mio amico, di cara e onorata memoria, raccontava una scena curiosa, alla quale era stato presente in casa d'un giudice di pace in Milano, val a dire molt'anni fa. L'aveva trovato tra due litiganti, uno de' quali perorava caldamente la sua causa; e quando costui ebbe finito, il giudice gli disse: avete ragione. Ma, signor giudice, disse subito l'altro, lei mi deve sentire anche me, prima di decidere. È troppo giusto, rispose il giudice: dite pur su, che v'ascolto attentamente. Allora quello si mise con tanto più impegno a far valere la sua causa; e ci riuscì così bene, che il giudice gli disse: avete ragione anche voi. C'era lì accanto un suo bambino di sette o ott'anni, il quale, giocando pian piano con non so qual balocco, non aveva lasciato di stare anche attento al contradittorio; e a quel punto, alzando un visino stupefatto, non senza un certo che d'autorevole, esclamò: ma babbo! non può essere che abbiano ragione tutt'e due. Hai ragione anche tu, gli disse il giudice. Come poi sia finita, o l'amico non lo raccontava, o m'è uscito di mente...

Julius Dessauer, DER JÜDISCHE HUMORIST. Budapest: Selbstverlag, 1879 (?) p. 122 [misnumbered p. 112].

ALLE HABEN RECHT. Zwei Männer, die in einem Streite begriffen waren, kamen zu einem Richter. Als der Kläger seine Rechtssache vortrug, sagte der Richter: Du hast recht; der Angeklagte brachte seine Vertheidigungsgründe vor, der Richter gab ihm auch recht. Da frug ein Richkterkollege diesen jungen Richter: Wie kannst Du doch beiden Parteien das Recht zusprechen? er antwortete ihm: Du hast auch recht!

Alexander Moszkowski, DIE UNSTERBLICHE KISTE. Berlin: Verlag der "Lustigen Blätter," Dr. Eysler & Co., 1908; p. 68.

Richter: Der Kläger hat Recht!
(Nachdem der Anwalt der Gegenpartei gesprochen:)
Der Beklagte hat auch Recht!
Beisitzer: Aber ich bitte Sie, es können doch nicht alle Beide Recht haben.
Richter: Der Herr Beisitzer hat auch Recht!

Manuel Nuél [Schnitzer], RABBI LACH UND SEINE GESCHICHTEN. Berlin: Hesperus, 1910; pp. 58-59.

Dieser selbe unweise Rabbi galt auch als übler Richter, und mit gutem Fug. Denn er war habsüchtig und ließ sein Urteil durch Geschenke bestechen.

Eines Tages kam Elkan Gelenkwasser zu ihm und trug ihm seinen Streit mit Markus Aschtopf vor, in dem der Rabbi die Entscheidung treffen sollte. Er brachte eine fette Gans mit.

(cont.)

Nuél, *cont.*

Also included in
Manuel Schnitzer's
RABBI LACH.
EIN KULTUR-
DOKUMENT IN
ANEKDOTEN.
Hamburg: Verlag W.
Gente, 1921; p. 80.

Der Rabbi sagte: "Elkan Gelenkwasser, es ist kein Zweifel. Ihr habt recht!"

Dann schlich sich Markus Aschtopf ins Haus. Er brachte zwei Gänse mit, und der Rabbi sagte:

"Markus Aschtopf, es ist kein Zweifel. Jetzt habt Ihr recht."

Des Rabbi Frau, die diese falschzüngigen Urteile mitangehört hatte, rief empört: "Du Spitzbube, du Schande unter den Rabbis, wie kannste erst Elkan Gelenkwasser und dann Markus Aschtopf sagen: 'Ihr habt recht'?...Wo doch nur einer kann recht haben?"

Da sagte der Rabbi: "Jetzt hast du recht!"

ALE GERECHT

Immanuel Olsvanger,
ROZINKESS MIT
MANDLEN. Zurich:
Die Arche, 1965 (orig.
pub. 1920);
p. 138.

The same text, dif-
fering only with
regard to spelling,
later appears in
Olsvanger's RÖYTE
POMERANTSEN.
New York: Schocken,
1965 (orig. pub.
1935);
p. 168.

Zu ejnem a row sanen gekumen zwej iden mit a dintêjre. Zwej schejne iden, mit berd, mit pejess, we ess badarf zu sajn. Di rebezn is gewejntach êjch gesessen in schtub. Macht der row zu ejnem fun di iden: "Nu, woss tajnet ir?" Sogt er, asêj un asêj is gewén di majsse, un er mus bazolen un er mus doss un er mus jenss; a kiser, er hot asêj fajn geret un asêj b'schajnperlach darwisen, as er wejss, woss er fordert, as der row hot em gemusst sogen: "Ir sajt gerecht". "Nu, un woss tajnet ir?" macht der row zum zwejten iden. Is ober der zwejter id êjch kejn nar nit gewén, un hot êjch gehat a maul af zum rejden, hot er darwisen b'schajn-perlach, as er wejss nit fun woss zu sogen, un as er is nit schuldig kejn kopike. Macht der row zum iden: "Ir sajt gerecht". Hot doss di rebezn nit gekent heren, macht si zu-n-em: "Solstu gesunt un schtark sajn! wi ken doss sajn, as bejde solen recht hoben? As ejner gewint, mus doch der anderer farliren". Macht der row zu der rebezn: "Du bist êjch gerecht".

J. Ch. Rawnitzky,
YIDISHE WITZN.
New York: Morris S.
Sklarsky, 1950
(orig. pub. 1923);
vol. 1, p. 145.

אויך גערעכט .303

איינער איז געקומען צום דראזשנער רב און זיך באַקלאָגט פאַר
אים אויף זיינעם אַ שותּף. אייסגעהערט די טענות זיינע, זאָגט אים
דער רב, אַז ער איז גערעכט.

דער איז אַוועקגעגאנגען, קומט נאכדעם דער צווייטער שותּף
און דערציילט דעם רב זיינע טענות, גיט אים דער רב אויך גערעכט.

די רביצין האָט עס געהערט, וואונדערט זי זיך, און נאכדעם
זי דער צווייטער שותּף איז אַוועקגעגאנגען פרעגט זי דעם רב:

— ווי קען דאָס זיין, אַז ביידע זאָלן זיין גערעכט?

דער רב האָט זיך אַ ביסל פאַרטראַכט און געענטפערט:

— וואָס מיינסטו, דו ביסט טאַקע אויך גערעכט.

EVERYBODY RIGHT

Jacob Richman,
LAUGHS FROM
JEWISH LORE.
New York and
London: Funk &
Wagnalls, 1926;
pp. 24-25.

The venerable rabbi was sitting in the capacity of Judge. The case involved thousands of rubles, and the controversy between the litigants was very spirited.

"One at a time," ordered the rabbinic Magistrate. "Reb Yossel, you are the plaintiff, let me hear what you have to say." Reb Yossel told a long and convincing story, at the end of which the rabbi gravely remarked: "You are perfectly right."

"Reb Moishe, now we'll hear what you have to say," said the divine to the defendant; and at the end of his story the minister again observed: "You are perfectly right."

"For Heaven's sake!" exclaimed the "rebitzin" (rabbi's wife), who had been witnessing the proceedings, "how can they both be right?"

"Well," drawled the sage, abstractly, "I think you too are right."

"YOU ARE ALSO RIGHT"

Solomon Michael
Neches,
"AS 'TWAS TOLD TO
ME"; A HUNDRED
LITTLE STORIES OF
THE OLD RABBIS .
Los Angeles, 1926;
pp. 9-10.

The same version
is found in Neches'
HUMOROUS TALES
OF LATER DAY
RABBIS. New York:
Dobsevage, 1938;
pp. 23-24.

Reb Moishelle Charif of Boiberick was known all over the "world" as a great Talmudist, and a very pious man, but was very much preoccupied in his studies, so that sometimes he took scant notice of worldly affairs; people say he would have forgotten many times even to eat, were it not for his dear old Rabbetzin who reminded him about it.

One day while Reb Moishelle was occupied in a deep study of a very tangled affair in the Talmud, there came to him a man complaining of the wrong his neighbor had done to him. Reb Moishelle heard his story and said to him:

"You are right."

Soon the man's neighbor came in and made a cross-complaint to the Rabbi, stating his side of the story; Reb Moishelle said to him also: "You are right."

At this the Rabbetzin, who had heard the proceedings, could not restrain herself any longer, and exclaimed with astonishment, "Oi Moishelle, Moishelle dear! How in the world can they both be right? One of them surely must be wrong!"

Whereat the Rabbi turned to her and said with mild surprise: "Yes, yes; you are also right."

JÜDISCHE
SCHWÄNKE.
Vienna: R. Löwit,
1928; pp. 147-148.

Zwei Juden bringen einem Rechtsstreit vor den Row. Wie gewöhnlich sitzt die Rebezen auch im Zimmer. Der Row fragt den einen: "Nun, was hast du zu sagen?" Der Jude erzält die Sache von A bis Z, begründet seine Ansprüche und erweist sein Recht in so wohlgesetzter Rede, dass der Row ihm sagt: "Du hast recht." Dann wendet er sich an den anderen Juden: "Nun, was hast du zu sagen?" Der zweite Jude, der auch nicht auf den Mund gefallen ist, beweist sein Recht ebenso eingehend und klar; er habe keinerlei Ansprüche zu erfüllen und dergleichen. Der Row sagt ihm: "Du hast recht." Der Rebezen geht das über die Hutschnur und sie sagt ihrem Mann: "Leben sollst du und gesund sein! Beide können doch unmöglich recht haben; hat der eine recht, so muss doch der andere unrecht haben."–"Da hast du auch recht"–begütigt der Row seine Frau.

AN IMPARTIAL JUDGE

Rufus Learsi,
THE BOOK OF
JEWISH HUMOR.
New York: Bloch,
1941; pp. 33-34.

Reprinted in Learsi's
FILLED WITH
LAUGHTER.
New York and
London: Thomas
Yoseloff, 1961;
pp. 102-103.

What is most important in the character of a judge? All will admit that impartiality is most important. The impartiality of the rabbi of Chelem was famous for miles around.

Two litigants came to him one day to settle their dispute. After listening long and patiently to the plaintiff, he said to him: "You are in the right."

Then he listened to the defendant and said to him: "You are in the right."

The litigants departed highly pleased, but the rabbi's wife, who was present, was puzzled. A mere woman, what would she understand of legal matters?

"How is it possible," said she, "that they should both be in the right?"

The rabbi pondered the question long and deeply. Finally he turned to his good wife and said:

"Shall I tell you something? You are also in the right."

EVERYBODY WAS HAPPY

S. Felix Mendelsohn,
LET LAUGHTER
RING.
Philadelphia: Jewish
Publication Society,
1941; p. 41.

The scholarly rabbi was interrupted in his deep study of the talmud by two litigants, Moses and Aaron, who came for the purpose of straightening out a serious business difference. Moses spoke first.

"After listening to that story," said the rabbi, "I am inclined to think that Moses is right."

Aaron spoke next.

(cont.)

Mendelsohn, *cont.*

"Now that I have heard the other side," said the rabbi, "I believe that Aaron is right."

The litigants were bewildered. The rebbitzin tried to save the situation.

"It is not my business to interfere," remarked the rebbitzin, "but how is it possible for both to be right?"

"Well, now," replied the rabbi, "it is perfectly evident that the rebbitzin too is right."

Harry Schnur, JEWISH HUMOR. London: Allied Book Club, n.d. [1945]; pp. 54-55.

The Rabbi is a good kind soul, always willing to see the other fellow's point of view. This makes him easy to live with, but does not qualify him as a judge–as shown when two men bring a case before him.

The plaintiff states his case so convincingly that the Rabbi immediately exclaims: "You are right!"

The defendant protests: "But you know that the Bible says that both parties must be heard. Let me put my case."

He proceeds to do so–again so convincingly that the Rabbi exclaims: "You are right."

The Rabbi's wife who has been present as a listener can no longer contain herself. "How can you say to both of them that they are in the right? One must be right, and the other is bound to be in the wrong."

The Rabbi says: "You, too, are right, my dear."

ALL RIGHT

Nathan Ausubel, TREASURY OF JEWISH FOLK-LORE. New York: Crown, 1948; p. 22. Also included in the 1980 Bantam edition on p. 24.

There was once a rabbi who was so open-minded that he could see every side of a question. One day a man came to him to request that he grant him a divorce.

"What do you hold against your wife?" asked the rabbi gravely.

The man went into a lengthy recital of his complaints. "You are right," he agreed when the man finished. Then the rabbi turned to the woman.

"Now let us hear your story," he urged.

And the woman in her turn began to tell of the cruel mistreatment she had suffered at her husband's hands.

The rabbi listened with obvious distress.

"You are right," he said with conviction when she finished.

At this, the rabbi's wife, who was present, exclaimed, "How can this be? Surely, both of them couldn't be right!"

The rabbi knitted his brows and reflected.

"You're right, too!" he agreed.

Joey Adams,
JOEY ADAMS
JOKE BOOK.
New York: Fell, 1952;
pp. 106-107.

Harry Hershfield loves to rib members of the bench. He tells the story about the happy judge who wanted to please everybody.

"My wife is a pain in the neck," said the plaintiff, "and I'm elevating it. She doesn't cook supper for me, she's out playing cards all night and she neglects our children. I want a divorce."

The jurist answered solemnly, "You're right."

The wife spoke up and said, "But, Your Honor, he stays away for days at a time. He comes home drunk and beats me! I want a hundred dollars a week and custody of the children."

The judge looked down and said, "You're right."

One of the laywers spoke up and said, "Judge, they can't both be right!"

The judge looked at him happily and said, "You're right, too!"

Ausor Rajower,
MASSES UND
CHOCHMES.
JUDISCHER
HUMOR.
Zurich: Scheffel-
verlag, 1959; p. 11.

Zum Rabbi kommt Jankele, um ihm von seinen Händeln mit Jizchok zu erzählen, und um ihn zu fragen, ob er richtig gehandelt habe.

"Du hast recht", antwortet ihm der Rabbi.

Und am gleichen Abend erscheint dann auch eben jener Jizchok, um seinerseits um des Rabbis Meinung in diesem Streit zu bitten.

"Du hast recht", beruhigt ihn der Rabbi.

Nachdem auch Jizchok gegangen ist, kann sich des Rabbis Weib, die sich alles schweigend mit angehört hat, nicht enthalten, ihm vorzuhalten:

"Wenn du in dieser Geschichte dem Jankele recht gibst, muss doch Jizchok im Unrecht sein? Und umgekehrt muss doch Jankele im Unrecht sein, wenn du Jizchok recht gibst? Beide können doch nicht recht haben!"

"Du hast auch recht", beschwichtigt sie der Rabbi.

Harry Hershfield,
LAUGH LOUDER,
LIVE LONGER.
New York: Grayson,
1959; p. 116.

Up to judge came the plaintiff and told his story. When he finished, His Honor said to him: "You're right." Then up came the defendant and gave his testimony, to which the judge said: "You're right." Then the clerk whispered to the judge: "Your Honor, they can't both be right." "You're right, also," whispered back the judge.

THE BALANCE OF JUSTICE

Martin Rywell,
LAUGHING
WITH TEARS.
Harriman:
Pioneer Press,
1960; p. 130.

The rabbi listened to the story of his grievances as he sought a divorce, and said, "According to your story, you are right." The wife protested and recited her version of the differences and the rabbi said, "According to your story, you are right." Whereupon the rabbi's wife who had overheard the procedure asked the rabbi, "I'm bewildered. How is it possible for both sides to be right?" "My dear wife," answered the rabbi, "You are also right."

Milton Rokeach,
THE OPEN AND
CLOSED MIND.
New York: Basic
Books, 1960; pp. 3-4.

One day there came to visit the town Rabbi a man and wife who were in dispute over a marital problem. In accord with tradition, the Rabbi was to hear boths sides of the argument and then decide who was right. He first heard the husband's side of the story and, when he was finished, the Rabbi said to him: "You are right." Then he heard the wife's side of the story. "You are right," the Rabbi said. When they both left, the Rabbi's wife stepped from her hiding place behind the draperies. She had overheard everything. "But how could they both be right?" she asked. The Rabbi answered: "You are right."

Hans and Renate
Nicklas,
SCHNORRER-
SCHADCHEN-
RABBI. Weisbaden:
Falken-Verlag Erich
Sicker, 1962; p. 82.

Zum Rabbi kommt ein Jude und bringt seine Klage vor. Der Rabbi hört sich geduldig die Klagerede an. Schliesslich entscheidet er: "Du hast recht."

Nach einer Weile erscheint der Beschuldigte. Auch er erklärt ausführlich den Vorfall–jedoch so, dass er im Recht erscheint. Der Rabbi hört wiederum geduldig die Rede an und sagt schliesslich: "Du hast recht."

Die Frau des Rabbiners hat die beiden Gespräche mit angehört und meint nun zu ihrem Mann:

"Was sind das für Entscheidungen, die du triffst! Es kann doch nur einer von den beiden recht haben!"

Der Rabbi: "Du hast auch recht!"

Salcia Landmann,
DER JÜDISCHE
WITZ. Breisgau:
Walter Verlag, 1960;
p. 160.

Ein Jude kommt zum Rabbi und führt Klage gegen seinen betrügerischen Lieferanten. Der Rabbi hört aufmerksam zu und erklärt dann: "Du hast recht."

Bald danach kommt der beschuldigte Lieferant und klagt seinerseits über den Ankläger. Der Rabbi hört wieder sehr aufmerksam zu und sagt wieder: "Du hast recht."

(cont.)

Landmann, *cont.*

Also in Landmann's JÜDISCHE WITZE. Munich: Deutscher Taschenbuch Verlag, 1982 (orig. pub. 1962); p. 89.

Die Frau des Rabbiners hat beide Entscheide mit angehört, und als der Lieferant weggegangen ist, sagt sie vorwurfsvoll zu ihrem Manne: "Es können doch niemals beide recht haben!" Da gibt der Rabbi zu: "Da hast du auch recht."

Hermann Hakel, OI, BIN ICH GESCHEIT! Munich: Südwest Verlag, [1965]; pp. 54-55.

Zwei Juden bringen einen Rechtsstreit vor den Rabbi. Der eine schildert den Fall: "Rabbi, in meinem Garten steht ein Apfelbaum. Ein Ast hängt hinüber in den Garten meines Nachbars. Aber der Baum ist meiner–dann gehören doch auch die Äpfel mir."

"Hast recht", sagt der Rabbi.

Doch der Nachbar sieht den Fall anders: "Rabbi, der Baum gehört jenem, da hat er recht. Aber die Äpfel, die in meinen Garten herüberhängen, sind doch meine Äpfel."

"Hast recht", sagt der Rabbi.

Der Schüler hat dem Streit und der Entscheidung aufmerksam zugehört. Jetzt sagt er verwundert: "Rabbi, du gibst dem einen recht und dem anderen recht. Es können doch nicht zwei recht haben an einer Sache."

Sagt der Rabbi: "Hast auch recht."

Lillian Mermin Feinsilver, THE TASTE OF YIDDISH. New York: Thomas Yoseloff, 1970; p. 69.

BIST OYCH GERECHT! (ironic).

You're right, too!

This is a famous punch line of an old tale about a rabbi who is asked to settle a dispute. To each of the two complainants he listens and comments, "You're right." When a third person exclaims that they can't both be right, he nods, "You're right, too." The implication is that no one is ever wholly right or wholly wrong.

Hermann Hakel, WENN DER REBBE LACHT. ANEKDOTEN. Munich: Kindler, 1970; p. 65.

Zu Reb Jossel von Drozne–einige sagen, es sei der Rebbe von Chelm gewesen–kamen zwei Juden und verlangten seine Entscheidung über einen Streitfall.

Der Rebbe hört den ersten an und sagt kurz und bündig: "Hast recht!" Der Rebbe hört den zweiten an und sagt wieder kurt und bündig: "Hast recht!"

Mischt sich die Rebbezin in die Verhandlung ein: "Reb Loksch, was heisst? Es können doch nicht beide recht haben?"

Antwortet ihr der Rebbe ebenso kurz und bündig wie zuvor: "Hast auch recht!"

Leo Rosten:
THE JOYS OF
YIDDISH.
London: W. H. Allen,
1970; pp. 101-102.

A husband and wife came to the learned *dayan* [rabbinical judge], wrangling and fuming. The *dayan* first asked the woman into his study, where she plunged into a recitation of her husband's unkindnesses and inconsiderateness.

"–and I can't stand it any more, rabbi! I want to leave him! I want a divorce!"

The *dayan* nodded gravely. "You're right," he said and sent her out.

Now her husband entered, ranting: "She probably told you such a *megillah* of lies I wouldn't recognize them! The truch is she's a lazy, no-good *yenta,* a terrible *baleboosteh*, she's mean to me and my friends, I should throw her out of the house! I want a divorce!"

"You're right," said the *dayan*.

The man left.

One of the *dayan*'s students, who had observed all this with a puzzled air, inquired: "But *rebbe:* you told her *she* was right, and you told him *he* was right; I don't see how both of them can be–"

"You're *right!*" said the *dayan*.

FIDDLER ON THE
ROOF (1971). Pro-
duced and directed
by Norman Jewison,
Screenplay by
Joseph Stein.

[Early in the film, the men of Anatevka are gathered around Tevye's wagon, Avram having just told them of an article in the newspaper about Jews being evicted from their homes in another village.]

Perchik	You should know what is going on in the outside world.
Mordcha	Why should I break my head about the outside world. Let the outside world break its own head! Well put! (Laughs)
Tevye	He's right. As the good book says, if you spit in the air, it lands on your face.
Perchik	Nonsense! You can't close your eyes to what's happening in the world!
Tevye	He's right.
Avram	*He's* right (pointing to Mordcha), and *he's* right (pointing to Perchik), they can't both be right!
Tevye	You know, you are also right.

NÅR ALLE HAR RET

Bronislaw
Aleksandrowicz,
JØDISK HUMOR
FRA POLEN OG
RUSLAND.
Copenhagen:
Gyldendal, 1973;
p. 20.

Chaim og Salman gik op til rabbineren for at lade ham afgøre, hvem af dem der havde ret i en sag, de længe havde skændtes om.

– Chaim, vil du forklare hvad det drejer sig om, sagde rabbineren.

Chaim forklarede sagen i alle dens detaljer og spurgte til sidst:

– Hvem har så ret?

– Det har du, svarede rabbineren, men nu er det din tur, Salman, til at fortælle, hvordan sagen hænger sammen.

Salman gav sin version af sagen og spurgte så:

– Hvem har så ret efter denne forklaring?

– Også du har ret.

Rabbinerens kone, der havde hørt det hele, spurgte overrasket:

– Er det muligt, at de begge to har ret samtidig?

– Ja, sagde rabbineren, også du, min kæreste, har ret.

Henry B. Berman,
HAVE I GOT A JOKE
FOR YOU. New
York: Hart, 1975;
p. 73.

Simon R. Pollack,
JEWISH WIT FOR
ALL OCCASIONS.
New York: A & W
Publishers, 1979;
p. 73.

A man and his wife came to the village rabbi. The woman poured out a long history of her misery at the hands of her husband. "I can't stand it!" she wound up with. "He's awful!"

The old rabbi took her hand and said, "You're right."

Next it was the husband's turn. His story was just as accusing. He complained tearfully about his wife's behavior, citing many misdeeds.

The rabbi patted the man gently on the back, and said to him, "You're right."

A student who had been permitted to listen to both interviews now approached the rabbi, and whispered, "How can it be, rabbi? You told her *she* was right, and now you tell him *he* is right. How can both of them be right?"

"Ah!" answered the rabbi. "You're right, too!"

DAS URTEIL

Alexander
Drozdzynski,
YIDDISCHE WITZE
UND SCHMONZES.
Dusseldorf: Droste
Verlag, 1976; p. 89.

Zwei Juden hatten einen Streit und kamen zum Rabbiner. Der Rabbi hörte den einen an und sagte:

"Du hast recht".

Dann hörte er den anderen an und sagte:

"Du hast recht".

Daraufhin fragte ihn seine Frau:

"Wie kommt es, dass du den beiden zerstrittenen Seiten recht gibst. Entweder die eine oder die andere Seite kann nur recht haben."

Darauf der Rabbi:

"Du hast auch recht."

William Novak and
Moshe Waldoks,
THE BIG BOOK OF
JEWISH HUMOR.
New York: Harper &
Row, 1981; p. 57.

The most famous of these stories has to do with the two
litigants who come before the rabbi. After hearing the first
testimony, the rabbi says, "It seems that you are right." But
after the second man speaks, the rabbi says, "It seems that
you are right too."

"How can this be?" says the rabbi's wife, who has been
listening to the arguments. "How can both of these men be
right?"

"Hm," says the rabbi. "You're right too."

Sanford Triverton,
COMPLETE BOOK
OF ETHNIC JOKES.
New York: Galahad,
1981; p. 205.

A man and his wife came to the village rabbi. The woman
poured out a long history of her misery at the hands of her
husband. "I can't stand it!" she wound up with. "He's awful!"

The old rabbi took her hand and said, "You're right."

Next it was the husband's turn. His story was just as
accusing. He complained tearfully about his wife's behavior,
citing many misdeeds.

The rabbi patted the man gently on the back, and said to
him, "You're right."

A student who had been permitted to listen to both
interviews now approached the rabbi, and whispered,
"How can it be, rabbi? You told her *she* was right, and now
you tell him *he* is right. How can both of them be right?"

"Ah!" answered the rabbi. "You're right, too!"

Henri Atlan,
A TORT ET A
RAISON. INTER-
CRITIQUE DE LA
SCIENCE ET DU
MYTHE. Paris: Seuil,
1986; p. 6.

Un maître rendait la justice entre deux plaignants devant
ses disciples. Au premier qui exposait son cas, le juge après
une longue réflexion décida de donner raison. Mais quand
le deuxième eut fini de plaider, le juge, encore après avoir
réfléchi longuement, lui donna aussi raison. Aux disciples
qui s'étonnaient alors que leur maître pût ainsi donner
raison aux deux versions contradictoires des mêmes faits, le
juge répondit, après une nouvelle et longue réflexion: "En
effet, vous aussi avez raison."

Kjeld Koplev,
GUDS UDVALGTE.
Copenhagen: Haase,
1988; p. 57.

Jøder bryder sig ikke om de store personlige uoverens-stemmelser. De er mere indstillet på at give alle ret for ikke at blive uvenner med nogen. Det viser historien om Salomon og Chaim, der ville have mange års strid ud af verden og derfor gik til deres rabbiner.

Først hørte han på Salomons udlægning af sagen.

– Så har du ret, sagde rabbineren, da Salomon var færdig.

– Ikke når du hører min, sagde Chaim og begyndte sin udlægning.

– Jo, du har også ret, var rabbinerens konklusion.

– Men de kan da ikke begge to have ret, brød rabbiner-ens kone ind. Hun havde overværet hele sagen.

– Jo, min kæreste, sagde rabbineren, –og du har også ret.

CHI HA RAGIONE?

Matilde Cohen
Sarano, STORIE
DI GIOCHÀ.
RACCONTI
POPOLARI
GIUDEO-
SPAGNOLI.
Florence: Sansoni,
1990. Told in
Hebrew to the author
in 1984 by Mishel
Nachum, born in
Turkey.

Due che stavano discutendo fra di loro vennero dal *chogia* [giudice] perché dicesse loro chi di loro due aveva ragione.

Il *chogia* sentì le ragioni dell'uno e gli disse:

– Hai ragione tu!

Sentì le ragioni dell'altro e gli disse:

– Hai ragione anche te!

Intanto uscì dalla cucina la moglie del *chogia,* che aveva sentito quello che stava dicendo, e gli disse:

– Come è possibile che tutti e due abbiano ragione!

– Hai ragione anche te! – le disse il *chogia.*

Chapter 2

Man versus God in a Classic Jewish Joke

Yossel stops in at Rabinovitch's shop and orders a pair of pants from him.

"But it's on one condition: that you deliver the pants to me tomorrow evening. I need them; I'm about to set out on a trip. Otherwise I'll go to Hirschberg."

"Count on me. I give you my word of honor that you will have them tomorrow evening."

But Rabinovitch is lazy and forgets his customer's order. Two years later, he remembers, hurriedly makes the pants and rushes off to deliver them. Yossel looks very displeased:

"Rabinovitch, you're some tailor! It takes you two years to make a pair of pants, while God needed only six days to create the world!"

"Yossel, please, don't compare me to God: take a look at the world, and just look at these pants!"

Raymond Geiger, *Nouvelles histoires juives* (Paris: NRF, 1925), p. 117; my translation.

The History and Variants of the Joke

The Joke in its Original Form

Presumably of East European origin – though only its flavor, rather than concrete evidence, points in that direction – this is one of the few classic Jewish jokes whose circulation in the West began in France, where it appeared in print for the first time in the mid 1920's as shown above (Geiger, 1925).

Although jokes often appear in a somewhat rudimentary form the first time they are in print, this story was fully elaborated from the very beginning and its original publication is as complete an expression as can be found of the principal and most satisfying form this joke has taken.

Here the joke begins and ends with a dialogue, contains a broken promise and concludes with a statement accompanied by a gesture. In none of the other forms of this story is the symmetry as complete, the punchline as well prepared or the same sense of closure provided at the end.

As it happens, the only other pure example of this original story is also French:[1]

Moshe stops in at the shop of Levy, his tailor.
- "I need a pair of paints, but it's urgent! I must have them tomorrow evening. Can you do it?"
- "Of course! What a miserable tailor I would be if I couldn't produce a pair of pants within twenty-four hours... Trust me: tomorrow evening they'll be ready!"
But the tailor is not really up to it and he has a lot of other things on his mind. He completely forgets about the pants. Six months later, he suddenly remembers, does the job and brings the pants to Moshe.
- "Levy, Levy – you're incredible! You promise me a pair of pants for the next day and you show up with them six months later! Don't you think they took a little long? And tell me: how can you take six months to make a pair of pants when God took only six days to create the world?"
- "Moshe, please. How can you compare me to God? Just look at the world! And look at these pants!"

Here, again, the punchline contains no explicitly valuative words regarding either the world or the pants, thereby leaving it entirely up

---

[1] *Popeck raconte les meilleures histoires de l'humour juif* (Paris: Mengès, 1978), p. 19; reprinted in *Encyclopédie internationale du rire* (Paris: Mengès, 1981), p. 197. My translation.

to the reader to grasp what the tailor means. Much of the charm of the joke results from by-passing explicit valuation, and some of that charm is lost in otherwise faithful retellings of the joke when references are made to "this phooey world" (Asimov, 1972) or to "the mess God made" and these "beautiful," "gorgeous," or "lovely" trousers (Ausubel, 1948; Spalding, 1969; Marks, 1985).

Two Future-Tense Variants

As the story appears in some anthologies, it is while the customer is still waiting interminably that he complains to the tailor. The joke appeared in this form for the first time in Vienna in 1933:[2]

A man orders a suit from a tailor, who delays doing the work for weeks on end and continues putting his customer off from one day to the next. When the customer's patience finally runs out, he says to the tailor: "God created the world in six days, while you take weeks and weeks to make a suit!" – "Ha," replies the tailor, "but what does the world look like and how is your suit going to look?"

Here, not only is the initial dialogue omitted, but also the tailor's finished product. Consequently, the reader has less to visualize and savor, and the joke provides a weaker form of closure.

There is another variant which also ends without the tailor proudly pointing to the product of his labor when the punchline is delivered. In this case, what had formerly been the initial and final dialogues are both rolled into one:[3]

Harry had heard of a tailor who was supposed to be a genius. A business associate who recommended him certainly wore good-looking suits. So Harry went downtown to see the man.
   –"Sure I can make a suit for you, mister. But it'll take me thirty days."

---

[2] J. Kreppel, *Wie der Jude lacht* (Vienna: Verlag "Das Buch," 1933), p. 2; my translation. Other examples of this variant can be found in anthologies by Adam (1966), Rosten (1970), Aleksandrowicz (1975) and Koplev (1988). The joke is also told in this form, though with more elaborate embroidery, by the character Nagg in Samuel Beckett's play, *Fin de partie* (1957); here the tailor is identified as an Englishman, with no ethnic tagging.
[3] Henry B. Berman, *Have I Got a Joke for You* (New York: Hart, 1975), p. 154. The joke is also found in Simon R. Pollack, *Jewish Wit for All Occasions* (New York: A & W Publishers, 1979), p. 154 – the Berman and Pollack books being identical in every respect except for the author's name and the title of the book.

-"Thirty days!" cried Harry in dismay. "Why it only took God six days to make the entire universe!"

-"*Nu*," shrugged the tailor, "and look at what he turned out."

The Returning Visitor Variant

In yet another version of the narrative – this one found in the earliest American publication of the joke – the customer is a visitor to the town in which the tailor lives. Once again, the initial dialogue is absent and the joke correspondingly poorer:[4]

A BOTCH VERSUS A MASTERPIECE

A wealthy Jewish merchant from Berlin came to a small Galician town on business and ordered a pair of trousers from a local tailor. The merchant remained in the town for two weeks but his trousers were still not ready.

Two years later business again brought the merchant to the same town.

This time the tailor delivered the trousers.

"That's certainly strange," remarked the merchant. "God created the whole world in six days but it took you two years to turn out one pair of trousers." "Pardon me," said the tailor, "your comparison is not a good one. Look carefully at the world and then look at these trousers."

The Second Punchline Variant

As mentioned earlier, much of the charm of the original story stems from a punchline in which essentials are left unspoken, and the joke is somewhat weakened when anthologists add remarks about "the mess God made" and the "beautiful" trousers, as though they were afraid the reader might not otherwise get the point.

However, these minor additions are nothing compared to what one anthologist did to this joke: namely, continuing the story beyond its original punchline, then diligently spelling out everything that

---

[4] S. Felix Mendelsohn, *The Jew Laughs* (Chicago: L. M. Stein, 1935), p. 31.

should have remained unspoken, and finally ending the joke with a second – or pseudo – punchline that is utterly anticlimactic:[5]

"So you've brought me my Passover clothes at last," the rich man barked at the perspiring tailor. "It certainly took you long enough! Here it is almost the eve of Passover and I was beginning to wonder if I would have to appear in *shul* in my old clothes. Don't stand at the door! Spread them out and let me see what sort of job you've done. I have to have things just right, you know."

Carefully the rich man examined the coat, the trousers, the vest. He was pleased, and his manner relented.

"If only you didn't take so long," he said in a softer voice. "The good Lord, you know," he continued with a patronizing smile, "took only six days to make this great big world of ours, and you it took two weeks to make a suit of clothes."

"Ah," said the tailor, "but look at my work, and look at the work of the Lord! Everything I have done is just right, the workmanship is without a flaw, the fit is perfect. But this world we live in! It's full of blemishes. I know that the holy books tell us the Almighty left the world imperfect on purpose. His desire is that we who live on it should finish and perfect it. Still, why must there be so much suffering in this world? So much cruelty? Why must His people Israel have to endure such a long and bitter exile? And I ask you further, why must there be so many poor people who don't deserve their riches? You know what I think?" he concluded, looking hard at his customer, "I think the Almighty could have taken a little more time, just a little more time."

The source of this additional punchline is undoubtedly the title Ausubel (1948) had given this joke in his anthology: "He should have taken more time"– Learsi using as his title, "Just a little more time." Adler (1969) followed in Learsi's misguided footsteps in allowing the original punchline to be overshadowed by a second one, his version of the joke ending this way: "That's true," replied the tailor, "But look at my suit of clothes and look at this world. Don't you think the good Lord could have taken another week?"

---

[5] Rufus Learsi, *Filled with Laughter* (New York and London: Thomas Yoseloff, 1961), pp. 196-197. Generally, Learsi [actually Israel Goldberg] is an excellent storyteller. It is only this particular joke that he manages to ruin.

Competing Jewish Conceptions of
Man's Relationship to God

In order to appreciate this joke[6] within its cultural matrix, it is essential to consider two radically different religious norms regarding the attitude required of man in his relationship to God. The reader is asked to bear with me for momentarily leading the discussion away from the joke itself.

Worshipful Reverence

One Jewish conception of man's relationship to God involves the view that man must be submissive and assume a posture of worshipful reverence. Nowhere in the Jewish tradition is this norm put forward more forcefully than in the Book of Job, written principally to undercut the view (placed in the mouths of Job's "comforters") that suffering is always merited. In this remarkable work, Job calls out to God for an explanation as to why he has been afflicted with one terrible misfortune after another. In speaking to Job from a whirlwind, God does not reply to Job's question, but rather brings him to the realization that man is too insignificant a creature to understand the order of the world. "Where wast thou when I laid the foundations of the earth?" God derisively asks. "Declare if thou hast understanding" (38:4). Repeatedly, God confronts Job with such humbling questions as:

"Hast thou entered into the springs of the sea? or hast thou walked in the search of the depth? Have the gates of death been opened unto thee? or hast thou seen the doors of the shadow of death? Hast thou perceived the breadth of the earth? declare if thou knowest all" (38:16-18).

"Canst thou lift up thy voice to the clouds, that abundance of waters may cover thee? Canst thou send lightnings, that they may go, and say unto thee, Here we are? Who hath put wisdom in the inward parts? or hath given understanding to the heart?" (38:34-36).

---

[6] All references to the joke from this point on will be to the original version, as represented in Geiger (1925) and Popeck (1978/1981).

"Doth the hawk fly by thy wisdom, and stretch her wings to the south? Doth the eagle mount up at thy command, and make her nest on high?" (39:27-28).

Having compelled Job in this way to recognize that the human mind cannot fathom the wonders of creation or the order of the universe, God speaks again, referring to Job's questioning of divine justice, and the following dialogue ensues:

"Shall he that contendeth with the Almighty instruct him? he that reproveth God, let him answer it."
Then Job answered the Lord, and said, "Behold, I am vile; what shall I answer thee? I will lay mine hand upon my mouth. Once have I spoken; but I will not answer: yea, twice; but I will proceed no further."
Then answered the Lord unto Job out of the whirlwind, and said, "Gird up thy loins now like a man: I will demand of thee, and declare thou unto me. Wilt thou also dis-annul my judgment? wilt thou condemn me, that thou mayest be righteous?" (40:2-8).

In his study of Job, Robert Gordis wrote: "The natural world, though it is beyond man's ken, reveals to him its beauty and order. It is therefore reasonable for man to believe that the universe also exhibits a moral order with pattern and meaning, though it is beyond man's power fully to comprehend. Who, then, is Job, to reprove God and dispute with Him?"[7]

While the Book of Job is unique in other respects, it is representative of one mainstream within Jewish thought, insofar as it affirms that the order of the universe lies beyond the scope of human understanding, just as the wonders of creation dwarf the possibilities of human labor. And because man is insignificant in these respects, any questioning of God's work is a presumptuous act, to be repented "in dust and ashes" (42:6).

Man as God's Equal

Another current within Jewish thought emphasizes that man's status in relation to God is that of an equal – in some ways, even a superior – partner in the ongoing process of creation; and that man has every right to question, judge and condemn God over the issue of injustice in the world.

---

[7] *The Book of God and Man. A Study of Job* (Chicago and London: University of Chicago Press, 1978; originally published 1965), p. 297.

This alternate and more radical current in Judaism will be illustrated briefly with reference to three issues that are relevant to the joke at hand.

THE SUPERIORITY OF MAN'S WORKMANSHIP

When Rabbi Akiba was asked by the Roman governor of Judea, Tineius Rufus, "Are the works of God more beautiful than those of flesh-and-blood?", Akiba answered that human art is superior, obviously not in areas that lie beyond the scope of human activity, but in the sphere of things within man's reach. The rabbi argued as follows:[8]

Bring me ears of grain and loaves of bread. Then he said to him, "Those [ears of grain] are the work of God, and these [loaves of bread] are the work of flesh-and-blood. Are they not more beautiful? Bring me hanks of flax and linens from Beth Shean! Those are the work of God and these are the work of flesh-and-blood. These are more beautiful."

In a book devoted to the Jewish conception of man as God's partner – perpetually "co-author and co-responsible for creation" along with God – Paul Giniewski commented on Akiba's courageous reply to Rufus, stating that Judaism views the world as "an arena open to the spirit of human enterprise, and where the work of man is more beautiful even than that of God, since God willed it to be so."[9] In this way, man's fulfillment of his own potential through the exercise of his skills, is seen as a process of completing and perfecting the work of God – even to the point of surpassing it in beauty.

---

[8] "Midrash Tanhuma Tazria," in Hans Bietenhard's edition of *Midrasch Tanhuma. B. R. Tanhuma über die Tora genannt Midrasch Jelammedenu* (Bern: Peter Lang, 1982), vol. 2, p. 56; my literal translation from the German. Akiba had sensed correctly that Rufus was trying to lay a trap form him with respect to the question of circumcision and answered accordingly. However the portion of his argument cited above was no mere tactic. Though they were friends at the time of this discussion, Rufus was to sentence Akiba to death and supervise his execution many years later. My source of information on Akiba is Louis Finkelstein's *Akiba. Scholar, Saint and Martyr* (New York: Atheneum, 1970).

[9] Paul Giniewski, *Les complices de Dieu* (Neuchâtel: A la baconnière, 1963), p. 136; my translation.

THE INDEPENDENCE OF HUMAN JUDGMENT

It is told in the Talmud that Rabbi Eliezer argued about a question of ritual purity with the majority of his colleagues on the rabbinical council. Unable to convince them of his point of view, yet certain that he was right, Eliezer said that if the *halacha* (religious law) was on his side, then let the carob-tree prove it. Immediately the carob-tree uprooted itself, to which the rabbi's colleagues replied, "No proof can be brought from a carob-tree." Eliezer then said, "If the *halacha* agrees with me, let the stream prove it," and the waters of the stream flowed backwards. Still his colleagues remained unimpressed, as they did when he called upon the walls of the schoolhouse to prove that he was right and the walls leaned over. Finally Eliezer called out:

"If the *halacha* agrees with me, let it be proved from Heaven!" Whereupon a Heavenly Voice cried out: "Why do ye dispute with R. Eliezer, seeing that in all matters the *halacha* agrees with him!" But R. Joshua arose and exclaimed: "It is not in Heaven." What did he mean by this? – Said R. Jeremiah: That the Torah had already been given at Mount Sinai; we pay no attention to a Heavenly Voice, because Thou hast long since written in the Torah at Mount Sinai, *After the majority must one incline.*

In other words, once the Torah has been given to man, all questions of interpretation are to be settled by a majority on the rabbinical council, without celestial interference! The best part of the story is yet to come, and concerns God's reported response to the rabbi's rejection of His intervention in this matter of interpretation. According to the Talmud,[10] the prophet Elijah happened to be with God in heaven at the time of the dispute. After the prophet had returned to earth

R. Nathan met Elijah and asked him: What did the Holy One, Blessed be He, do in that hour?– He laughed (with joy), he replied, saying, "My sons have defeated Me, My sons have defeated Me."

---

[10] "Baba Mezi'a," 59b in the volume devoted to this book in *The Babylonian Talmud*, ed. Rabbi Dr. I. Epstein (London: Soncino Press, 1935), pp. 352-353. More ample commentary on this passage will be found in the volume devoted to "Bava Mezi'a" in *The Talmud* (Jerusalem and Tel Aviv: El-'Am, 1969), pp. 180-182. It is also discussed by Immanuel Olsvanger in *Contentions with God. A Study in Jewish Folklore* (Cape Town: T. Maskew Miller, 1921), p. 14, and by Erich Fromm in *You Shall Be as Gods. A Radical Interpretation of the Old Testament and Its Tradition* (New York: Holt, Rinehart & Winston, 1966), pp. 77-79.

Here, God is conceived of as delighting in man's independence, even to the point of enjoying the rabbi's refusal of His participation in their discussion.

CHALLENGING AND JUDGING GOD

In one of the most remarkable passages of the Old Testament, in which Abraham is informed of God's plan to destroy Sodom, the patriarch presumes to ask, "Wilt thou also destroy the righteous with the wicked?" and then continues:

Peradventure there be fifty righteous within the city: wilt thou also destroy and not spare the place for the fifty righteous that are within? That be far from thee to do after this manner, to slay the righteous with the wicked: and that the righteous should be as the wicked, that be far from thee: Shall not the judge of all the earth do right? And the Lord said, If I find in Sodom fifty righteous within the city, then I will spare all the place for their sakes (Genesis 18:23-33).

Abraham continues in this manner until God agrees to spare Sodom if there are 45, 40, 30, 20 or even 10 righteous souls within the city.

In commenting on this passage, Erich Fromm wrote: "In courteous language, yet with the daring of a hero, Abraham challenges God to comply with the principles of justice. His is not the attitude of a meek supplicant but that of the proud man who has a right to demand that God uphold the principle of justice" (op. cit., p. 28). For Fromm, this daring to challenge God is representative of the "radical humanist" current within Judaism, in which "man becomes God's partner and almost his equal" (p. 47).

In essentially the same spirit, a number of Hasidic stories deal with injustice in the world as a failure on God's part to live up to his contractual responsibilities to man. One such tale involves a humble tailor who strikes a bargain with God on Yom Kippur, the solemn day of atonement for sins committed during the past year. The "Berdichever" in this story is Rabbi Levi Yitzchok of Berdichev (c. 1740-1810) who was noted for his kindliness:[11]

---

[11] Louis I. Newman, *The Hasidic Anthology* (New York: Schocken, 1975; originally published in 1934), p. 57. The same story is found in Nathan Ausubel, *Treasury of Jewish Folklore* (New York: Crown, 1948) pp. 160-161. In a Yiddish folktale entitled "Berl the Tailor," Isaac Loeb Peretz told the story of a little tailor who is ready to summon God to a rabbinical court, and whose boycotting of a Yom Kippur service – held by Rabbi Levi Yitzchock of Berdichev – results, with the rabbi's aid, in God's giving in to the tailor's

After Yom Kippur the Berdichever called over a tailor and asked him to relate his argument with God on the day before. The tailor said: "I declared to God: You wish me to repent of my sins, but I have committed only minor offenses; I may have kept left-over cloth, or I may have eaten in a non-Jewish home, where I worked, without washing my hands.

But Thou, O Lord, hast committed grievous sins: Thou has taken away babies from their mothers and mothers from their babies. Let us be quits: mayest Thou forgive me, and I will forgive Thee."

Said the Berdichever: "Why did you let God off so easily? You might have forced Him to redeem all of Israel!"

At times, this outlook led to its ultimate consequence: the convening of a *Din Torah* or rabbinical court, in order to place God on trial for the unmerited suffering of his subjects. If after weighing the evidence, the rabbis found God guilty, they might instruct Him to put an end to famine,[12] or an oppressive edict that had just been issued by the Austrian emperor might miraculously be withdrawn in the very hour the verdict against God was handed down.[13]

Such trials were also held during the Holocaust. Elie Wiesel was present at one of them, while imprisoned in a concentration camp. He wrote: "inside the kingdom of night, I witnessed a strange tribunal. Three rabbis – all erudite and pious men – decided one winter evening to indict God for allowing his children to be massacred."[14] Another commentator, Eliezer Berkowitz, told of a *Din Torah* held in the ghetto of Lodz in 1943, after twenty-two thousand Jews had been sent off to a concentration camp, and God was called upon by the rabbinical court to stop the undeserved punishment. Berkowitz added: "It is the very reality of the relationship, the intimacy between the partners of the covenant, that not only allows but, at times, requires the Jew to contend with the divine 'Thou.'"[15]

---

demand that God forgive the sins of man against man, as well as those between man and God.

[12] This was the outcome of a tribunal convened by Arye Leib of Shpole (or Spola), who died in 1811. An account of this trial is given by Elie Wiesel in *Souls on Fire. Portraits and Legends of Hasidic Masters* (New York: Vintage Books, 1973), p. 47.

[13] For accounts of this legendary trial, see Martin Buber, *Tales of the Hasidim. Early Masters* (New York: Schocken Books, 1961; originally published in 1947), pp. 258-259; and Louis I. Newman, *Hasidic Anthology* (op. cit.), pp. 58-59.

[14] Elie Wiesel, *The Trial of God (as it was held on February 25, 1649 in Shamgorod). A Play in Three Acts,* translated by Marion Wiesel (New York: Random House, 1979). This quote is from the introductory section entitled "The Scene" and explains the genesis of the play.

[15] Eliezer Berkowitz, *With God in Hell. Judaism in the Ghettos and Concentration Camps* (New York and London: Sanhedrin Press, 1979), pp. 127-128.

For some believers, the conclusion to be drawn in the face of the unrelenting massacre was to pass a bitter sentence against God. In a moving Yiddish poem by Itzik Manger (1901-1969), entitled "The Lovers of Israel in the Death Camp Belshitz," God is called to account for the "heaps of ashes on the ground," as a result of His not having "guarded His vineyard." The poem concludes as follows:[16]

> Reb Meir of Przemysl leaning on his heavy stick,
> Waits, feverish with pain:
> "Friends, let us all lift our voices, and repeat in refrain:
>
> 'Creator of the worlds, You are mighty and terrible beyond all doubt.
> But from the circle of true lovers of Israel, we Galicians,
> Forever shut you out!'"

Two Interpretations of the Joke

When the tailor says: "How can you compare me to God? Just look at the world! And look at these pants!", there are two radically different attitudes we may hold toward his statement, each of those attitudes in turn resting on assumptions as to why he speaks as he does and whether or not his remarks about God violate cultural prescriptions. I will try to outline concisely each of the two possible readings of the joke.

Tactical Manoeuvre

The tailor can be seen as a businessman who has broken a promise, risks losing a sale and a customer, and finds himself subjected to an elaborate reproach, against which any defense seems unimaginable.

With this in mind, we can easily see his statement in the punchline as a tactical manoeuvre designed to help him to complete the business transaction by promoting the virtues of his merchandise while at the same time enabling him to gain the upper hand in his

---

[16] *An Anthology of Yiddish Literature,* edited by Joseph Leftwich (The Hague and Paris: Mouton, 1974), p. 282.

relationship to an indignant customer. In this perspective, the sales-
manship and face-saving properties of the remark discredit it in our
eyes. We see through it for what it is: namely a *pseudo*-philosophical
posture used by a clever operator who knows how to turn an
unfavorable situation to his own advantage.

However, it is not only in its shrewdness as a ploy that the tailor's
remark strikes us as funny; it is also comically deviant with respect to
the religious norm requiring of man an attitude of worshipful
reverence toward God (as illustrated above in relation to the Book of
Job). In this respect, the tailor's remark – brushing off the comparison
with God as though it were an insult – comes across as outrageously
arrogant.

When the joke is understood in this perspective, we are therefore
implicitly invited to view the statement made in the punchline as
being ludicrous and deplorable in its lack of respect for God, just as it
is a clever move in a purely tactical sense.

Exemplary Deviance

Sarah Blacher Cohen[17] is the only commentator who has discussed
the meaning of this joke, which in her view

> functions as a form of camouflaged blasphemy, permitting the Jew to give witty
> expression to his disappointment at divine promises not kept and to comically censure
> himself for his own hubris at challenging God.[...] The joke disparages the reliability of the
> tailor for his failure to keep his word and for his ingenious way of deflecting criticism
> from himself. But above all, it castigates him for his impudence to see himself as the rival
> of God, as the better craftsman whose hand-sewn pair of pants is a better piece of
> handiwork than God's creation. But the joke also finds fault with God for his shoddy
> workmanship, for his creation of an imperfect world.

Although Cohen goes so far as to say that God's workmanship is
flawed according to the premises of the joke, she nevertheless
maintains that the tailor's attitude is presented as unjustified. And so
it is, when viewed from the standpoint found, for example, in the
Book of Job.

---

[17] Sarah Blacher Cohen, "Introduction: The Varieties of Jewish Humor," in *Jewish Wry:
Essays on Jewish Humor* (Bloomington and Indianapolis: Indiana University Press, 1987),
pp. 3-4.

However, when viewed in another perspective, this joke can be understood as implicitly inviting us to *applaud* the tailor's outlook – whether his "Just look at the world!" is taken as a comment on God's workmanship or as a tacit indictment of God for allowing injustice to flourish. In either case, the tailor's remarks are still deviant with respect to the norm requiring an attitude of worshipful reverence; only now, a *positive* value is ascribed to that deviance, which is held out to us as commendable.

In other words, the joke can be understood from a standpoint located in the more radical current of Judaism – the current affirming: a) the superiority of man's workmanship; b) the independence of human judgment; and c) man's right to challenge and judge God (as illustrated above).

When the joke is viewed in this perspective, the tailor's remark about the relative merits of his own work and that of God, is presented to us as utterly sincere and as rich in resonances, which connect particularly with the historical experience of the Jewish people. The very words, "Look at the world," are reminiscent of two Yiddish proverbs which implicitly deplore the injustice God allows to prevail in the world: "'The world goes on its ancient way' – that's just why it looks the way it does!" and "Ruler of the Universe: look down from heaven and take yourself a look at your world!"[18]

What is left unspoken in the tailor's words, "Look at the world," could fill a library. And needless to say, what is alluded to in these words has deeply tragic dimensions.

This highly indirect evocation of the tragic within the framework of a joke is in itself a sign that the joke is to some degree a means for sharing a moment of recognition of this somber side of human life – and also for sharing a sense that that aspect of our existence does not prevent us from engaging in a playful interaction concerning it.

Furthermore, immediately following the tacit evocation of adversity, the joke points to something which can be seen as one way of making up in part for the unfavorable conditions of existence, on a modest – even a comically modest – scale: namely the pants of which the tailor is so proud, and which might symbolize mastery and

---

[18] "'*Olom ke'minhogo noheg'–deriber zet takeh di velt azoy oys!*" and "*Riboyne-shel-oylem: kuk arop fun'm himl un kuk dir on dayn velt!*" Lillian Mermin Feinsilver, *The Taste of Yiddish* (New York and London: Thomas Yoseloff, 1970), pp. 220 and 138, respectively. The first half of each of these proverbs in Hebrew.

accomplishment in an area of life over which the individual can maintain full control, no matter what is going on in the world at large.

In these respects, a pessimistic picture of the world is taken as a spring-board for affirming nothing less than the ascendency of the human spirit in the face of adversity. How apt it was for Israel Knox to describe Jewish humor as often embodying a sense of "tragic optimism."[19]

On the Open-Endedness of the Joke

As I have tried to show, the punchline of this joke can be understood in two very different ways, both of which are represented within the basic triad: 1) as a pseudo-philosophical posture designed to promote the successful conclusion of a business transaction, and which is comical both in its shiftiness and its arrogance; and 2) as an admirable affirmation that the fruits of human labor are potentially superior to God's work, and are in some sense a compensation for those un-favorable conditions in the world over which we have no control.

These opposite meanings of the joke reflect a polarity within Jewish thought, which is summed up beautifully by a saying attri-buted to a Hasidic master, Rabbi Bunam:[20]

Everyone must have two pockets, so that he can reach into the one or the other, according to his needs. In his right pocket are to be the words: "For my sake the world was created," and in his left: "I am earth and ashes."

We find here in a nutshell the opposing currents of Jewish thought described above. But while this saying embraces both attitudes in a way that explicitly and simultaneously acknowledges the validity of each of them, our joke – as was also shown to be the case with "Rabbinic Judgment"– allows us alternately to perceive first one and then the other of its two meanings, like a reversible figure.

With "Rabbinic Judgment," a certain resonance exists between the exemplary deviance meaning, according to which the rabbi's con-

---

19 Israel Knox, "The Traditional Roots of Jewish Humor," *Judaism* 12, 3 (Summer 1963), p. 331.

20 Martin Buber, op. cit., *Later Masters*, pp. 249-250. An alternate formulation is found in Robert Gordis, op. cit., p. 131: "A man should carry two stones in his pocket. On one should be inscribed, 'I am but dust and ashes.' On the other, 'For my sake the world was created.' And he should use each stone as he needs it." Rabbi Bunam of Pshysha died in 1827.

ception of the truth allows for the validity of two or more logically incompatible statements, and the manner in which the joke itself functions, inviting us to view the same imaginary event in radically
different ways.

In the case of the joke comparing the tailor's work to that of God, a
resonance of a different kind is in play. Here, each of the two interpretations to which the joke lends itself, is rooted in a corresponding conception of man's relationship to God. In this respect, the joke's reversibility enables it to straddle two competing currents within Jewish
thought, tacitly playing them off against one another and giving each
its due.

Arthur Szyk's illustration of the joke in *Le juif qui rit*,
published in 1926 by Albin Michel.

PUBLICATION HISTORY

Raymond Geiger,
NOUVELLES
HISTOIRES JUIVES.
Paris: NRF, 1925;
p. 117.

Rabinovitch reçoit la visite de Iossel qui lui commande un pantalon.

– Mais c'est à la seule condition que vous me le livrerez demain soir. J'en ai besoin: je pars en voyage. Sinon, j'irai chez Hirschberg.

– Comptez sur moi. Je vous donne ma parole d'honneur que vous l'aurez demain soir.

Mais Rabinovitch est paresseux, il oublie la commande du client. Deux ans plus tard, il s'en souvient, fait en hâte le pantalon et court le livrer. Iossel a l'air mécontent:

– Rabinovitch, vous êtes un tailleur extraordinaire! Il vous faut deux ans pour faire un pantalon, alors qu'il n'a fallu que six jours à Dieu pour créer le monde!

– Iossel, je vous en prie, ne nous comparez pas, Dieu et moi: voyez le monde et voyez-moi ce pantalon!

JUSTIFICATION

Arthur Szyk,
LE JUIF QUI RIT, 2e
série. Paris: Albin
Michel, 1927; p. 217.

– Comment! Dieu a mis six jours pour créer le monde, et vous avez mis quatre semaines pour confectionner un pantalon?

– Sans doute, Feb? Mais aussi, regardez le monde–et regardez-moi ce pantalon!

J. Kreppel,
WIE DER JUDE
LACHT.
Vienna: Verlag "Das
Buch," 1933; p. 2.

Ein Mann bestellte beim Schneider einen Anzug. Der Schneider zögerte wochenlang mit der Anfertigung und vertröstete den Besteller immer wieder von heute auf morgen und von morgen auf übermorgen. Als dem Besteller schließlich die Geduld riss, sagte er zum Schneider: Gott erschuf die Welt in sechs Tagen, Sie aber brauchen für einen Anzug Wochen und Wochen! – "Ha"– erwiderte der Schneider – "wie schaut aber Gottes Welt aus und wie wird Ihr Anzug aussehen!"

A BOTCH VERSUS A MASTERPIECE

S. Felix Mendelsohn,
THE JEW LAUGHS.
Chicago: L. M. Stein,
1935; p. 31.

A wealthy Jewish merchant from Berlin came to a small Galician town on business and ordered a pair of trousers from a local tailor. The merchant remained in the town for two weeks but his trousers were still not ready.

Two years later business again brought the merchant to the same town.

This time the tailor delivered the trousers.

"That's certainly strange," remarked the merchant. "God created the whole world in six days but it took you two years to turn our one pair of trousers." *(cont.)*

| Mendelsohn, *cont.* | "Pardon me," said the tailor, "your comparison is not a good one. Look carefully at the world and then look at these trousers." |

| Henry Schnur, JEWISH HUMOR. London: Allied Book Club, n.d. [1945]; p. 57. | A client orders a pair of trousers from Solomon the tailor. Solomon promises prompt delivery, but he takes his time. Two months pass, three months, and only after four months are the trousers ready. |

The customer is displeased. "Look here, Solomon, God has created the whole world in six days, and you need four months for a pair of trousers."

"Yes–but look at the world, and look at these trousers."

HE SHOULD HAVE TAKEN MORE TIME

| Nathan Ausubel, TREASURY OF JEWISH FOLKLORE. New York: Crown, 1948; p. 16. | The rabbi ordered a pair of new pants for the Passovers holidays from the village tailor. The tailor, who was very unreliable, took a long time finishing the job. The rabbi was afraid that he would not have the garment ready for the holidays. |

On the day before Passover the tailor came running all out of breath to deliver the pants.

The rabbi examined his new garment with a critical eye.

"Thank you for bringing my pants on time," he said. "But tell me, my friend, if it took God only six days to create our vast and complicated world, why did it have to take you six weeks to make this simple pair of pants?"

"But, Rabbi!" murmured the tailor triumphantly, "just look at the mess God made, and then look at this beautiful pair of pants!"

| Samuel Beckett, FIN DE PARTIE. Paris: Éditions du Minuit, 1957; pp. 36-37. | NAGG.-Écoute-la encore. *(Voix de raconteur.)* Un Anglais – *(il prend un visage d'Anglais, reprend le sien)* – ayant besoin d'un pantalon rayé en vitesse pour les fêtes du Nouvel An se rend chez son tailleur qui lui prend ses mesures. *(Voix du tailleur.)* Et voilà qui est fait, revenez dans quatre jours, il sera prêt." Bon. Quatre jours plus tard. *(Voix du tailleur.)* "Sorry, revenez dans huit jours, j'ai raté le fond." Bon, ça va, le fond, c'est pas commode. Huit jours plus tard. *(Voix du tailleur.)* "Désolé, revenez dans dix jours, j'ai salopé l'entre-jambes." Bon, d'accord, l'entre-jambes, c'est délicat. Dix jours plus tard. *(Voix du tailleur.)* "Navré, revenez dans quinze jours, j'ai bousillé la braguette." Bon, à la rigueur, une belle braguette, c'est calé. |

(cont.)

Beckett, *cont.*

(Un temps. Voix normale.) Je la raconte mal. *(Un temps. Morne.)* Je raconte cette histoire de plus en plus mal. *(Un temps. Voix de raconteur.)* Enfin bref, de faufil en aiguille, voici Pâques Fleuries et il loupe les boutonnières. *(Visage, puis voix du client.)* "Goddam Sir, non, vraiment, c'est indécent, à la fin! En six jours, vous entendez, six jours, Dieu fit le monde. Oui Monsieur, parfaitement Monsieur, le MONDE! Et vous, vous n'êtes pas foutu de me faire un pantalon en trois mois!" *(Voix du tailleur, scandalisée.)* "Mais Milord! Mais Milord! Regardez–*geste méprisant, avec dégoût)* – le monde... *(un temps)* ... et regardez–*(geste amoureux, avec orgueil)* – mon PANTALON!"

JUST A LITTLE MORE TIME

Rufus Learsi,
FILLED WITH
LAUGHTER.
New York and
London: Thomas
Yoseloff, 1961;
pp. 196-197.

"So you've brought me my Passover clothes at last," the rich man barked at the perspiring tailor. "It certainly took you long enough! Here it is almost the eve of Passover and I was beginning to wonder if I would have to appear in *shul* in my old clothes. Don't stand at the door! Spread them out and let me see what sort of job you've done. I have to have things just right, you know."

Carefully the rich man examined the coat, the trousers, the vest. He was pleased, and his manner relented.

"If only you didn't take so long," he said in a softer voice. "The good Lord, you know," he continued with a patronizing smile, "took only six days to make this great big world of ours, and you it took two weeks to make a suit of clothes."

"Ah," said the tailor, "but look at my work, and look at the work of the Lord! Everything I have done is just right, the workmanship is without a flaw, the fit is perfect. But this world we live in! It's full of blemishes. I know that the holy books tell us the Almighty left the world imperfect on purpose. His desire is that we who live on it should finish and perfect it. Still, why must there be so much suffering in this world? So much cruelty? Why must His people Israel have to endure such a long and bitter exile? And I ask you further, why must there be so many poor people who don't deserve their riches? You know what I think?" he concluded, looking hard at his customer, "I think the Almighty could have taken a little more time, just a little more time."

Salcia Landmann, "On Jewish Humor," THE JEWISH JOURNAL OF SOCIOLOGY 4, 2 (December 1962), p. 204.

And, finally, a joke which, in its profundity and bitterness, seems to have undertones of Schopenhauer and Indian philosophy:

A traveller, arriving in a Galician town, orders a pair of trousers from a Jewish tailor. Three months later he leaves, without the trousers. After seven years he happens to pass through the same place again and, lo and behold, the tailor comes to deliver the trousers. "Well," the traveller exclaims, astounded, "God created the world in seven days – but you take seven years for a pair of trousers!" "True," the Jew agrees, quite unimpressed, "but look at the world – and look at my trousers."

Theodor Reik, JEWISH WIT. New York: Gamut, 1962; p. 207.

...an engineer comes to a little town in Galicia and orders a pair of trousers from the Jewish tailor. When a few weeks have passed, the trousers are still not ready; the engineer has to leave. When he returns to the town after seven years and the tailor brings him the pair of trousers, the customer says, "God has created the whole world in seven days and you need seven years to make some trousers?" But the tailor gently stroking his work replies: "Yes, but look at the world and then look at these trousers!"

Adam, L'HUMOUR JUIF. Paris: Denoël, 1966; pp. 51-52.

Moshé le tailleur, reçoit un jour la visite d'un client qui lui commande un pantalon. Moshé prend les mesures et demande au client de revenir la semaine suivante pour prendre livraison du pantalon. Huit jours plus tard, le client revient, mais le pantalon n'est pas prêt.

Le client n'est pas content, mais Moshé lui dit:

– Écoutez, si vous voulez du travail bien fait, qu'est-ce que c'est que quelques jours de plus, revenez vendredi prochain.

Le vendredi suivant, le client revient, le pantalon n'est toujours pas prêt. Alors le client, furieux:

– Enfin, Moshé, je ne comprends pas! Dieu a fait le monde en six jours, et toi en trois semaines, tu n'est pas fichu de faire un pantalon!

Alors Moshé:

– Oui, Il a fait le monde en six jours, mais quel pantalon vous allez avoir!

Bill Adler,
JEWISH WIT
AND WISDOM.
New York: Dell,
1969; pp. 143-144.

It was only two days before Passover, and the wealthy Jewish banker was furious with his tailor for not having finished his new suit sooner.

"Well," he ranted, "it certainly took you long enough! I was beginning to wonder if I would have to go to the synagogue in my old clothes. Don't just stand there, spread them out and let me see what kind of a job you have done. I demand perfection in everything, you know."

The tailor meekly displayed the new clothes. When he had carefully inspected the coat, the vest, and the trousers, the banker finally softened, for the new suit was, indeed, beautifully made.

"If only you hadn't taken so long," he said in milder tones. "The Lord, you know, only took six days to make this entire world of ours, while it took *you* two whole weeks to make this suit of clothes."

"That's true," replied the tailor, "but look at my suit of clothes, and look at this world. Don't you think the good Lord could have taken another week?"

Henry D. Spalding,
ENCYCLOPEDIA OF
JEWISH HUMOR.
New York: Jonathan
David, 1969; pp. 14-
15.

A wealthy merchant ordered a pair of new pants from the local tailor, with the stipulation that the work be finished within a week.

"Remember," said the merchant, "I must leave town next week and I will be away for six weeks on an extended buying trip. And I want those trousers for the journey."

But the tailor, an unreliable fellow, did not have the pants ready on time, and the merchant was compelled to leave without them.

Immediately upon his return he went to the tailor shop and was greeted warmly. "Here are your new pants," the tailor said proudly, holding them aloft for the customer to admire. "I just finished them."

"You just finished?" gasped the merchant. "Look, I want to ask you a question."

"*Nu*, ask!"

"Why is it that God Almighty was able to create the world – this whole universe – in only six days, but it takes you six weeks to make a simple pair of pants?"

"What kind of comparison is that?" snorted the tailor. "Just look at the mess God made, and then look at this gorgeous pair of pants *I* made!"

Leo Rosten,
THE JOYS OF
YIDDISH.
London: W. H. Allen,
1970;
p. 312.

Mr. Abraham, driven to desperation by the endless delayings of the tailor who was making him a pair of trousers, finally cried, "Tailor, in the name of heaven, it has already taken you six *weeks* !"

"So?"

"*So*, you ask? Six weeks for a pair of pants? *Riboyne Shel O'lem!* It took God only six days to create the universe"

"*Nu ,*" shrugged the tailor, "look at it..."

Harvey Mindess,
THE CHOSEN
PEOPLE. Los
Angeles: Nash,
1972; pp. 36-37.

A man orders a pair of pants from a tailor. It takes him six weeks to complete the job. Incensed, the customer berates him. "God it took only six days to create the whole world, and you it takes six weeks to make a pair of pants!"

"Yes," replies the tailor, "But look at these pants – and look at the world!"

Isaac Asimov,
TREASURY OF
HUMOR. New York:
Vallentine-Mitchell,
1972; pp. 268-269.

Jones had ordered a suit from a neighborhood tailor who had been highly recommended to him, but considerable time had passed and the suit had not yet been delivered.

In rather a passion, Jones stepped into the tailor's shop to have it out. He said, "See here, Mr. Levy, you promised to let me have the suit in two weeks, and four weeks have already passed."

"I'm working. I'm working," said Mr. Levy. "The suit is hang-ing right there. It's almost finished."

"*Almost* finished?" But why does it take you so long, Mr. Levy? The good Lord made the whole world in only six days."

Mr. Levy put down his needle, stood up, and said, "Come here, mister. I want you should feel the material on this suit I am making for you. Okay? Now I want you should come to the window and take a look at this phooey world."

HVAD SER BEDST UD?

Bronislaw
Aleksandrowicz,
JØDISKE ANEK-
DOTER. Copenhagen:
Nordisk Bogforlag,
1975; p. 26.

Chaimovitz bestiller en habit, som skrædderen lover færdig i løbet af en uge. Da han kommer for at hente tøjet, er det endnu ikke færdigt.

– Hør nu, siger han til skrædderen. – Gud brugte kun en uge til at skabe verden. Og du kan ikke engang sy en ny habit på den samme tid.

– Nej, svarede skrædderen! Men se så, hvordan verden ser ud. Og se så på min habit, når den i overmorgen blir færdig.

Henry B. Berman, HAVE I GOT A JOKE FOR YOU. New York: Hart, 1975; p. 154. Simon R. Pollack, JEWISH WIT FOR ALL OCCASIONS. New York: A & W Publishers, 1979; p. 154.

Harry had heard of a tailor who was supposed to be a genius. A business associate who recommended him certainly wore good-looking suits. So Harry went downtown to see the man.

-"Sure I can make a suit for you, mister. But it'll take me thirty days."

-"Thirty days!" cried Harry in dismay. "Why it only took God six days to make the entire universe!"

-*Nu*," shrugged the tailor, "and look at what he turned out."

Alexander Drozdzynski, JIDDISCHE WITZE UND SCHMONZES. Dusseldorf: Droste Verlag, 1976; pp. 156-157.

Ein Kunde hat bei einem jüdischen Schneider ein paar Hosen bestellt. Es dauert aber sechs Wochen, bis die Hosen endlich fertig sind. Der Kunde, verärgert über die lange Wartezeit, sagt zum Schneider:

"Euer Gott brauchte sechs Tage, um die ganze Welt zu schaffen, und Sie brauchen sechs Wochen, um ein paar lumpige Hosen zu machen?"

Darauf der Schneider:

"Bitte, schauen Sie, wie sieht die Welt aus und wie meine Hosen!"

POPECK RACONTE LES MEILLEURES HISTOIRES DE L'HUMOUR JUIF. Paris: Mengès, 1978; p. 19.

Also included in ENCYCLOPÉDIE INTERNATIONALE DU RIRE. Paris: Mengès, 1981; p. 197.

Mosché se rend chez Lévy, son tailleur.

- J'ai besoin d'un pantalon, mais c'est urgent! Il me le faut absolument pour demain soir. C'est possible?

- Évidemment! Quel piètre tailleur je serais si je n'étais pas capable de fabriquer un pantalon en 24 heures... Sur ma vie, demain soir ce sera prêt!

Mais Lévy n'est pas très courageux et, de plus, il est distrait. Il oublie complètement de faire le pantalon... Et ne s'en souvient que 6 mois plus tard il se met au travail et va porter le vêtement à Mosché.

- Mon cher Lévy! Vous êtes fabuleux... Vous me promettez un pantalon pour le lendemain et vous me le livrez six mois plus tard... Cela ne vous semble-t-il pas un peu longuet? Et dites-moi comment se fait-il que vous mettiez six mois pour faire un pantalon quand Dieu a mis six jour pour créer le Monde?

- Mosché! Ne me comparez pas à Dieu... Voyez le Monde! Et voyez mon pantalon...

Leo Rosten, HOORAY FOR YIDDISH. New York: Simon & Schuster, 1982; p. 169.

The story is of told of the great pianist Leopold Godowski, who was having a suit made for a national tour.

Driven to desperation by the endless delays of the tailor, Godowski finally cried, "Tailor, in the name of heaven! It has already taken you six *weeks*."

"So?"

"So? Six weeks for a pair of pants? It took God only six days to create the universe!"

"*Nu*," sighed the tailor, "look at it."

Alfred Marks, A MEDLEY OF JEWISH HUMOR. London: Robson Books, 1985; pp. 111-112.

A man who needed a pair of trousers for an impending holiday went to his local tailor to be measured.

"That's all, Sir," said the tailor, putting his tape-measure away. "I'll have them ready for you in four days."

"I'm sorry, Sir," said the tailor, "I've made a mess of the seat. Come back next week."

A week later, the man returned.

"Forgive me," said the tailor, "but your trousers are still not ready. You'll have to come back after your holiday."

The man was furious, but realized that it was no use arguing. He returned to the tailor on the day he got back from holiday, four weeks later.

"You'll never believe it," said the tailor, "but I've had a lot of trouble with the flies. Come back tomorrow and they'll be perfect."

The man couldn't hold back his anger any longer. "For God's sake, man, this is too much, too much. Six days, I repeat, six days it took the Almighty to create the whole world. *The world, I say!* Yet you are not capable of making a single pair of trousers in six weeks!"

"Please, sir, please," replied the tailor. "You've been unfair. I mean, look at the mess God made of the world–and then look at my *lovely* trousers!"

Kjeld Koplev, GUDS UDVALGTE. Copenhagen: Haase, 1988; p. 35.

Unge fremadstormende og meget utålmodige Levinson, råbte desperat til skrædderen.

– I himlens navn, hvornår er de bukser færdige? Det har allerede taget dig seks uger nu.

– Og hvad så?

– Og hvad så? Seks uger for et par bukser. Det tog kun Gud seks dage at skabe Jorden.

–Se på resultatet og se så på mine bukser, når de engang er færdige.

Ferruccio Fölkel,
NUOVE STORIELLE
EBRAICHE. Milan:
Rizzoli, 1990; p. 73.

Un ingegnere viennese, tale Isacco Funkenstein, viene mandato per lavoro in una cittadina della Galizia dove ordina a un suo amico, il sarto Fischer, un paio di pantaloni. Purtroppo i pantaloni non sono pronti in tempo e Funkenstein deve rientrare a Vienna.

Sette anni dopo l'ingegnere ritorna nella stessa cittadina e il suo amico Fischer gli porta i pantaloni appena finiti. Dice l'ingegnere: "L'Altissimo ha creato il mondo in sette giorni e a te, per un paio di pantaloni, ti ci sono voluti sette anni."

Fischer, accarezzando affettuosamente i pantaloni, risponde: "Hai forse ragione, ma guarda il mondo intorno a te dopo sette anni e guarda questi pantaloni!"

The title page of Y. L. Lazarus' *Enzyklopedia fun yidishe witzn*
published by Pardes in New York in 1928.

Chapter 3

The Ten Commandments Joke and the Issue of Ethnic Self-Disparagement

"Do you know why," the narrator asks, "there are *two* Tablets of the Law? Of course you don't! I'll tell you why. When God had finished working out the Ten Commandments, he engraved them on a *single* stone, which was the normal procedure. Then armed with his work, he set out to offer it to various nations.

'Would you like it?' he asked the French.

'First tell us what it is,' the French replied with some mistrust.

'Rules to live by, such as: "Thou shalt not covet thy neighbor's wife."'

'Thanks anyway,' said the French. 'That would be the end of our fun!'

Then God went to see the Germans.

'Would you like it?'

'What is it?'

'Rules to live by, such as: "Thou shalt not kill."'

'No way!' said the Germans, 'how could we make war then?'

God then tried the English, Italians, Greeks, Arabs and Chinese: no one wanted his work, and God was disheartened. It was then that he offered it to the Jews, who asked him right away:

'What does it cost?'

'Nothing,' God hastened to answer. 'It's perfectly free.'

'Well, in that case,' said the Jews, 'we'll take *two*.'"

Albert Memmi, *La libération du juif* (Paris: Payot, 1966), pp. 42-43; my translation.

The History and Variants of the Joke

The Forerunner: a Joke about Jews

Although in virtually all the subsequent re-tellings of the joke, the punchline would be spoken by a Jewish character, a Scot is cast as the primary comic figure in the earliest printed version I have been able to find of the story, published in 1927. The Scot is, however, played off against a Jew, whose accent and role as easy prey make him the story's secondary comic figure:[1]

A DEAL WITH ISAAC

An Aberdonian, in London, in need of a new suit, asked a friend if he could recommend a good tailor. "Oh yes," replied his friend, "Isaac Ikestein is a good man but you will have to offer him half whatever price he quotes and you will get a bargain."

The Aberdonian went to Isaac. "How much for a good suit?" he asked. "Four pounds," said Isaac. "That's ower much," replied the Aberdonian, "I'll gie ye twa pounds." "Two pounds–that is not enough," said Isaac, "but seeing you are a new customer, I vill let you have it for three pounds." "Thirty shillings or the deal's off," said the Aberdonian. "Vell now, that is too little, but as I don't vant to lose a customer I vill say two pounds, vat yu say to that?" "I'll gie ye a pound but nae mair," replied the Aberdonian. "Oh, come now," replied Isaac, "You are too hard, let us say thirty shillings: I don't vant to lose your pizness." "Fifteen shillin's or naething," replied the Aberdonian. "Vell, this is awful," said Isaac, "you are the hardest customer I have ever had, I vill give you the suit for nodings." "In that case," replied the Aberdonian, "I'll tak twa."

A shorter version of essentially the same joke, appeared one year later in an anthology of after-dinner stories – this time, with a Jew in the role of ungrateful opportunist:[2]

"I know how you feel about accepting any gratuities from a concern you buy of," said the general manager to the Jewish customer, "so I suggest that you give me a trifling sum, say a quarter, for this box of Christmas cigars. That will take the disgrace off." "In that case," said Israel Rosenbloom, "I'll take three boxes. Here's seventy-five cents."

---

[1] Allan Junior, *The Aberdeen Jew* (Dundee and London: Valentine, 1927), p. 13.
[2] James Schermerhorn, *Schermerhorn's Stories* (New York: George Sully, 1928), p. 220.

It is significant that in this early form of the joke, the punchline could be spoken by a Scot or Jew interchangeably. This is a property Christie Davies (1986) calls "switchability," and which is indicative of stories that should *not* be classified as Jewish jokes. Davies rightfully defines Jewish jokes as so firmly anchored in traditions specific to Jewish culture that no substitution to another ethnic group, with a reputation for thrift or shrewdness, would be possible without spoiling the joke.[3]

What we have then in this story, as it first appeared in anthologies of humor in the late 1920's, is a "joke about Jews," rather than a "Jewish joke." And this remains the case, even when the story makes its way into Jewish anthologies, essentially unchanged, as in the following examples from 1966[4] and 1987,[5] respectively:

Little Isaac, aged 10, is the most resourceful of poverty-stricken Ezechiel's children. When his only pair of shoes finally wears out, his father tells him: "Here's some money. Go buy yourself a new pair, and don't spend too much. I'm going to give you a tip: offer the salesman half of whatever price he asks."

Isaac runs to the shoe store. He tries on a pair of shoes which fits him perfectly and asks the price:

"Forty francs."

"That's far too much! Twenty francs!"

The salesman, moved by the child's impoverished air, says to him:

"All right, i'll do what I can: what about thirty francs?"

"That's too much! Fifteen francs!"

"All right, I'll let you have them for twenty francs; I'll lose money on the deal, but never mind..."

"No! Ten francs!"

Finally, worn out by this discussion, the salesman says:

"Listen, Isaac, you can have the shoes for free."

To which Isaac replies:

"I'll take two pair!"

The Jerusalem builder, having obtained a lucrative government contract, wanted to give an official a television set. The official refused it, saying that he could not accept a bribe.

"In that case," said the builder, "I'll sell it to you for two pounds."

The official gave it thought and finally said, "I'll take two."

---

[3] Christie Davies, "Jewish Jokes, Anti-Semitic Jokes, and Hebredonian Jokes," in *Jewish Humor*, ed. Avner Ziv (Tel Aviv: Papyrus, 1986), pp. 75-96.

[4] Adam, *L'humour juif* (Paris: Payot, 1966), p. 81; my translation.

[5] Michael Dines, *The Second Jewish Joke Book* (London: Futura, 1987), pp. 40-41.

Even when told by one Jew to another, and even when an Israeli setting is used as in the last example cited, it remains a "joke about Jews," with no real roots in Jewish culture.

Transformation into a Jewish Joke

In the early 1960's, someone, whose name we will never know, invented the "Ten Commandments" joke by combining the non-Jewish forerunner discussed above, with an ancient Jewish legend about the Gentiles' refusal of the Torah. This legend can be traced back to the *Mekilta de-Rabbi Ishmael*, a rabbinic commentary on the Book of Exodus, believed to have been compiled as early as the 4th Century A.D., and first printed in Constantinople in 1515. This is the form the legend had some sixteen centuries before the "Ten Commandments" joke was devised:[6]

And it was for the following reason that the nations of the world were asked to accept the Torah: In order that they should have no excuse for saying: Had we been asked we would have accepted it. For, behold, they were asked and they refused to accept it... [The Lord] appeared to the children of Esau the wicked and said to them: Will you accept the Torah? They said to Him: What is written in it? He said to them: "Thou shalt not murder." They then said to Him: The very heritage which our father left us was: "And by thy sword shalt thou live." (Gen. 27.40). He then appeared to the children of Amon and Moab. He said to them: Will you accept the Torah? They said to Him: What is written in it? He said to them: "Thou shalt not commit adultery." (Deut. 5.18) They, however, said to Him that they were all of them children of adulterers, as it is said: "Thus were both the daughters of Lot with child by their father" (Gen. 19.36). Then He appeared to the children of Ishmael. He said to them: Will you accept the Torah? They said to Him: What is written in it? He said to them: "Thou shalt not steal" (Deut. 7.17). They then said to Him: The very blessing that had been pronounced upon our father was:: "And he shall be as a wild ass of a man: his hand shall be upon everything" (Gen. 16.12)... But when He came to the Israelites and: "At His right hand was a fiery law unto them" (Deut. 33.2), they all opened their mouths and said: "All that the Lord hath spoken will we do and obey" (Ex. 24.7).

---

[6] *Mekilta de-Rabbi Ishmael*, translated and edited by Jacob Z. Lauterbach (Philadelphia: Jewish Publication Society of America, 1976; originally published in 1933), vol. 2, "Tractate Bahodesh," pp. 234-235. Essentially the same account is also found in Louis Ginzberg, *The Legends of the Jews* (Philadelphia: Jewish Publication Society of America, 1947; orig. pub. 1911), vol. 3, pp. 80-81.

It is here that our unknown jokester found the narrative structure and set of roles he used in the "Ten Commandments" joke, which begins with two or more refusal-sequences modeled directly on those in the rabbinic legend:

a) God asks a Gentile nation whether it wishes to accept His law;
b) the nation asks what is written in it;
c) God cites a commandment;
d) the nation refuses, on the grounds that observing the commandment
   would be incompatible with its way of life.

In the "Ten Commandments" story, the Jewish acceptance-sequence which follows these Gentile refusal-sequences, begins like the one in the legend, but is brilliantly rescripted to feed into the punchline of the "joke about Jews" that had been in circulation since the 1920's. This recycling of the punchline logic of a mildly anti-Semitic story, to provide a comic closure within an old rabbinic narrative, resulted in a joke that is firmly anchored in traditions specific to Jewish culture.

In the non-Jewish forerunner, some product or other – cigars, a suit, a pair of shoes or television set – was offered by a person whose identity was unimportant, to an individual Jew who might just as well have been a Scot. In the "Ten Commandments" joke, we have a story focusing on what is probably the single most important event in the historical mythology of the Jews: the giving of the Law at Mount Sinai. Now the "giver" in the story is God, the object transmitted is the very cornerstone of the Jewish religion, and the "taker" is depicted as the Jewish people or its leader. The "switchability" that characterized the forerunner, is excluded here: no other group could logically be portrayed as accepting the Ten Commandments.

Even though the story's cultural frame of reference is now specific to the Jewish ethnic community, *some* substitutions still remain possible, as illustrated by the fact that the joke developed along slightly divergent lines in Europe and the United States.

In what I will call the European variant, which appeared in print for the first time in Paris in 1966,[7] the key number in the punchline is two, referring to the tablets; the Gentile nations represented are West European – the "adulterous French" and "warlike Germans"; and God

---

[7] Albert Memmi, *La libération du juif* (Paris: Payot, 1966), pp. 42-43. This variant subsequently appeared in Ben Eliezer, *The World's Best Jewish Jokes* (London: Angus & Robertson, 1984), p. 36, and Alfred Marks, *A Medley of Jewish Humour* (London: Robson Books, 1985), p. 63.

finally offers the tablets to the Jews as a collective entity. In the U.S. variant, first cited in an American journal in 1971,[8] the key number is ten, referring to the commandments, the Gentile nations are biblical, such as "thieving Babylonians" and "idolatrous Egyptians," and it is to Moses that the final offer is made.

The following are representative samples of the two variants:

EUROPEAN VARIANT	AMERICAN VARIANT
Albert Memmi, *La libération du juif*	Isaac Asimov, *Treasury of Humor*
(Paris: Payot, 1966)	(New York: Vallentine-Mitchell, 1972)

"Do you know why," the narrator asks, "there are *two* Tablets of the Law? Of course you don't! I'll tell you why. When God had finished working out the Ten Commandments, he engraved them on a *single* stone, which was the normal procedure. Then armed with his work, he set out to offer it to various nations.

'Would you like it?' he asked the French.

'First tell us what it is,' the French replied with some mistrust.

'Rules to live by, such as: "Thou shalt not covet thy neighbor's wife."

'Thanks anyway,' said the French. 'That would be the end of our fun!'

Then God went to see the Germans.

'Would you like it?'

'What is it?'

'Rules to live by, such as: '"Thou shalt not kill."

'No way!' said the Germans, 'how could we make war then?'

During the period when the Israelites were suffering in Egyptian bondage, God traveled over the earth seeking those who might follow his mild law. He came across an Arab and said to him, "Would you like to follow My commandments?

The Arab frowned suspiciously. "Like what, for instance?"

"One is: Thou shalt not kill!"

The Arab said, "You must be mad. Follow that commandment, indeed! My profession consists in lying in wait for camel trains, slaughtering the merchants when they arrive, and confiscating all their goods. A commandment like that would just about ruin the whole system of private enterprise.

God turned away and traveled to Babylonia. There He accosted a merchant and said, "Would you like to follow My commandments?"

The Babylonian said, "For example?"

"Thou shalt not steal!"

---

[8] Alan Dundes, "A Study of Ethnic Slurs: The Jew and the Polack in the United States," *Journal of American Folklore* 84 (1971), pp. 186-203; reprinted in *Cracking Jokes. Studies of Sick Humor Cycles and Stereotypes* (Berkeley: 10 Speed Press, 1987), p. 123. The American variant later appeared in Isaac Asimov, *Treasury of Humor* (New York: Vallentine-Mitchell, 1972), pp. 328-329, and Elizabeth Petuchowski, *Das Herz auf der Zunge. Aus das Welt des jüdischen Witzes* (Freiburg: Herder, 1984), pp. 120-121.

God then tried the English, Italians, Greeks, Arabs and Chinese: no one wanted his work, and God was disheartened. It was then that he offered it to the Jews, who asked him right away:

'What does it cost?'

'Nothing,' God hastened to an-swer. 'It's perfectly free.'

'Well, in that case,' said the Jews, 'we'll take *two*.'"

"Friend," said the Babylonian, "I am sorry. My entire living is made up of buying cheap and selling dear, of misrepresentations and dishonesty. If I cannot steal, I cannot live."

Rather discouraged, God turned westward, and in Egypt, He found a bearded old man haranguing the ruler of the land in an attempt to get him to free certain slaves.

God called to him. "Moses," He said, "would you like to follow My command-ments?"

And Moses said, "How much do they cost?"

"Why, nothing," said God. "I'm giving them away free."

"In that case," said Moses, "I'll take ten."

The American variant follows the rabbinic account more closely in evoking biblical rather than West European nations in the refusal-sequences. In my view, however, the European variant makes a better joke because the stereotypes involved for the Gentile nations come across more clearly *as* stereotypes than those depicting Middle Eastern peoples in the American variant.

The Issue of Ethnic Self-Disparagement

Though Freud never knew the "Ten Commandments" joke, it is a perfect illustration for his widely quoted remark about Jewish humor, made in passing in 1905: "Incidentally, I do not know whether there are many other instances of a people making fun to such a degree of its own character."[9]

Attempts to explain this property of Jewish humor have resulted in an on-going discussion – at times a debate – in the literature. Five major explanations have been proposed, each of which is intrinsically interesting and should be known by anyone studying the "Ten Commandments" story or any other Jewish joke involving ethnic self-

---

[9] Sigmund Freud, *Jokes and Their Relation to the Unconscious* (Harmondsworth: Penguin, 1981; orig. pub. 1905), p. 157.

disparagement.[10] For that reason, I will provide a thumbnail sketch of those explanations, not as a preparation for applying them to the joke at hand – the reader can do that him/herself to whatever degree it seems appropriate – but in order to establish a frame of reference in relation to which the analysis I will propose can be situated. In other words, I will be proposing a *sixth* explanation for ethnic self-disparagement in Jewish jokes, and want to give the reader the necessary background for seeing how my approach differs from those already found in the literature.

Five Explanations: A Review of the Literature

MASOCHISM

The simplest explanation for self-disparaging Jewish jokes is undoubtedly Bergler's (1956) view that Jews derive a masochistic pleasure from making fun of themselves. He noted that "people who have little contact with Jews cannot 'understand' Jewish jokes," because of "the direction of aggression inward, instead of outward." Bergler believed that this masochism was conditioned by "the seclusion, poverty, absence of opportunity and bitterness of life in the ghetto," as well as "the persecution and bias encountered outside the ghetto."[11]

This view was partially subscribed to by Reik (1962), who corrected what he saw as Bergler's one-sidedness, and argued that "masochistic self-humiliation" is one of two poles between which Jewish wit oscillates – the other pole being "paranoid superiority-feelings."[12]

The masochism explanation might also be linked to discussions of "Jewish self-hatred." Lewin (1941) suggested that when members of an under-privileged minority feel frustrated by their lower status, their frustration gives rise to an aggressivity that cannot be directed

---

[10] A distinction can be maintained between ethnic and personal self-disparagement in Jewish humor. If a Jewish joker makes fun of the Jewish people, ethnic self-disparagement is in play; if he ridicules his own person, as in the Groucho Marx joke to be discussed in Chapter 5, the self-disparagement is personal, even if it is exercised within the framework of Jewish humor.

[11] Edmund Bergler, *Laughter and the Sense of Humor* (New York: International Book Corp., 1956), pp. 111-112.

[12] Theodor Reik, *Jewish Wit* (New York: Gamut, 1962), p. 233.

against the privileged majority, and which "is likely to be turned against one's own group or against one's self."[13] In the process, these members of a minority group – for example, Jews who feel trapped in their lesser status – are "greatly influenced by the low esteem the majority has for them" (p. 226) and tend to "see things Jewish through the eyes of the unfriendly majority" (p. 230).

A DEFENSIVE STRATEGY

Considering the apparent masochism of Jewish humor to be only a mask, enabling the Jew to blunt the dangerous hostility of his persecutors, Grotjahn (1957) wrote:[14]

...one can almost see how a witty Jewish man carefully and cautiously takes a sharp dagger out of his enemy's hands, sharpens it so that it can split a hair in mid-air, polishes it so that it shines brightly, stabs himself with it, then returns it gallantly to the anti-Semite with the silent reproach: Now see whether you can do it half so well. [...]

Aggression turned against the self seems to be an essential feature of the truly Jewish joke. It is as if the Jew tells his enemies: You do not need to attack us. We can do that ourselves- and even better.

Reik also believed that the self-ridicule in Jewish jokes can involve a *"pseudo-*masochism," designed to enhance the Jew's chances of survival in a hostile world (p. 222). Memmi (1966) concurred:

...describing his own quirks and oddities with humor, [the Jew] sollicits a benevolent complicity, he disarms the person he is speaking to. So, you accuse me of being greedy, stingy, shrewd? Alright, I describe myself as preoccupied with money, calculating, etc. You see what a good sport I am! But at the same time you must admit that it can't be that serious, since I am the first to joke about it. And what is amusing can hardly be very dangerous (pp. 41-42).

---

[13] Kurt Lewin, "Self-Hatred Among Jews," *Jewish Record* 4, 3 (June 1941), pp. 219-232. For a more recent work on this subject, see Sandor L. Gilman, *Jewish Self-Hatred. Anti-Semitism and the Hidden Language of the Jews* (Baltimore: Johns Hopkins University Press, 1986).

[14] Martin Grotjahn, *Beyond Laughter* (New York: McGraw-Hill, 1957), pp. 22-23, 25. Essentially the same arguments are developed in Grotjahn's "Jewish Jokes and Their Relation to Masochism" (1961), reprinted in *A Celebration of Laughter*, ed. Werner M. Mandel (Los Angeles: Mara Books, 1970), pp. 135-144.

SOCIAL DIFFERENTIATION

Katz and Katz (1972)[15] dealt with the apparent paradox of the "anti-Jewish Jewish joke" in America by suggesting that stories in which the butt speaks in Yiddish dialect, do not involve *self*-ridicule, but rather the ridiculing of and dissociation from an embarrassing subgroup within the Jewish community. Katz and Katz referred to

the uneasy situation of the second generation American Jew who still strongly regarded himself as part of the Jewish community, and was aware of being so regarded by others, but who wished to separate himself sharply from the unassimilated immigrant, whose ways he viewed not only as old fashioned and irrelevant but, most important, as an obstacle to his own efforts toward acceptance by the majority culture.

Ben Amos (1973)[16] also denied that Jewish humor involves any masochistic attack upon oneself, and argued that social differentiation is the process in play:

It becomes apparent that within the communicative event of joke telling in the Jewish society, there is no social identification between the ridiculer and the ridiculed. The narrator is not the butt of his story, and self-degradation could not possibly be a classical form of Jewish humor. Rather, joking serves as a vehicle for verbal aggression toward those from whom the narrator distinguishes himself unequivocally.

LAUGHING AT ONE'S ENTRAPMENT IN A GENTILE WORLD

When discussing Jewish humor in the context of Eastern Europe at about the turn of the century, rather than the contemporary situation in the U.S., Katz and Katz suggested that the Yiddish joke often

evokes amusement at the usually ineffectual although sometimes valiant and frequently ingenious attempts of the Jew in Czarist Russia and Poland to get along while trapped in an essentially hostile society that makes no sense to him, of which he basically does not approve, and in which he does not normally aspire to full participation (p. 216).

---

[15] Naomi and Eli Katz, "Tradition and Adaptation in American Jewish Humor," *Journal of American Folklore* 84 (1971), p. 219.

[16] Dan Ben-Amos, "The 'Myth' of Jewish Humor," *Western Folklore* 32, 2 (1973), p. 123.

In all of these stories one can find a strong element of laughing at oneself, an appreciation of the ludicrous position in which Jews found themselves – or even put themselves – while attempting to function in what was to them an absurd environment (p. 217).

In illustrating this point, Katz and Katz cited the following story, about a Russian Jew trying to circumvent the Czarist residence laws which excluded Jews from many regions:[17]

A man by the name of Rabinovitsh was once traveling with a passport that carried another [fictitious] name. When the train reached a check-point, the documents were collected for inspection. By the time the official came to return the passports Rabinowitsh had in his anxiety forgotten the name on his document. Finally his turn came to step up and claim the passport. "Well, what's your name?" asked the official. The befuddled traveler reflected for a moment and replied, "One thing is sure – it isn't Rabinovitsh!"

SELF-TRANSCENDENCE

Yet another approach focuses on Jewish humor as means for "ridiculing out of existence the foibles and incongruities in Jewish character" (Ausubel 1953)[18] or for "rising above one's deficiencies by frankly admitting and enjoying them" (Mindess 1971).[19] In commenting on this last view, Goldstein (1976) added that in joking about his inadequacies, the Jew "objectifies" them, "so that they become temporarily part of the non-self, objects to be toyed with" (p. 110). More recently, Ziv (1986) gave this approach its fullest

---

[17] Versions of this joke can be found in the following anthologies: Immanuel Olsvanger, *Rosinkess mit Mandlen* (Zurich: Der Arche, 1965; orig. pub. 1921), p. 46; J. Ch. Rawnitzki, *Yidishe Witzn* (New York: Morris S. Sklarsky, 1950; orig. pub. 1923), vol. 1, p. 23; Jacob Richman, *Laughs from Jewish Lore* (New York and London: Funk & Wagnall's, 1926), pp. 84-85; *Jüdische Schwänke* (Vienna: R. Löwit, 1928), pp. 202-203; Immanuel Olsvanger, *Röyte Pomerantsen* (New York: Schocken, 1935; orig. pub. 1935), p. 53; S. Felix Mendelsohn, *Let Laughter Ring* (Philadelphia: Jewish Publication Society, 1941), pp. 31-32; Harry Schnur, *Jewish Humor* (London: Allied Book Club, [1945]), pp. 35-36; Salcia Landmann, *Der jüdische Witz* (Breisgau: Walter, 1960), p. 296; and Martin Rywell, *Laughing with Tears* (Harriman: Pioneer Press, 1960), p. 88.

[18] Nathan Ausubel, "Why Jews Laugh," in *A Treasury of Jewish Humor* (Garden City: Doubleday, 1953), pp. xviii-xix.

[19] Harvey Mindess, *Laughter and Liberation* (Los Angeles: Nash, 1971); cited by Jeffrey H. Goldstein, "Theoretical Notes on Humor," *Journal of Communication* 26, 3 (Summer 1976), p. 110.

expression, while linking it to the defensive strategy explanation already cited:[20]

Self-disparaging humor that makes possible self-criticism, and enables a man to take a courageous look at his own negative aspects, and those of the group or people with which he identifies. Self-disparaging humor is a sign of maturity and of self insight. Recognition of one's own shortcomings, readiness to accept and even laugh at them, demonstrate, paradoxically enough, a sense of self-confidence. In this way, self-disparaging humor actually evokes sympathy, and staves off aggression by its listener.

An interesting variant of this view was proposed by the Jewish writer, Romain Gary (1974),[21] who described the function of humor in his work as that of cutting the "self" down to size. Although it focuses more on personal than on ethnic self-disparagement, this quote is nevertheless a fitting conclusion to our review of explanations for self-disparagement in a Jewish context:

"I" is unbelievably pretentious. It has no idea as to what will happen to it in ten minutes yet it takes itself seriously in a tragic mode, it speaks like Hamlet, soliloquizes, calls upon eternity and even has the alarming nerve of writing the works of Shakespeare. If you want to understand the role played by the smile in my work – and in my life – think of it as a kind of settling of accounts with the "I" we all have, with its extravagant pretensions and its plaintive love affair with itself. Laughter, mockery, derision are all enterprises of purification, of clearing the way, they prepare for future measures of health. The very source of popular laughter and of all comedy is this pin-point which bursts the balloon of the "I," swelled up with its own importance.[...] The comic calls us back to humility. The "I" always loses its pants in public.

Years ago, Arthur Koestler asked me: "Why are you always telling stories against yourself?" Koestler is one of the most intelligent men of the era and I was stupefied to hear this question coming from him. I do not tell stories against myself, but against the "I", against our little kingdom of the "I".

---

[20] Avner Ziv, "Psycho-Social Aspects of Jewish Humor in Israel and in the Diaspora," in *Jewish Humor*, ed. Avner Ziv (Tel Aviv: Papyrus, 1986), p. 56.
[21] Romain Gary, *La nuit sera calme* (Paris: Gallimard, 1974), pp. 12-13, 231; my translation.

Ethnic Self-Disparagement in the "Ten Commandments" Joke

FINAL PRELIMINARIES

In the forerunner of the "Ten Commandments" joke – for example in the Schermerhorn version cited on p. 72 above, in which a Jewish customer takes advantage of a Gentile manager by asking for three boxes of cigars at the give-away price – positive and negative qualities are distributed as they usually are in anti-Semitic humor, with Jewishness identified as scheming, ungrateful, insatiable, etc., while the non-Jewish role is a model of tact and generosity.

In the "Ten Commandments" joke, however, the behaviors attributed to Gentile nations, such as adultery and killing, represent offences of a much graver nature than the relatively innocent one of wanting to get something for nothing. In this comparative respect, the self-portrayal involved in the joke is only moderately negative, since the Gentile norm from which Jewish behavior is seen to deviate is far from positive, according to the implicit value system of the joke.

This story has other resonances as well which mitigate the self-disparagement, and make it possible to suggest – as Memmi has – that this story, like all Jewish jokes when told by Jews, is essentially a defence ("un plaidoyer") in favor of the Jewish people. From Memmi's point of view, the "Ten Commandments" story opens onto an almost tragic portrayal of Jewish life:

in managing in fact to extract *two* Tablets of the Law from the divine partner, the Jews thought they had gotten a good deal. But was this really the case? Isn't it disconcerting that the other peoples had refused the present? Beyond the appearance that the gift was free of charge and of the advantageous deal, wasn't the price to be paid ultimately quite high? To forego having fun, courting the neighbor's wife, making war... a lot could be said about the real meaning of this bargain, which in fact was a purely spiritual one. We can just make out, beyond the contours of the joke, the bitterness of the Jew confronting the austerity of his life. In any case, we are far from the simple, amusing description of the cleverness of the Jew in doing business, though that is also here (pp. 43-44, my translation).

In suggesting that the *underlying* theme of this story is Jewish acceptance of the Law, which in turn can be seen as a heavy burden, Memmi spoke of resonances that help enlist our sympathy for the embodiment of Jewishness in the joke.

But even if we keep in mind the relative innocence of the Jewish offence, as well as the deeper resonances Memmi spoke of, we can

still wonder why a story told by Jews about themselves should end
with essentially the same negative image of the Jew as that found in
the anti-Semitic forerunner of the story.

In order to make real headway with this problem, we will have to
look at the joke in an entirely different perspective – and one which
will take into account, not only the representation of Jewishness in
this story, but the portrayal of the Gentile nations as well.

THE PARODISTIC DIMENSION

An example from the sphere of cinema will help pave the way for our
looking at the "Ten Commandments" joke in a different light.

Near the beginning of a Neil Simon film called *The Cheap Detective*
(1978, directed by Robert Moore), the following dialogue occurs in
the office of a San Francisco private detective, played by Peter Falk
speaking with a Bogart lisp to his beautiful client played by Madeline
Kahn, who had given her name as Denise Manderley:

FALK. Your name isn't Denise Manderley, is it?
KAHN. No, it's Wanda Coleman.
FALK. Then why does your driver's license say Gilda Dabney.
KAHN. I believe my life is in danger. That's why I've taken so many precautions. My real
     name is Chloe Lamarr.
[...]
FALK. Alright, can we stop playing games now? It isn't Manderley or Coleman or Dabney
     or even Lamarr, is it? The initials on this handkerchief are A.P. What does A.P. stand
     for?
KAHN. Alma Chalmers.
FALK. Chalmers begins with a C. This is a P.
KAHN. Palmers. Alma Palmers.
FALK. Listen. You give me the run around one more time and I'm gonna slap you around
     this office. I don't even care what your name is any more. Just make one up, so I know
     what to call you.
KAHN. Vivian Purcell.
FALK. That's better.
KAHN. Carmen Montenegro. (Falk slaps his desk in disgust.)

This dialogue is funny, even to viewers unfamiliar with the films
spoofed in *The Cheap Detective*. But in order to understand what is
going on here, it helps to know that Falk and Kahn are caricatures of
Bogart and Mary Astor in *The Maltese Falcon* (1941, directed by John

Huston). At the start of this film classic, Astor gives her name as Wonderly to Sam Spade, the private detective played by Bogart. She later phones him and asks him to meet her at her apartment, which is listed under the name of LeBlanc. When Spade arrives, the following dialogue occurs:

ASTOR. Mr. Spade, I – I have a terrible, terrible confession to make... That story I told you yesterday was just a story.
BOGART. Oh, that we – didn't exactly believe your story, Miss, er, – What is your name, Wonderly or LeBlanc?
ASTOR. It's really O'Shaughnessy, Brigid O'Shaughnessy.

If, while watching *The Cheap Detective*, we realize that screenwriter Neil Simon was playing with and parodying bits of dialogue and character types from Bogart movies, then we also understand that we are not to take anything in *The Cheap Detective* at face value; what we are really invited to enjoy at any point in this film is the fun it pokes at *The Maltese Falcon* and *Casablanca*, by picking out in memorable scenes whatever comes across as most striking – like the Wonderly/LeBlanc/O'Shaughnessy business – and inflating it preposterously.

The relationship of the "Ten Commandments" story to its anti-Semitic forerunner, is in some ways comparable to what the *The Cheap Detective* film does to *The Maltese Falcon*, in the sense that the Jewish joke picks up the salient features of the "joke about Jews" and blows them up to gigantic proportions. In this respect, the "Ten Commandments" joke is a parody of the anti-Semitic forerunner.

However, the situation is more complex, for several reasons.

One difference concerns the harmlessness of the things made fun of by the Neil Simon film – such as Astor's multiple aliases in the original – in contrast to the potentially vicious and repressive uses of ethnic stereotypes. In this respect, more is at stake in the parodying of racist jokes than in spoofs of classic movies.

Furthermore, the object of parody in the case of the films cited above, was a serious movie and the bits selected for parodistic transformation were not originally intended to elicit laughter, while the Schermerhorn and other forerunners of the "Ten Commandments" joke were already supposed to be funny. It is one thing to parody a serious representation and quite another to parody a joke.

It is probably for that reason that *The Cheap Detective* comes across so unequivocally as a parody from start to finish, while the "Ten Commandments" joke is fundamentally ambiguous in that respect: no unmistakable cues can be provided, telling us whether the real butt of the joke is the ethnic group unfavorably portrayed in the punchline, or people who subscribe to the stereotypes evoked.

What all of this suggests is that a Jewish joke which appears to be ethnically self-disparaging, is constructed in such a way that we are left in doubt as to whether the stereotypes and clichés it transmits – about Jews and any other groups – are implicitly endorsed or ridiculed by the story, and whether the joke is an exercise in or parody of ethnic (self-)disparagement. In any event, the joke at least partially undercuts its own representation of Jews and other groups by leading us to wonder whether that representation shouldn't be seen as a parody of standard stereotypes, and not as a comically exaggerated but still essentially valid depiction of the way Jews and others actually behave.

In the case of the "Ten Commandments" story, we cannot tell whether the joke earnestly proposes such characterizations as the "adulterous French" and "warlike Germans"– as well as the image of Jewish shrewdness – or implicitly invites us to see all of those constructs as negative stereotypes the joke is parodistically over-fulfilling in order to make fun of them. We are given both options. Racist jokes, on the other hand, are open to only one possible inter-pretation, though anyone challenged for expressing racist attitudes by telling such a joke will invariably pretend that the joking framework undercuts – rather than transmits – the racist message ("It was only a joke!").

The openness of the "Ten Commandments" joke to radically different interpretive possibilities makes the story a reversible figure, though not of the type already seen in the "Rabbinic Judgment" story. There, we were left in doubt as to how the behavior of the comic figure should be accounted for: as role-fiasco, a tactical manoeuvre or a case of exemplary deviance. Here we are in doubt as to whether the story should be taken at face value, as a self-contained fiction im-plicitly endorsing its own content despite the joking framework, or as a parody of other narratives, in which case it disowns – and invites us to disown – the images it pretends to propose.

While I would not suggest that this is the only viable approach to the ethnic self-disparagement found in many Jewish jokes, it sets in relief an aspect of these jokes that has not yet been described in the literature on Jewish humor. This approach might therefore be con-sidered as a supplement to those explanations for self-disparagement that have already been proposed in the literature, and which were briefly outlined above.

AN ADDITIONAL STRATEGY

Parody is not the only means by which Jewish jokes can undercut the destructive potential of stereotypes. Another strategy for achieving the same end can be seen in a joke that was widely circulated in the early 1940's:[22]

After months of persuasion the Fuehrer finally permitted Dr. Schacht to demonstrate his pet theory about the Jews. The Nazi party was bent on going through with the program of Aryanization at a rapid pace, but Dr. Schacht pleaded caution. "The Jews are excellent businessmen and the Reich still needs them," maintainted Dr. Schacht, and in order to prove his point he took Hitler on a brief shopping tour on Leipzigerstrasse.

They stopped at a store run by an Aryan and asked for a teacup for a left-handed person. The proprietor said that he did not have any. They went to another Aryan store and received the same reply.

The Fuehrer and Dr. Schacht then entered a Jewish store and repeated their request. The Jew went to the back of the store and returned in a few minutes.

"I have only one such cup left," said the Jew, "and it will cost fifty percent more than the ordinary cup."

The two dignitaries told the proprietor that they would return a little later. Upon emerging from the store, Dr. Schacht said: "What did I tell you? The Jew is a cleverer businessman than his Aryan competitor."

"Clever nothing," bellowed the Fuehrer. "The Jew was just lucky enough to have a cup for a left-handed person."

As usual, the Jew is portrayed as a shrewd businessman – only here, that quality is *destigmatized* by the joke, which is constructed like a kind of intelligence test which the "Aryan" merchants fail while the Jewish shopkeeper passes it with flying colors. Consequently, the qualities the Jew exhibits in his tactical maneouvre are defined for us – and by someone near the top of the Nazi hierarchy! – as being admirable, expressive of superior intelligence, and a precious asset for the Reich, while "Aryan-ness" is identified with intellectual mediocrity, and Hitler with downright stupidity.

At a time when the stereotype of Jewish cunning and greed was being used to justify the destruction of European Jewry, this joke

---

[22] S. Felix Mendelsohn, *Let Laughter Ring* (New York: Jewish Publication Society, 1941), pp. 120-121. Hjalmar Schacht, considered Hitler's "financial wizard," was president of the Reichsbank until 1939. The publication history of this joke will be found on pp. 222-229 below.

contributed in its own small way to the neutralization of that stereotype.

Jokes of this type are more praiseworthy than they are funny. On the whole, it is through parodistic overfulfillment of racist stereotypes that Jewish humor most successfully removes the venom from them.

The Parodistic Triad

Sets of Interpretive Counterparts

In the punchline of the "Ten Commandments" joke, the Jews who say "We'll take two!" can be seen in two different ways: a) in terms of tactical manoeuvre, if we take the joke at face value, as a story about differences between Jews and other peoples; and b) as parodistically overfulfilling the negative stereotype of Jewish shrewdness, if we understand the story as a parody of anti-Semitic jokes.

As it turns out, the parodistic option just mentioned is one of three positions on what might be called a parodistic triad, each of which has its counterpart on the basic triad. Just as tactical manoeuvre and parodistic *over*fulfillment of a *negative* stereotype go hand in hand, so do role-fiasco and parodistic *under*fulfillment of a *positive* stereo-type, as well as exemplary deviance and the parodistic *over*fulfillment of a *positive* stereotype. The following table may help the reader to visualize these alignments:

BASIC TRIAD	PARODISTIC TRIAD
role-fiasco	underfulfillment of a positive stereotype
tactical manoeuvre	overfulfillment of a negative stereotype
exemplary deviance	overfulfillment of a positive stereotype

The following joke, which was one Freud found meaningful in relation to a personal dilemma,[23] will help to illustrate the alignment of role-fiasco with its parodistic counterpart. In this case, the stereotype played with and parodied is that of the rabbi gifted with "the wisdom of Solomon":[24]

"Wise Rabbi, you must give me your advice, I am in great difficulty. I have a rooster and a hen and must slaughter one of them. If I slaughter the rooster, the hen will complain; if I slaughter the hen, the rooster will complain. What should I do?"

"I understand, Aaron," said the wise rabbi, "this is a very difficult case. Give me time until tomorrow to think about it."

The next day the man asked his question again and was given the following answer: "You must slaughter the hen."

"But Rabbi, then the rooster will complain?!"

– "So, let it complain!"

Here, we can see the rabbi as pretending to solve a problem he is incapable of even grasping – the role-fiasco position; or we can see the joke as playing with and making fun of narratives which celebrate rabbinic wisdom – in which case we have a parodistic under-fulfillment of a positive stereotype.

The final set of counterparts – exemplary deviance and parodistic overfulfillment of a positive stereotype – can be illustrated with the following joke, which involves issues that will require a fuller discussion:[25]

A great tidal wave was rushing towards the land. In two days this huge wave was going to inundate all the continents. Evacuation was futile, since the wave was higher than all the mountains. Earth was doomed.

So with the end of the world imminent, the big TV networks decided to donate their time to the clergy to calm the populace. Perhaps a panic might be averted.

So Pope John gets on and he makes the sign of the cross and says a couple of Hail Marys, and all the cardinals are praying and there's this guy swinging the incense around under the golden canopy and the Pope is standing there in all the glory of St. Peter's and he says, "Your duty as sons and daughters of Rome is to confess your sins and meet your maker with clean souls. We have stationed priests at every street corner where they will

---

[23] The joke is cited in Sigmund Freud's *Aus den Anfängen der Psychoanalyse. Brief an Wilhelm Fliess* (London: Imago, 1950), pp. 299-301, in a letter dated May 28, 1899. Freud's comments on the joke in relation to a conflict between marriage and career, are briefly discussed in Elliot Oring, *The Jokes of Sigmund Freud. A Study in Humor and Jewish Identity* (Philadelphia: University of Pennsylvania Press, 1984), p. 30.

[24] Alexander Moszkowski, *Die unsterbliche Kiste* (Berlin: Verlag der "Lustigen Blätter," 1908), pp. 78-79; my translation.

[25] Ed Cray, "The Rabbi Trickster," *Journal of American Folklore* 77 (1964), p. 335. The publication history of this joke will be found on pp. 230-232 below.

stay on duty for the next two days so that you may confess and take the last Sacrament. *Pax vobiscum.*"

From New York comes the Protestant in his business suit and buttoned-down collar. He gets up and takes off his horn-rimmed glasses and says, "It's really up to you as individuals to meet this great crisis with dignity and peace of mind. I would stress also that you think positively that this tidal wave is not the end, but a beginning of a new life."

Finally, the little reb gets on and he shrugs, "Nu. Ve got two days to learn how to live under water."

This is one of many jokes which play on ethnic or national differences – typically setting up the representatives of two initial groups as holding "normal" attitudes, while the spokesman for the third group expresses an outlook which deviates radically from the other two and makes us laugh.

In the "Global Catastrophe" joke, normalcy means giving up in the face of hopeless odds. This is identified as the Christian position, and is not in any way deprecated as it is expressed. Set in sharp relief against this Christian acceptance of the inevitable, which can be seen as "tragically ennobling,"[26] is the outlook the joke playfully defines as the Jewish alternative, and which can be perceived in two different ways.

One is to view the rabbi's comically deviant outlook as exemplary. In introducing this joke, Feinsilver cites a Yiddish proverb which she then comments upon: "*Az me ken nit aribergeyn, geyt men arunter.* If you can't climb over, you tunnel under. (You find a way. This proverb pinpoints one of the keys to Jewish survival – never say die!"[27] In another context (p. 35), she cites other proverbs equally expressive of an outlook that is diametrically opposed to fatalistic resignation: "*Az me vil, ken men iberkeren di ganste velt* (If you want to, you can turn over the whole world); *Az me mus, ken men* (If you have to, you can); *Me gefint zich an eytse* (You find a way out)." The same spirit is found in Joseph Heller's indirect allusion to the joke in his novel, *God Knows*, in the following dialogue between two biblical figures:[28]

"It was his destiny, David."

"That's bullshit, Samuel," I told him. "We're Jews, not Greeks. Tell us another flood is coming and we'll learn how to live under water. Character is destiny."

---

[26] Kurt Schlesinger, "Jewish Humor as Jewish Identity," *International Review of Psycho-Analysis* 6 (1979), p. 322.

[27] Lillian Mermin Feinsilver, *The Taste of Yiddish* (New York: Thomas Yoseloff, 1970), p. 68.

[28] Joseph Heller, *God Knows* (London: Black Swan, 1985), p. 79.

Finally, Kurt Schlesinger – who cites the joke in a version in which the Jewish outlook is preceded by the statements of an Englishman, a Frenchman and an American – comments on the story in the following terms:

> The first three speakers are in the tragic-heroic tradition. They fight, suffer and die and hypothetically define themselves as tragic heroes. The Jew also defines himself as fighting and suffering, but he refuses to accept death as a final outcome. At the critical moment he alters not the rules of reality but his stance toward them. He does not accept or willingly submit to a hypothetical death as the final, ennobling cloture. He feels free to hypothesize a creative solution of an underwater life. Taken literally, this is unreal. As a metaphor defining attitudes, it has most realistic correlates. Much of the humorous tension here comes precisely from the awareness of the truth that is ambiguously expressed in this fantasy. Survival depends on creating your own world. The ghetto was such a world in which people learned to live underwater. We witness a triumph of the absurd as the postulated, tragic heroism of the others is trumped by the Jew's refusal to bow to reality in order to survive in it (p. 322).

Taking into account the historical experience of the Jewish people, and the Jewish emphasis on resourcefulness and refusal of fatalism, as illustrated for example in the Yiddish proverbs cited above, there can be no doubt that we are invited to applaud the rabbi's problem-solving stance. This is also Cohen's reading of the joke[29] as showing that

> Jews refuse to succumb to the dire circumstances. Abandoning the stance of tragic heroism, they create an alternative to an ennobling death. They learn to fashion their own reality. Though they are often gasping for air in their underwater existence, they somehow manage to survive, for humor is their life preserver.

But it is precisely because: a) that outlook is so stereotypically Jewish; b) the rabbi is so over-equipped with resourceful optimism; and c) his solution is so far-fetched, that an additional reading – not proposed by any commentator – should also be taken into account: namely the possibility of seeing this joke as playing with a positive Jewish stereotype by pushing those qualities it celebrates to the most absurd limits. This overfulfillment of a positive stereotype would thus be the parodistic counterpart of exemplary deviance.

In combining the basic with the parodistic triad, we have expanded our repertory of interpretive frameworks from three to six. The relationship between the two triads might be represented schema-

---

[29] Sarah Blacher Cohen, *Jewish Wry. Essays on Jewish Humor* (Bloomington and Indianapolis: Indiana University Press, 1987), pp. 13-14.

tically as follows, with counterparts aligned at opposite ends of the star:

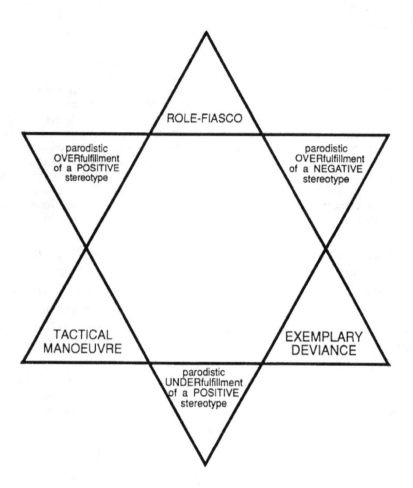

Types of Reversibility

As shown in Chapter 1, the "Rabbinic Judgment" story is open to three interpretive options, all located on the basic triad, and involving different ways of accounting for the rabbi's behavior, from within the framework of the fiction: role-fiasco, tactical manoeuvre and exemplary deviance.

The "Ten Commandments" joke exhibits a somewhat different type of reversibility, since the story can be understood in terms of one position on the basic triad – tactical manoeuvre – and its counterpart on the parodistic triad: overfulfillment of a negative stereotype.

Both types of reversibility – within and between triads – can be in play in our experience of a single joke. The following example will help to clarify what that double reversibility amounts to:[30]

In a little town in Galicia, some Jews come to ask the rabbi to perform a miracle. The shames [sexton] of the synagogue has just died, and the rabbi is to resuscitate him.
 – Alright, says the rabbi. Let's go to the shames' house.
When they arrive at the home of the deceased, the rabbi asks for a glass of good red wine. He empties it, and with a thundering voice, he commands the dead man to rise up and walk. The body just lies there.
 – Bring me a glass of burgundy!
He drinks the burgundy and commands the dead man to come back to life: the shames doesn't budge.
 – Bring me a bottle of champagne!
He drinks half the bottle and then tries once again, but still in vain.
 – Well, says the rabbi, now that's what I call being dead!

The most obvious way in which the rabbi's behavior can be understood is in terms of role-fiasco, as an embodiment of a ludicrously ill-advised attempt to perform a feat he himself should have known from the start he could never pull off. The drinks he takes, presumably to mobilize his supernatural powers, and the commands he issues, are all empty theatrics. And when his failure is a fait accompli, the comment he makes is as hair-brained as the whole enterprise had been: he is *impressed* by how dead the body remains.

A second possibility is to view the rabbi as a rather shifty character who has seized upon an opportunity: that of getting himself provided with a quantity of liquid refreshment. Perfectly lucid as to the inevitable outcome of the event, the rabbi plays the townspeople along, conning them into satisfying his thirst, after which he shrugs off the whole affair with his oddball comment. When the rabbi's behavior is seen in these terms of tactical manoeuvering, the joke might be related to the Yiddish proverb: "*Der rebbe trinkt aleyn oys dem vayn un heyst dernoch di andere freylach zayn* – The rabbi drains the bottle and tells the others to be gay."[31]

We now arrive at the third interpretive option: namely the parodistic counterpart of the role-fiasco position. In this perspective, the joke would be seen as playing with and parodistically under-

---

30 Raymond Geiger, *Nouvelles histoires juives* (Paris: Gallimard, 1925), pp. 36-37; my translation. The publication history of this joke will be found on pp. 201-203 below.
31 Hanan J. Ayalti, *Yiddish Proverbs* (New York: Schocken, 1971; orig. pub. 1949), pp. 58-59.

fulfilling a positive stereotype: that of the wonder-working rabbi, able to perform miraculous cures and other supernatural feats, just as Jesus had been able to raise Lazarus from the dead by crying out with a loud voice: "Lazarus come forth!" (John 11: 43-44). The "Dead Shames" joke is one of many stories making fun of tales about wonder-working rabbis – tales that had begun to circulate in connection with the founder of the Hasidic movement, the Baal Shem Tov (Israel Ben Eliezer, 1700-1760), and which even proponents of Hasidism tried to dissociate from the essence of the movement.[32]

Seen in this third perspective, the failure enacted in the "Dead Shames" joke is viewed – not as an object of ridicule in itself – but as part of an exercise in playing with the positive stereotype of the wonder-working rabbi, by underfulfilling those expectations that are specific to it. Jokes susceptible of this kind of reading often end with the same kind of thud, following an elaborate build-up, that is found in shaggy-dog stories.

The various types of reversibility described in this section might be represented graphically in this manner:

Rabbinic Judgement	Ten Commandments	Dead Shames
three positions in the basic triad	one position in the basic triad + its counterpart in the parodistic triad	two positions in the basic triad + the parodistic counterpart of one of them
role-fiasco tactical man-oeuvre ← → exemplary deviance	parodistic overfulfillment of a negative stereotype ← → tactical manoeuvre	role-fiasco ← → parodistic underfulfillment of a positive stereotype tactical manoeuvre

---

[32] "The more learned Hasidic Rabbis cared little for miracles, and explained the true facts when among their own group. They permitted, however, the circulation of tales of wonder-working among the common people in the belief that thereby they might become attached to an ethical life." Louis I. Newman, *The Hasidic Anthology. Tales and Teachings of the Hasidim* (New York: Schocken, 1963; orig. pub. 1934), p. 261.

PUBLICATION HISTORY

Forerunner

Allan Junior,
THE ABERDEEN JEW.
Dundee and London:
Valentine, 1927; p.13.
Illustration by Gregor
McGregor.

An Aberdonian, in London, in need of a new suit, asked a friend if he could recommend a good tailor. "Oh yes," replied his friend, "Isaac Ikestein is a good man but you will have to offer him half whatever price he quotes and you will get a bargain."

The Aberdonian went to Isaac. "How much for a good suit?" he asked. "Four pounds," said Isaac. "That's ower much," replied the Aberdonian, "I'll gie ye twa pounds." "Two pounds – that is not enough," said Isaac, "but seeing you are a new customer, I vill let you have it for three pounds." "Thirty shillings or the deal's off," said the Aberdonian. "Vell now, that is too little, but as I don't vant to lose a customer I vill say two pounds, vat yu say to that?" "I'll gie ye a pound but nae mair," replied the Aberdonian. "Oh, come now," replied Isaac, "You are too hard, let us say thirty shillings: I don't vant to lose your pizness." "Fifteen shillin's or naething," replied the Aber-donian. "Vell, this is awful," said Isaac, "you are the hardest customer I have ever had, I vill give you the suit for nodings." "In that case," replied the Aberdonian, "I'll tak twa."

James Schermerhorn,
SCHERMERHORN'S
STORIES. New York:
George Sully & Co.,
1928; p. 220.

"I know how you feel about accepting any gratuities from a concern you buy of," said the general manager to the Jewish customer, "so I suggest that you give me a trifling sum, say a quarter, for this box of Christmas cigars. That will take the disgrace off." "In that case," said Israel Rosenbloom, "I'll take three boxes. Here's seventy-five cents."

Adam, L'HUMOUR
JUIF. Paris: Denoël,
1966; p. 81.

Le petit Isaac, 10 ans, est le plus débrouillard des enfants du pauvre Ezéchiel. Comme son unique paire de souliers est hors d'usage, son père lui dit:

(cont.)

Adam, *cont.*

– Tiens, voilà de l'argent. Va t'acheter une paire neuve, et ne dépense pas trop. Je vais te donner un truc: tu offriras au marchand la moitié de ce qu'il te réclamera.

Isaac court chez le marchand de chaussures. Il essaye une paire qui lui convient parfaitement et demande le prix.

– Quarante francs.

– C'est beaucoup trop cher! Vingt francs!

Le marchand, attendri par l'aspect misérable d'Isaac, lui dit:

– Bon, je vais faire un effort: trente francs, ça va?

Isaac se met alors à pleurer et marmonne entre deux sanglots:

– C'est trop cher! Quinze francs!

– Allez, prends-les pour vingt francs; j'y perds, mais enfin...

– Non! Dix francs!

Alors le marchand, épuisé par cette discussion:

– Écoute, Isaac, tes chaussures, je te les donne!

Alors Isaac:

– J'en prendrai deux paires!

ROBERT CASTEL
RACONTE...
Paris: Mengès, 1978;
p. 222.

Stéphano, qu'il a une grosse affaire d'olives cassées et d'anchois, demi-sel et gros sel, et même sans sel, offre à Boogie, le représentant, avec qui il vient de traiter un gros marché de boîtes vides, une bouteille d'anisette Cristal.

–Merci, dit Boogie, en refusant, mais ma maison m'interdit formellement d'accepter un cadeau de qui que ce soit.

–Bon, admet Stéphano en riant. Faisons une affaire. Je vous la vends pour 1 F.

–1 F, fait Boogie. C'est différent. Dans ces conditions j'en prends cinquante bouteilles.

Michael Dines,
THE SECOND JEWISH
JOKE BOOK.
London: Futura, 1987;
pp. 40-41.

The Jerusalem builder, having obtained a lucrative government contract, wanted to give an official a television set. The official refused it, saying that he could not accept a bribe.

"In that case," said the builder, "I'll sell it to you for two pounds."

The official gave it thought and finally said, "I'll take two."

Jay Allen, 500 GREAT JEWISH JOKES. New York: Signet, 1990; p. 60.

The salesman was trying to close a big sale with Harvey Weinberg, a vice-president of a major electronics firm. As negotiations came down to the wire, the salesman mentioned that he'd toss in a brand-new Mercedes if the deal was signed.

Weinberg was indignant. "So who do you think you're dealing with, some slimy politician? I can't accept a bribe."

The salesman said, "Well, in that case, we won't make it a gift. Suppose I sell you the Mercedes for a hundred dollars."

"In that case," Weinberg replied, "I'll take two."

The Ten Commandments

Albert Memmi, LA LIBÉRATION DU JUIF. Paris: Payot, 1966; pp. 42-43.

"Savez-vous pourquoi, demande le narrateur, il existe *deux* Tables de la Loi? Vous ne le savez évidemment pas! Je vais vous l'expliquer: Dieu, après avoir mis au point les dix commandements, les a gravés d'abord sur une seule pierre. Ce qui était plus normal. Puis, muni de son oeuvre, il s'en alla la proposer à différents peuples.

"– En voulez-vous? dit-il aux Français.

"– Mais d'abord, qu'y a-t-il dedans? lui demandèrent les Français avec méfiance.

"– Des règles de vie: par exemple: 'Tu ne convoiteras pas la femme de ton voisin...'

"– Ah! non, merci bien, dirent les Français, il n'y aurait plus moyen de s'amuser!

"Dieu s'en alla voir les Allemands:

"– En voulez-vous?

"– Qu'y a-t-il dedans?

"– Des règles de vie; par exemple: 'Tu ne tueras pas.'

"– Diable! dirent les Allemands, mais comment faire la guerre, alors?

"Dieu fit ainsi le tour des Anglais, des Italiens, des Grecs, des Arabes et des Chinois: personne ne voulait de son oeuvre; et Dieu fut très embarrassé. C'est alors qu'il la proposa aux Juifs. Les Juifs, aussitôt, lui demandèrent:

"– Combien ça coûte?

"– Rien, répondit Dieu avec empressement. Rien, c'est gratuit.

"– Ah! bien, dirent les Juifs: alors, vous nous en donnerez *deux.* "

Isaac Asimov,
TREASURY OF
HUMOR. New York:
Vallentine-Mitchell,
1972; pp. 328-329.

During the period when the Israelites were suffering in Egyptian bondage, God traveled over the earth seeking those who might follow his mild law. He came across an Arab and said to him, "Would you like to follow My commandments?" The Arab frowned suspiciously.

"Like what, for instance?"

"One is: Thou shalt not kill!"

The Arab said, "You must be mad. Follow that commandment, indeed! My profession consists in lying in wait for camel trains, slaughtering the merchants when they arrive, and confiscating all their goods. A commandment like that would just about ruin the whole system of private enterprise.

God turned away and traveled to Babylonia. There He accosted a merchant and said, "Would you like to follow My commandments?"

The Babylonian said, "For example?"

"Thou shalt not steal!"

"Friend," said the Babylonian, "I am sorry. My entire living is made up of buying cheap and selling dear, of misrepresentations and dishonesty. If I cannot steal, I cannot live."

Rather discouraged, God turned westward, and in Egypt, He found a bearded old man haranguing the rule of the land in an attempt to get him to free certain slaves.

God called to him. "Moses," He said, "would you like to follow My commandments?"

And Moses said, "How much do they cost?"

"Why, nothing," said God. "I'm giving them away free."

"In that case," said Moses, "I'll take ten."

Marvey Mindess,
THE CHOSEN
PEOPLE. Los
Angeles: Nash,
1972; p. 10.

When God wrote the Bible, He offered it to the Egyptians. They asked what was in it, so He explained about The Ten Commandments. "No thanks," they said. "We're not interested."

So He offered it to the Babylonians. They, too, asked what was in it, and when He explained about The Ten Commandments, they too declined.

Then He offered it to the Jews. "How much does it cost?" they wanted to know. And when He told them it was for free, they immediately replied, "In that case, we'll take two."

Ben Eliezer, THE WORLD'S BEST JEWISH JOKES. London: Angus & Robertson, 1984; p. 36.

Why were the Ten Commandments written on two separate tablets? Well, God offered them first to the Germans. "Impossible!" they replied. "What's this stuff about thou shalt not kill? It's natural to kill!" And they refused. .So then God offered them to the French. "What's this rubbish about thou shalt not commit adultery?" they exclaimed. "It's in our blood! It's l'amour!" And they refused too.

So eventually God offered them to the Jews.

"How much are they?" asked the Jews.

"They're free," came the reply.

"In that case we'll take two!"

Elizabeth Petuchowski, DAS HERZ AUF DER ZUNGE. AUS DAS WELT DES JÜDISCHEN WITZES. Freiburg: Herder, 1984; pp. 120-121.

Gott kam eines Tages nach Babylon und rief aus:

"Hört, ihr guten Leute, ich habe hier ein Gebot, das ich gern fortgäbe."

Ein Babylonier erkundigte sich:

"Was steht denn drin?"

"Du sollst nicht stehlen."

"Nein, danke," sagte der Babylonier.

Gott ging nach Ägypten, das Gebot anzubieten.

Ein Ägypter erkundigte sich:

"Was steht denn drin?"

"Du sollst keine anderen Götter vor mir haben."

"Nein, danke," sagte der Ägypter.

Da ging Gott in die Wüste und sagte zu Moses:

"Ich habe hier ein Gebot für dich."

Moses fragte:

"Was soll das kosten?"

"Nichts."

"Ich nehme zehn."

Alfred Marks, A MEDLEY OF JEWISH HUMOR. London: Robson Books, 1985; p. 63.

An elderly Jew explained to his grandson why the Ten Commandments were written on two tablets of stone instead of one.

At first God had approached the French to see if they wanted the Commandments. "Never," said the French, "we cannot accept 'Thou shalt not commit adultery'- it is part of our culture!"

So then God went to Scotland to see if they would like the Commandments there. "How can we love our neighbors," asked the Scots, "when we live next to the English?" And the Scots, too, turned them down.

In the end God went to the Jews and asked if *they* wanted the Commandments.

"How much?" said the Jews.   *(cont.)*

Marks, *cont.*

"They're free," said God.
"We'll take two," said the Jews.

Alan Dundes, "The Jew and the Polack in the U.S.: A Study of Ethnic Slurs" (1971), in CRACKING JOKES. STUDIES OF SICK HUMOR CYCLES AND STEREOTYPES. Berkeley: 10 Speed Press, 1987; p. 123.

God comes down to a Babylonian one day. He says, "Say, I have a commandment; I'd like to give it to you." And the Babylonian says, "Well, what is it?" "Thou shalt not steal." And the Babylonian says, "Well, no thanks." So God went over to an Egyptian and offered him the same deal. And when the Egyptian heard it, he said, "No thanks." And then God met Moses and God said, "I have a commandment for you." And Moses said, "Well, how much is it going to cost me?" "Nothing." And Moses says, "I'll take ten."

Salcia Landmann, DIE KLASSISCHEN WITZE DER JUDEN. Berlin and Frankfurt: Ullstein, 1989; pp. 47-48.

Wussten Sie schon, wie die Zehn Gebote an die Juden gekommen sind? Das war so: In der uralten Zeit kam ein Engel aus dem Himmel und landete bei den Deutschen: "Liebe Leute, Jungfrauen und Ritter! Ich komme zu euch mit Zehn Geboten, die der grosse Gott euch allen schickt. Das erste Gebot lautet 'Du sollst nicht töten', das zweite..."

"Waaas! Zu uns kommst du mit einem Gebot, nicht zu töten?! Zu uns, den kriegerischen Rittern!? Hinaus mit dir! Verschwinde!"

Der Engel fliegt weiter und landet bei den Russen: "Ihr Brüderchen, ich habe für euch die Zehn Gebote mitgebracht, die euch Gott schickt. Sie lauten: 'Du sollst nicht töten', 'Du sollst dich nicht betrinken', 'Du sollst...'"

"Waaas! Zu uns kommst du mit solchem Quatsch: 'Du sollst dich nicht betrinken'?! Hinaus mit dir!"

Enttäuscht fliegt der Engel weiter und landet bei den Rumänen: "Gott schickt mich zu euch mit den Zehn Geboten. Ich will sie euch vorlesen: 'Du sollst nicht töten', 'Du sollst dich nicht betrinken', 'Du sollst nicht stehlen', 'Du sollst...'"

"Was?! Hör mal, Kleiner, wem sagst du da, dass er nicht stehlen soll? Einem Rumänen? Ha, ha, ha! Geh raus! Fort mit dir! Verschwinde!!"

Müde, traurig fliegt der arme Engel weiter und landet bei den Juden: "Hört zu, Leute! Ich bringe euch Zehn Gebote, die der grosse Gott den Menschen schickt. 'Du sollst nicht töten', 'Du sollst nicht stehlen', 'Du...'"

"Lass das, lass das! Sag uns zuerst einmal, was die Sache kosten soll!"

"Das kostet doch nichts! Gar nichts! Es ist umsonst!"

"Umsooonst? Dann gib sie her!"

Chapter 4

The Ultimate Jewish Mother Joke

Mrs. Markowitz was walking along the beach with her grandson when suddenly a wave came and washed the three-year-old boy out to sea.

"Oh, Lord!" cried the woman. "If you'll just bring that boy back alive I'll do anything. I'll be the best person, I'll give to charity. I'll go to temple. Please, God! Send him back!"

At that moment, a wave washed the child back up on the sand, safe and sound. His grandmother looked at the boy and then up to the heavens.

"Okay!" she exclaimed. "So where's his hat?"

Larry Wilde, *The Official Jewish Joke Book* (New York: Pinnacle, 1974), pp. 70-71.

The History and Variants of the Joke

The Original Anti-Semitic Anecdote

In the following story, which appeared in a book of anecdotes published in London in 1822, the reader will recognize the rudiments of our classic Jewish joke:[1]

THE MOSAIC MOTHER

On one of the nights when Mrs. Siddons first performed at the Drury Lane, a Jew boy, in his eagerness to get to the first row in the shilling gallery, fell over into the pit, and was dangerously hurt. The managers of the theatre ordered the lad to be conveyed to a lodging, and he was attended by their own physician; but notwithstanding all their attention, he died, and was decently buried at the expense of the theatre. The mother came to the playhouse to thank the managers, and they gave her his clothes and five guineas, for which she returned a curtsey, but with some hesitation added, they had forgotten to return her the shilling which Abraham had paid for coming in.

According to the implicit value system of this story, the theater managers are exemplary: they assume responsibility, though the accident was not their fault; they provide medical care and subsequently a proper burial, apparently without hesitating to cover the expenses; and they are generous in their dealings with the mother, giving her five guineas, and without a mention of the expenses they had incurred. It is in contrast to these admirable qualities that the mother's request for the shilling refund comes across as so outrageous, especially since – according to the premises of the joke – she shows no overt signs of grief and is apparently more indifferent to the loss of her child than to the opportunity for getting an extra shilling out of the situation. This mercenary concern eventually overshadows the original purpose of the visit, which was to thank the theater managers.

Everything the managers embody is ascribed a positive value here and is implicitly presented as being non-Jewish. Similarly the mother's ultimately ungrateful, unfeeling and avaricious nature is linked to being Jewish (as is the child's reckless rushing to the first row in the shilling gallery, in order to get the most for his money).

---

[1] *Anecdote Library, Being the Largest Collection of Anecdotes Ever Assembled in One Volume* (London: Whittaker, p. 340).

Curiously, another anti-Semitic joke which illustrates the same image of the Jewish parent as heartless and mercenary, is also based on the idea of a child falling from the gallery into the orchestra pit of a theater:[2]

Levy had his family at the theatre. When his little son fell out of the gallery into the orchestra circle, he cried out to the falling child: "Isidore, come oud of dose expensive seats quick!"

In view of the way the "Mosaic Mother" story polarizes attributes into a positive cluster on the Gentile side and a negative one on the Jewish side, it is clear that the circulation of this anecdote outside the Jewish community afforded the teller and hearer (or writer and reader) an opportunity to share a feeling of amused superiority vis-à-vis Jewishness. Furthermore, three aspects of the story all contribute to its *not* coming across as a joke: a) its references to a specific theater and actress; b) its style of objective reporting, with no cues suggesting playful fabulation; and c) the death of the child. Not only does this anecdote confirm and perpetuate a negative stereotype of Jewishness, but it even allows the reader or listener to wonder whether the story might not be a factual account of a real incident.[3]

Since the anecdote does not appear in such collections as George Coleman's *Circle of Anecdote and Wit* (1821) and W. Carew Hazlitt's *Jests, Old and New* (1887), its circulation may have been rather limited in 19th Century England. In any event, it appears to have been virtually forgotten until it surfaces again in the form of a new "rescuer variant" in the 1920's.

---

[2] James Schermerhorn, *Schermerhorn's Stories* (New York: George Sully & Co., 1928), p. 220.

[3] On the remote possibility that an actual incident was the basis for this anecdote, I consulted histories and records of the Drury Lane and even contacted the theater's present administration. Naturally, not a shred of evidence could be found. I mention this to illustrate the point that even someone who should know better could mistake this anecdote for a possibly factual account.

In all fairness to the editors of the book in which the anecdote appeared, I should also mention that in another section of the *Anecdote Library*, the editors deplored the religious hatred to which the Jews in England had been subjected, stating that "the cruelties and oppressions occasioned by this prejudice is one of the darkest stains on our national character" (*Persecution of the Jews in England*, p. 649).

The Rescuer Variant: A Transitional Form

A small boy of Jewish persuasion playing at the end of a pier fell off and was finally rescued with great difficulty by an intrepid swimmer.

Half an hour later, while leaving the pier, after resting from his exhaustive effort, the rescuer was touched on the shoulder by a man.

"Are you the man vot saved my boy, Ikey's life?" he asked.

"Yes," said the still breathless hero.

"Vell," said the indignant father, "vere's his cap?"[4]

In this second phase in the evolution of the story, with its new seaside setting, the child's plunge into the orchestra pit has been replaced by his falling into the water; the theater managers have given way to a rescuer who succeeds in saving the child from drowning – exhausting himself in the process; and the mother's request for the shilling refund has become the father's even more outrageous reproach to the rescuer for not having recovered the drowning child's hat.

The various attributes are distributed in much the same way as in the original anecdote: a positive cluster is implicitly identified as non-Jewish and includes the rescuer's heroic exploit as well as the gratitude and relief the situation calls for (and both we and the rescuer are led to expect); a negative cluster, tagged as Jewish, consists in the father's ungrateful, unfeeling and materialistic nature. Consequently, the image of the Jew is no more flattering here than in the anecdote of 1822. Nor is that negative representation of Jewishness in any way undercut by the the story, though it now comes across unmistakably as a joke because of such changes as the survival of the child, the elimination of all trappings of objective reporting, and the inclusion of a dialogue in which the father's lines are tagged as comical by virtue of his accent, even before the punch-line is sprung.

There is no reason to believe that this new variant is of Jewish origin. It seems unlikely that the person who transcribed the joke as it appeared in the 1925 anthology (cited above) was Jewish, since no Jewish jokester would have written "a small boy of Jewish persuasion," just as the euphemistic "Mosaic" and overly blunt "Jew boy" in the original anecdote are types of ethnic tagging English Jews would hardly use.

We are still dealing with a "joke about Jews" rather than a "Jewish joke." Here, again, Davies' concept of "switchability," already men-

---

[4] *The Best Jewish Stories* (London: Grant Richards, 1925), pp. 63-64.

tioned in Chapter 3, is particularly useful. As Davies showed, the comic figure in this story – as published by Junior (1927) and Lettslaff (1938) – could be "switched" from a Jew to a Scotsman without spoiling the joke. In the case of a true Jewish joke, the story is so firmly anchored in traditions specific to Jewish culture that no such substitution to another ethnic group, with a reputation for thrift or shrewdness, would be possible.[5] The only addition I would make to Davies' characterization of this story is that it is not *yet* a Jewish joke, and could appropriately be seen as transitional in that respect.

The Miracle Variant: An Authentic Jewish Joke

With its final transformation, occurring in the United States in the 1970's, the story which had begun as an anti-Semitic anecdote becomes one of the finest Jewish jokes we have today.

The Wilde version of 1974 is the earliest in print:

> Mrs. Markowitz was walking along the beach with her grandson when suddenly a wave came and washed the three-year-old boy out to sea.
>
> "Oh, Lord!" cried the woman. "If you'll just bring that boy back alive I'll do anything. I'll be the best person, I'll give to charity. I'll go to temple. Please, God! Send him back!"
>
> At that moment, a wave washed the child back up on the sand, safe and sound. His grandmother looked at the boy and then up to the heavens.
>
> "Okay!" she exclaimed. "So where's his hat?"

Now, there is no longer an encounter between representatives of Jewish and Gentile culture and consequently no polarization within the joke's implicit value system into clusters of Jewish and non-Jewish characteristics. The positive role that was previously filled by Gentiles – the theater managers or rescuers in earlier variants – is now attributed to the most elevated figure within the Jewish universe: namely God. And in this final variant, the Jewish parent plays a crucial role in setting the rescue operation in motion, by appealing to God in the belief – which turns out to be justified – that He controls the very forces of nature that had carried the child away in the first place and can therefore also bring him back again.

In contrast to later retellings of the joke, Wilde's version is the only in which the grandmother promises to change her life as part of a

---

[5] Christie Davies, "Jewish Jokes, Anti-Semitic Jokes, and Hebredonian Jokes," in *Jewish Humor*, ed. Avner Ziv (Tel Aviv: Papyrus, 1986), pp. 75-96.

contractual arrangement with God – the grandmother vowing to become "the best person," "give to charity" and "go to temple," in exchange for God's deliverance of the child. This promise implies, among other things, that: a) the grandmother does not at present live up to the religious and moral prescriptions of Jewish life; b) God would consider that promised amendment of her ways to be a sufficient reason for rescuing her grandson; and c) at least in the grandmother's view of the order of the universe, there is a causal relationship between one's behavior and the disasters or salvation sent by God.

All of this can be related to beliefs that prevailed in the East European *shtetl*, where it was reportedly common to regard natural catastrophes and pogroms as acts of God brought on by the people's failure to live up to their religious duties – just as, according to the Bible, God had sent the Flood and had also destroyed the cities of Sodom and Gomorrah as a punishment for sinfulness. In their book on life in the *shtetl*, Zborowski and Herzog cite the following account:

"Whenever there was an epidemic in the shtetl they used to blame it on the people's sins. They tried to find the guilty ones and would expose them to the public. The Rov would pin up leaflets wherever people could see them saying that *the reason our children are dying is because the people are not pious enough:* they don't go to shul; they don't keep kosher too well; and because the women don't go to the mikva [...] Another method for getting rid of an epidemic, was to get two orphans if possible and marry them off on the cemetery. This was done as a mitzva for God to show Him the good deeds the people are doing and by pleasing Him thus He would call back the plague." In this sense pogroms are treated also as acts of God.[6]

If a child's life was endangered by illness, the *shtetl* mother might deal with that as a matter between her and God. The mother of a gravely ill child in Sholem Aleichem's tale, "The Little Pot" (1901), does just that: "'Dear God,' I pleaded with the Eternal One, 'do you want to punish me? Punish me in any way you like, but don't take my child from me.' And God heard me, He granted my wish, the boy became well again."[7]

---

[6] Mark Zborowski and Elizabeth Herzog, *Life is with People. The Jewish Little-Town of Eastern Europe* (New York: International Universities Press, 1952), p. 224; emphasis added.

[7] *Tevye's Daughters*, trans. Frances Butwin (New York: Crown, 1949), p. 186.

The mother's resources in such situations were viewed as potent:[8]

> The ideal shtetl mother, toiling constantly for her family, is an eternal fountain of sacrifice, lamentation, and renewed effort. When misfortune strikes she cries out with tears and with protests, but her efforts never flag.
> Parental love is also expressed in worrying [...]
> The intensity of one's worry shows the extent of identification, another proof of love. "Oh, it should have happened to me!" cries the mother whose child has hurt himself. "It should be to me and not to you!" and she wrings her hands – "breaks her fingers"– over his scratched face. Even before anything happens, a good mother worries about it *and there is magic in her worry.* It not only proves her love but it may keep the misfortune away.

This almost magical power is present in all of the versions of the "Miracle" variant, since the mother or grandmother manages to mobilize God in each of them; but as already mentioned, it is only in Wilde's version that God is set in motion by the grandmother's promise to change her life. In the Novak and Waldoks (1981) and Dines (1986) versions of the joke, the promise disappears entirely and is replaced by "wailing." All that is left of the original vow in the most recent retellings of the joke is the grandmother's promise of eternal gratitude (Lanigan 1990) or that she will never ask for anything again (Joke-meisters 1990). While all of these are acceptable "set-ups" for the punch-line, their lack of a strong form of contractuality leaves the joke without the center of gravity it has in Wilde's version.

One interesting alternative is, however, found in Koplev's (1988) version. Although no promise is made, a contractual dimension is still evoked since the basis for the mother's plea is that she has always lived up to God's commandments and that the present disaster is therefore undeserved. In this way, she reproaches God for having failed to live up to His contractual obligations, incurred as a result of her obedience to the law:[9]

> Sara was sitting with her child at the shore of the Red Sea. A gigantic wave washed in over her and swept the child away.
> – What have I done to you, Sara cried out to heaven where she thought God must be. – Nothing, right? I have fulfilled my obligations, performed all the rituals, attended every religious service, lived according to the laws in the Talmud and Torah. Why are you taking my child from me?

---

[8] Zborowski and Herzog, p. 294; emphasis added.

[9] Kjeld Koplev, *Guds Udvalgte. Jødisk vid fra Moses til Woody Allen* (Copenhagen: Haase, 1988), p. 13; my translation.

A moment passed as Sara continued her denunciation, and then a new wave cast the child right back into her arms again. Sara sat there looking at her-first born, now lying safe and sound in her lap. Then she turned her face toward God again.
– And the hat. What happened to it. The child was wearing a hat, wasn't he?

The only other recent innovation worth mentioning is the way the miracle itself is managed in Lanigan's (1990) retelling, where it is given a pseudo-biblical form:[10]

"...Please, please, just return my grandson and I'll be eternally grateful."
With that, a cloud suddenly formed in the sky and a giant hand reached down from it and deposited her grandson next to her, safe and sound.
Clasping her hands together the woman looked up. "He had a hat."

Interpretive Options

When the grandmother exclaims "He had a hat!", she comically deviates from the behavior expected of her in the situation at hand: namely an expression of gratitude and – in the Wilde version I will take as the basis for this discussion – an acknowledgment that it is now her turn to fulfill her part of the bargain.

The most obvious way to account for the grandmother's behavior is to see it as expressive of stereotypic Jewish penny-pinching, already discussed in relation to the earlier variants of the story. However, I think that reading overlooks the important ways in which the Jewish joke differs from its anti-Semitic forerunners. I will therefore leave that reading aside and concentrate instead on interpretive options specific to the "Miracle" joke, which in my view has shifted emphasis away from behavioral differences between Jews and Christians, and onto: a) the special qualities of the Jewish mother-figure; and b) Jewish conceptions of the relationship between man and God.

The Jewish mother

One way to understand the grandmother's behavior at the end of the joke, is to see it in tactical terms: having successfully manoeuvered

---

[10] Suds Lanigan, *A Minister, a Rabbi and a Priest* (New York: St. Martin's Press, 1990), pp. 17-18.

God into saving her grandson, she now – as a matter of strategy – declares His performance of the miraculous rescue to be flawed. That gives her the right to assume a superior and critical stance toward Him, rather than the humble and thankful one she owes Him; and it also releases her from having to fulfill her half of the bargain (becoming "the best person," etc.).

This clever operator, capable of getting the better of anyone in any situation, is made of essentially the same stuff as the Jewish mother whose "black belt" display of psychological jujitsu is celebrated in the following story that began to circulate in the early 1960's:[11]

A mother gives her son two shirts as a present. Eager to show his appreciation, he wears one of them the next time he sees her. She takes one look at it and says: "What's the matter? The other one you didn't like?"

The mother in this story engages in a brilliant tactical manoeuvre designed to engender feelings of guilt, inadequacy and failure in her offspring. This isn't necessarily deliberate or even conscious on her part; it is what she is programmed to do. An encounter with her is essentially a series of moves in a game that only she can win: no one can please her, and the greater the effort to do just that, the more certain the failure will be.

The mother's unbeatable performance in the "Shirts" joke may be impressive; but it is vastly outdone by the grandmother in our "Miracle" story, the point of which could be stated this way: *no one can satisfy a Jewish mother, not even God producing a miracle in compliance with her most desperate prayer.*

Having formulated that meaning of the joke, we are still free to under-stand it in two very different ways.

One involves taking the joke at face value, as implicitly stating: "This is, with some comic exaggeration, the way Jewish mothers actually operate." Seen in this perspective, the joke endorses its own depiction of Jewish motherhood.

The other possibility is to think of the joke as implicitly telling us: "Here is a story to top all previous Jewish mother stories." Seen in this way, the joke is an exercise in playing with and parodistically overfulfilling the stereotype of the Jewish mother no one can please. In this respect, it could be seen as both inspired by and attempting to outdo the "Shirts" joke, as a kind of tall tale through which we participate in the "folklorization" of the Jewish mother – an ongoing

---

[11] For the publication history of this joke, see pp. 233-235 below.

process that seems to have reached its peak in the United States in the 1960's and 1970's.[12]

What we have then, with respect to the unsatisfiable Jewish mother-figure in the story, is a set of two interpretations which constitute a reversibility in our experience of the joke: one accounting for her behavior as a tactical manoeuvre, the other accounting for the joke itself as parodistically out-distancing earlier representations of the Jewish mother by pushing the stereotype to new heights of absurdity.

Both of these options invite us to marvel at the Jewish mother's tactical prowess, one as a fact of life, the other in the manner of a tall tale. Both are affectionate,[13] though she treats God unfairly and the stereotype is a negative one. Neither of them, however, in any way proposes her as a role model.

The Relationship of Man and God

In a section in Chapter 2 devoted to competing Jewish conceptions of man's relationship to God, I tried to show that according to one current within Jewish thought, found for example in the Book of Job, man must assume a posture of worshipful reverence toward God, while another more radical current conceives of man as an equal partner in the ongoing process of creation, and as fully entitled to question, judge and condemn the Creator. Among the examples cited to illustrate this radical current was Abraham's boldness in arguing with God over the destruction of Sodom, and the convening of rabbinical courts to bring God to trial for allowing His children to be massacred during the Holocaust.

---

[12] A key text in this process of "folklorization" is Dan Greenberg's *How to Be a Jewish Mother. A Very Lovely Training Manual* originally published in 1964 and subsequently reprinted (Los Angeles: Price, Stern and Sloan, 1975).

[13] In citing the "Shirts" joke, Grotjahn (1970, traces the psychological origins of the story to an aggressive attitude toward the mother (pp. 139-140). Mindess (1972) also cites the same and related jokes as exemplifying a hostile attitude: "...it does not take a psychologist to see that much of the humor directed against [the Jewish mother] represents an attempt on the part of her grown up babies to assert their independence by parading their contempt" (p. 80). In my own view, neither the "Shirts" nor "Miracle" joke is aggressive or contemptuous toward the Jewish mother. These jokes have "got her number" in the sense that they describe her celebrated technique for instilling guilt, etc., but I believe that the spirit in which she is described is indulgent and affectionate.

To whatever degree we understand the "Miracle" joke in the context of the view calling for worshipful reverence, the grandmother's behavior is outrageous, not only in its lack of gratitude but also in the disrespect she expresses toward the Almighty. God has miraculously saved her grandchild, and all she can do is complain about a missing hat - either as a tactical manoeuvre (described above), or because she does not know any better, in which case a role-fiasco would be in play, of the type involving defective reasoning as to the attitude demanded by the situation at hand.

However, the joke can also be understood within the framework of the more radical Jewish conception of man's relationship to God, in which case the grandmother's comic deviance would be an admirable display of *chutzpah* [cheek]. And just as a positive value would be ascribed to the grandmother's behavior, God's conduct would take on a negative quality in this perspective.

This reading of the joke may not seem very plausible at first, but consider God's role in the fiction. If He could replace the little boy on the beach in response to the grandmother's promises, then it is logical to assume that *He could have prevented the three-year-old's being swept out to sea in the first place.* That God should have allowed such a thing to happen is what is most outrageous in the framework of this story – far more outrageous than the grandmother's complaint. In fact, considering what God had permitted to happen, the grandmother is letting Him off easily when she complains about the missing hat! In this context, the religious meaning of bareheadedness – a lack of respect for God – may have a special relevance.[14]

Naturally, all of this lies beneath the surface of the joke, as a kind of undercurrent which in some ways balances and completes the more obvious meanings of the story, and invests it with resonances of a tragic nature, linking it – however remotely – to situations in which the desperate prayers of Jewish mothers remained unanswered.

Once again, we are faced with a reversibility in our understanding of the joke - this time involving a religious perspective within which the grandmother's behavior in relation to God may be seen either as

---

14 "Jewish custom has for ages required [...] men to cover the head in order to show their humiliation and reverence before God." *The Jewish Encyclopedia* (New York: KTAV, n.d.), vol. 2, p. 530, under the entry "Bareheadedness." The same entry (p. 532) also includes the following anecdote: "The mother of Rab Nahum bar Isaac, having been told by an astrologer that her son would become a thief, kept his head always covered in order that the fear of God might always be with him; but on one occasion, as he was sitting under a palm tree, his head covering fell off, and when he looked about, the desire to steal dates came upon him (Shab. 156b)."

an exemplary deviance, as role-fiasco or in terms of the tactical manoeuvre described earlier.

The full range of interpretive options to which this joke is open, might be represented schematically as follows:

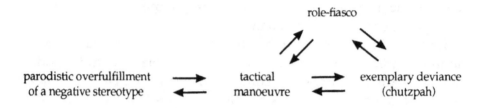

A Final Note

The boundaries between a Jewish joke and human nature can at times be difficult to locate.

For example, the following scene in the 1981 film, *Continental Divide*,[15] might have been inspired by the "Miracle Joke"– or it might simply deal with the same patterns of response that the joke was rooted in. Ernie (John Belushi), a Chicago journalist on his way up a steep mountain to interview an eagle researcher, awakens to find himself surrounded by bears:

ERNIE. Dear Lord, I know this might sound a touch hypocritical – after the way I've been, roughly since birth. But if you could swing things, just this once, so I can get out of here... uneaten... (bear growls) I promise I'll never aks for anything, or complain about anything. Just please don't let these hairy mother...
GUIDE (shouting roughly at the bears). Goddamit, get out of here! Go on! Get out of here. You goddam wet-nosed son-of-a-bitch! Get out of here! Go on, beat it! (The bears, who had been rummaging in the packs, run away.)
GUIDE (to Ernie). That was one of the other things you had to worry about.
ERNIE (gets up, brushes himself off). Thank you Lord. I won't forget that. Nor my promise. (Looking through his pack.) Oh, no. (Desperately) Oh, no! The bears stole all my cigarettes. For that I could have stayed in Chicago. Oh...

Even more striking in this context is an incident which occurred in Denmark in 1990. An 18 year-old high school student, working in a

---

[15] The film was directed by Michael Apted and written by Lawrence Kasdan, with Steven Spielberg as executive producer.

deep ditch he and his father had dug, was buried up to his neck when the walls of the ditch suddenly collapsed around him. The situation was desperate. An emergency-rescue team arrived on the scene, and the boy was finally pulled up to safety, leaving one boot behind at the bottom of the hole his body had been lodged in. When his father noticed that a boot was missing as his son was being pulled up from the ditch, he asked the rescue team if they couldn't get a hold of the missing boot, too.[16]

When Jewish humor is at its best, it is impossible to tell where the joke ends and reality begins.

---

[16] I am indebted to Hélène Wehner Rasmussen for showing me the newspaper article in which this event was reported. *Aarhuus Stiftstidende* , October 21, 1990, section 3, p. 2: "Jeg tænkte kun på at overleve" ("All I thought about was surviving").

PUBLICATION HISTORY

Refund Variant

THE MOSAIC MOTHER

ANECDOTE
LIBRARY.
London: Whittaker,
1822; p. 340.

On one of the nights when Mrs. Siddons first performed at
Drury Lane, a Jew boy, in his eagerness to get to the first
row in the shilling gallery, fell over into the pit, and was
dangerously hurt. The managers of the theatre ordered the
lad to be conveyed to a lodging, and he was attended by
their own physician; but notwithstanding all their attention,
he died, and was decently buried at the expense of the
theatre. The mother came to the playhouse to thank the
managers, and they gave her his clothes and five guineas,
for which she returned a curtsey, but with some hesitation
added, they had forgotten to return her the shilling which
Abraham had paid for coming in.

Rescuer Variant

THE BEST
JEWISH STORIES.
London: Grant
Richards, 1925;
pp. 63-64.

A small boy of Jewish persuasion playing at the end of a
pier fell off and was finally rescued with great difficulty by
an intrepid swimmer.

Half an hour later, while leaving the pier, after resting
from his exhaustive effort, the rescuer was touched on the
shoulder by a man.

"Are you the man vot saved my boy Ikey's life?" he
asked.

"Yes," said the still breathless hero.

"Vell," said the indignant father, "vere's his cap?"

Arthur Szyk
LE JUIF QUI RIT.
Paris: Albin Michel,
1927; p. 211.

SECOURS AUX NOYÉS

Le père. – C'est vous qui avez retiré le petit de l'eau?
Le pêcheur. – Oui, monsieur.
Le père (sévèrement, à son fils). – Et ton chapeau?

"WHAUR'S HIS BONNET?"

Allan Junior,
CANNY TALES FAE
ABERDEEN. Dundee:
Valentine, 1927; p. 17.
Illustration by Gregor
McGregor.

There was great excitement on Deeside. A boy had fallen in the river and had been rescued just in time by a passer-by. When things had calmed down a bit the hero was approached by the boy's father and questioned:
'Are you the man that saved my laddie?'
'Yes.'
'Whaur's his bonnet?'

THANKS

Ike'nsmile Lettslaff,
JOKES, JOKES, JOKES.
London: Universal
Publications, 1937;
pp. 48-49.

A Jewish lad was playing on the end of Southend pier and fell into the water. A well-known local swimmer jumped in and rescued the youngster after an exhausting time. About an hour afterwards the swimmer, fully rested, left the pier. Outside he was tapped on the arm by an excited old Jew, who asked him: "Are you the man vot saved Mo's life?"
"Yes," said the surprised swimmer.
"Vell, vere's his cap?"

Harry Hershfield,
NOW I'LL TELL ONE.
New York: Greenberg,
1938; p. 121.

McGregor took little Sandy out for a walk. Crossing a bridge near the park, the boy broke away for a moment and fell into the deep lagoon below. McGregor put up a great cry for help. Into the water dived an attendant and, after a hard struggle against the current, brought the boy safely to shore. The now exhausted hero simply waved non-chalantly to McGregor and said, "Well, there's your boy." "Yes," answered the father, "But where's his hat?"

Harry Hershfield,
LAUGH LOUDER
LIVE LONGER. New
York: Grayson, 1959;
p. 84.

"Help save my little son!" cried the panicky mother. Into the swirling water jumped a passerby. After a dangerous struggle, the brave one brought the youngster ashore – as the hero started to collapse from his efforts, the mother tapped him on the shoulder. "I hate to bother you – but where's his hat?"

Hervé Nègre ,
DICTIONNAIRE DES
HISTOIRES DRÔLES.
Paris: Fayard, 1973;
vol. 1, p. 131.

Un gosse arrive tout mouillé et pleurnichant vers son père:
   – Papa! Je suis tombé dans la rivière!
   – Hein? fait le père. Et qui t'en a sorti?
   – C'est un gentil monsieur qui a plongé tout habillé et qui m'a ramené sur le quai...
   – Ah, oui? Et où est-il ce monsieur?
   – Il est là-bas au bord, en train de se sécher...
Alors le père se précipite vers le sauveteur qui est tout grelottant et il lui dit:
   – C'est vous qui avez sorti mon fils de la flotte?
   – Oui, dit l'autre. Mais, vous savez, c'est tout naturel!
   – Ah, oui? Vous trouvez ça naturel? Et sa casquette, qu'est-ce que vous en avez fait?

INGRATITUDE

Leo Rosten ,
GIANT BOOK OF
LAUGHTER.
New York: Crown,
1985; p. 289.

The Padraic Hannegans of Sydney, Australia, were taking a holiday at the sea near Wollongong. Mrs. Hannegan was playing in the water with her little son, Carson. Suddenly, an unexpected, powerful wave rolled in, knocked the boy down, and, roaring back, scooped the child up and carried him out to sea.

"Carson! My boy! " screamed Mrs. Hannegan. "Help! Help!"

People leaped to their feet. Several waded into the water. But all stood frozen, for they could not see the lad who was being sucked out to sea.

"Help! My boy! Drowning!" shrieked Mrs. Hannegan.

From his high tower, a lifeguard leaped down to the sand, hurled his torpedo-buoy ahead in the direction he has seen the boy being carried, and with powerful strokes swam out, reached the lad, slung him across the orange torpedo, and propelled both onto a huge wave that carried all three back to shore.

Mrs. Hannegan smothered her son, who was coughing, but definitely alive, in her arms.

The lifeguard beamed. "Fit as a fiddle, he is, mum."

(cont.)

Rosten, *cont.*

Mrs. Hannegan noticed something, drew herself up, and, with considerable indignation, declared: "He-was-wearing-a-hat!..."

Ben Eliezer,
MORE OF THE
WORLD'S BEST
JEWISH JOKES.
London: Angus &
Robertson, 1985;
p. 52.

Little Moishe goes skating on the lake while his mother stands by, watching over him. Suddenly, through a crack in the thin ice, little Moishe vanishes.

"Oy veh!" shrieks his mother, "mine Moishe! In front of my very eyes."

Eventually a policeman comes, strips naked and dives into the icy water. Again and again, blue from the cold, he dives in and eventually finds Moishe. The policeman manages to revive him, wraps him in his own clothes and rushes him to the hospital where little Moishe eventually recovers.

Moishe's mother goes up to the policeman afterwards and says, "So? Where's his hat? He had a hat!"

Miracle Variant

Larry Wilde ,
THE OFFICIAL
JEWISH JOKE BOOK
New York: Pinnacle,
1974; pp. 70-71.

Mrs. Markowitz was walking along the beach with her grandson when suddenly a wave came and washed the three-year-old boy out to sea.

"Oh, Lord!" cried the woman. "If you'll just bring that boy back alive I'll do anything. I'll be the best person, I'll give to charity. I'll go to temple. Please, God! Send him back!"

At that moment, a wave washed the child back up on the sand, safe and sound. His grandmother looked at the boy and then up to the heavens.

"Okay!" she exclaimed. "So where's his hat?"

William Novak &
Moshe Waldoks,
THE BIG BOOK
OF JEWISH HUMOR.
New York: Harper &
Row, 1981; p. 225.

It was a hot day at Jones Beach. Bessie Cohen was there with her three-year-old grandson; she had bought him a cute little sailor suit with a hat, and she watched with delight as he played with his toys at the edge of the water.

Suddenly a giant wave swept onto the shore and before Bessie could even move, the boy was swept out into the cold Atlantic.

Bessie was frantic. "I know I've never been religious," she screamed to the heavens. "But I implore You to save the boy! I'll never ask anything of you again!"

(cont.)

Novak & Waldoks, *cont.*

The boy disappeared from view, and Bessie was beside herself. He went under a second time, and Bessie began to wail. As he went under for the third time, she screamed mightily, appealing to God to save the boy's life.

Her final supplication was answered, as the sea suddenly threw the child onto the shore.was badly shaken but clearly alive. Bessie picked him up and put him down gently on a blanket, far from the water. After looking him over, she turned her face toward the heavens, and complained loudly, "He had a *hat!*"

Michael Dines, THE JEWISH JOKE BOOK. London: Futura, 1986; p. 11.

Grandmother takes her young grandson to the beach and watches him as he paddles. Suddenly a giant wave hurls the boy out to sea. The grandmother starts wailing to God and another huge wave washes him back on to dry land. The grandmother raises a clenched fist and shouts to God.

"He had a hat!"

Kjeld Koplev, GUDS UDVALGTE. JØDISK VID FRA MOSES TIL WOODY ALLEN. Copenhagen: Haase, 1988; p. 13.

Sara sad med sit barn ved bredden af det Røde Hav. En kæmpebølge skyllede ind over hende og rev barnet med sig.

– Hvad har jeg gjort dig, skreg Sara op mod den himmel, hvor hun mente, at hendes Gud måtte befinde sig. – Ingenting, vel? Jeg har passet mit, overholdt alle ritualerne, gået til samtlige gudstjenester, levet efter forskrifterne i Talmud og Torah. Hvorfor tager du så mit barn fra mig?

Der gik et øjeblik, mens Sara fortsatte sine forbandelser, så kom en ny bølge og kastede barnet tilbage i armene på hende igen. Sara sad lidt og så på sin førstefødte, der lå frelst og uskadt i hendes favn. Så vendte hun atter ansigtet mod Gud.

– Og huen. Hvor bliver den af. Barnet havde en hue på, ikke?

THE JOKEMEISTERS.
New York: St. Martin's
Paperbacks, 1990;
p. 106.

An elderly Jewish woman takes her grandson to Miami Beach in the off-season. She sets up her umbrella and lawn chair while the boy goes down to play along the shore.

Suddenly a twelve-foot wave rises from the sea, envelops the boy, and sweeps him out to sea. The woman races down to the water's edgre, but the boy has disappeared without a trace.

The woman drops to her knees, clasps her hands, and peers heavenward. "Please, Lord," she prays, "my little Moishe, my only grandson, dear Lord I pray that you return him to me. I promise you, never again will I ask for anything in my whole life if you'll only deliver my grandson back to my arms."

A moment later there's a thunderclap. Another huge wave washes over the shore, and when it recedes there is the boy, not only alive but standing on his own two feet.

The woman looks at the boy, and then to the heavens again. "A hat, Lord, he was wearing a hat."

Suds Lanigan,
A MINISTER, A RABBI
AND A PRIEST. New
York:
St. Martin's Press, 1990;
pp. 17-18.

A grandmother was sitting on the beach in Miami sunning herself and watching her two-year-old grandson play in the wet sand. Suddenly a huge wave rolled in, washing over everything. When the grandmother recovered from her shock, she looked down at the water's edge.

"My grandson is gone!" she shrieked, and started running to the water. Despite the help of the lifeguards and others, the child could not be found.

The grandmother began beating her breast and wailing. Pounding the sand, she looked up at heaven and cried, "Oh, Lord, I've never asked you for anything in my life. I've been a good woman. Please, please, just return my grandson and I'll be eternally grateful."

With that, a cloud suddenly formed in the sky and a giant hand reached down from it and deposited her grandson next to her, safe and sound.

Clasping her hands together the woman looked up. "He had a hat."

Groucho Marx. Photo © National Broadcasting Company

Chapter 5

The Original Function of Groucho Marx's Resignation Joke

Groucho Marx sent the following wire to a Hollywood club he had joined: "Please accept my resignation. I don't want to belong to any club that will accept me as a member."

Introduction

In Chapter 3, a classic example of ethnic self-disparagement was studied in some detail. In that context, I argued that Jewish jokes evoking anti-Semitic stereotypes actually undercut those stereotypes by parodistically overfulfilling them. In hearing a joke like "Ten Commandments," we are left in doubt as to whether we are expected to believe in the validity of the disparaging characterizations – of the adulterous French, warlike Germans and bargain-obsessed Jews – or to view the very process of depicting peoples in that way as in itself a ridiculous enterprise which deserves to be mocked. If a story of that kind were taken at face value, as though it were a racist joke, the whole point of the humor would be missed.

It is equally important to refrain from taking jokes that play on personal self-disparagement at face value, as though they were unequivocally sincere expressions of the way in which the jokester actually perceives him- or herself. Sometimes the self-presentation involved is based on a fictional persona, propped up as a target of ridicule, such as the character Jack Benny played in his radio and television shows, when he gave new meaning to the concept of stinginess. The most memorable radio sketch was the one in which Benny is stopped by a mugger who says something like, "All right, buddy, your money or your life," after which the continuing silence becomes funnier with every passing second. To mistake the fictional character who can't decide whether he cares more about his own life or the money he is carrying at the moment, for the person pretending to be that character, would be stupid, even if one didn't know that in his private life, Benny was notoriously generous in giving to charities.

It is also common for professional entertainers to base their jokes on a potential liability for their career – turning that liability into an asset. This is what George Burns has done for decades, with self-disparaging jokes that call the audience's attention to the state of his aging body and his presumed loss of sexual viability. For example at a show he did in 1974, at the age of 78, he made such cracks as: "At my age, the only thing about me that still works is my right foot – the one I dance with," and "The only thing that gets me excited is if the soup is too hot." Through these jokes, the comedian turns to his own advantage a condition which might otherwise interfere with his continued acceptance as a vital entertainer. Some comediennes use jokes disparaging their sexual attractiveness in much the same way, such as Phyllis Diller's "I never made *Who's Who* but I'm featured in *What's That*," and "Have you ever seen a soufflé that fell? – nature sure slammed the oven door on me."

One of the all-time classics of self-disparaging humor is Groucho Marx's famous telegram. In reconstructing the situation in which the comedian actually used the telegram, I will try to show in a kind of "case study" of the joke, that the last thing on Groucho's mind was any concern with his own failings as a human being. But first, a brief discussion of the way in which the joke was used by Woody Allen, will help to set the stage for our analysis.

Annie Hall

Soon after the opening credits of *Annie Hall* (1977), Woody Allen tells the "Resignation Joke" while facing the camera, in his role as Alvy Singer:[1]

The – the other important joke for me is one that's, uh, usually attributed to Groucho Marx but I think it appears originally in Freud's *Wit and its Relation to the Unconscious.* And it goes like this – I'm paraphrasing: Uh... "I would never wanna belong to any club that would have someone like me for a member." That's the key joke of my adult life in terms of my relationships with women.

This "key joke" functions here as a self-diagnostic tool enabling our hero – as well as the viewer – to conceptualize a particular neurotic pattern in the life of a person who allows his feelings of unworthiness to prevent him from wanting any woman who would want him. This self-diagnostic use of the joke is further developed in a subsequent scene in which Alvy Singer interrupts his love-making with Allison Portchnik, and succeeds in engaging her in a discussion of John F. Kennedy's assassination. When Allison says: "You're using this conspiracy theory as an excuse to avoid sex with me," Alvy replies:

Oh, my God! (*Then, to the camera*) She's right! Why did I turn off Allison Portchnik? She was – she was beautiful. She was willing. She was real... intelligent. (*Sighing*) Is it the old Groucho Marx joke? That – that I – I just don't wanna belong to any club that would have someone like me for a member? (pp. 22-23)

---

[1] *Four Films of Woody Allen* (London: Faber & Faber, 1983), p. 4. I have taken the liberty of correcting the typography of the title of Freud's book.

As already seen, Alvy attributed this joke to Sigmund Freud's *Wit and its Relation to the Unconscious* (1905). Actually, neither the joke itself nor any likely forerunner appears in that book. Alvy's creator was probably thinking of a joke which had appeared in Theodor Reik's *Jewish Wit* in the following form:[2]

Every day in a coffee house, two Jews sit and play cards. One day they quarrel and Moritz furiously shouts at his friend: "What kind of a guy can you be if you sit down every evening playing cards with a fellow who sits down to play cards with a guy like you!"

Alvy's confusion of Reik's book with Freud's takes nothing away from Woody Allen's brilliant use of the joke in *Annie Hall*.

Virtually nothing has been written about the "Resignation Joke" in the literature on Groucho Marx. This is surprising, considering the notoriety enjoyed by the joke, especially since interest in it was revived by Woody Allen in 1977. Furthermore, none of the commentators who discuss the joke at all – Sheekman,[3] McCaffrey,[4] Wilson[5] and Arce[6] – raise the question as to why Groucho sent the famous telegram and what purpose it was intended to fulfill.

---

[2] Theodor Reik, *Jewish Wit* (New York: Gamut Press, 1962), pp. 57-58. For the publication history of this joke, see pp. 189-190 below.

[3] In his introduction to *The Groucho Letters* (New York: Simon & Schuster, 1967), Arthur Sheekman wrote of the joke: "There, in a few satirical words, is one of the most astute and revealing observations about the self-hating, socially ambitious human animal" (p. 8).

[4] For Donald W. McCaffrey, the joke was a *non sequitur*, resulting from "a chain reaction of delightful pseudo-logic that almost sounded valid." *The Golden Age of Sound Comedy* (South Brunswick and New York: Barnes, 1973), p. 74.

[5] Christopher Wilson described the "Resignation Joke" as an example of *shared ridicule*, through which "the joker derides himself and his audience simultaneously [...] The message of shared disparagement being–'If you don't mind me, you've got no taste!'" Wilson was also the first to identify the joke as "a variant of the famous Jewish joke–'What sort of a shmuck do you think I am? I'm not going to sit down and play cards with the sort of shmuck who'd sit down and play cards with me." *Jokes: Form, Content, Use and Function* (London: Academic Press, 1978), p. 190.

[6] In his introduction to *The Groucho Phile* (London: W. H. Allen, 1978), Hector Arce was the first to set the telegram in its social context: Referring to the Friar's Club of Beverly Hills, Arce wrote that Groucho "had some misgivings about the quality of the members, doubts which were verified a few years later when an infamous card-cheating scandal erupted there. When he decided to drop out of the group, he wrote: 'Gentlemen: Please accept my resignation. I don't care to belong to any social organisation that will accept me as a member'" (p. xv).

The situation in which the telegram was sent will now be reconstructed, after which the original function of the "Resignation Joke" will be described, and an attempt will be made to account for its effectiveness in fulfilling that intended function.

The Friar's Club Incident

We have two sources of information concerning the context in which Groucho Marx first used the "Resignation Joke." The earlier of these sources is the biography written by the comedian's son, Arthur Marx, who provided the following account:[7]

> [The actor, Georgie] Jessel has always been able to make Father laugh, and as a favor to him, he joined the Hollywood chapter of the Friar's Club a couple of years ago. But Father doesn't like club life, and, after a few months, he dropped out. The Friars were disappointed over losing him, and wanted to know why he was resigning. They weren't satisfied with his original explanation – that he just didn't have time to participate in the club's activities. He must have another, more valid reason, they felt.
>
> "I do have another reason," he wrote back promptly. "I didn't want to tell you, but since you've forced the issue, I just don't want to belong to any club that would have me as a member."

Since this biography appeared in 1954, "a couple of years ago" would place the incident somewhere in the vicinity of 1950-1952, assuming that a year or two may have elapsed between the writing and the publication of the book.

The other account we have was written by the comedian himself in the autobiography that was published in 1959. Much unpleasantness had apparently been omitted from the earlier record, perhaps out of discretion, in order to avoid offending anyone, or because any public criticism leveled at the club had to come from Groucho himself, and not his son. And even here, Groucho took the precaution of withholding the name of the club, which appears under the same alias ("Delaney") that is jokingly applied to a number of parties portrayed in the autobiography in an unfavorable light.

Groucho begins by telling of his general aversion for clubs, and this is consistent with the earlier description in his son's book, though here the aversion is concretized to a fuller extent:[8]

---

7 Arthur Marx, *Life with Groucho* (New York: Simon & Schuster, 1954), p. 45.

8 Groucho Marx, *Groucho and Me* (New York: Bernard Geis, 1959), p. 320.

I'm not a particularly gregarious fellow. If anything, I suppose I'm a bit on the misanthropic side. I've tried being a jolly good club member, but after a month or so my mouth always aches from baring my teeth in a false smile. The pseudo-friendliness, the limp handshake and the extra firm handshake (both of which should be abolished by the Health Department), are not for me. This also goes for the hearty slap-on-the-back and the all-around, general clap-trap that you are subjected to from the All-American bores which you would instantly flee from if you weren't trapped in a clubhouse.

In the remainder of his account, specific grievances Groucho had against the Friar's Club (alias "Delaney Club") come to light:

Some years ago, after considerable urging, I consented to join a prominent theatrical organization. By an odd coincidence, it was called the Delaney Club. Here, I thought, within these hallowed walls of Thespis, we would sit of an evening with our Napoleon brandies and long-stemmed pipes and discuss Chaucer, Charles Lamb, Ruskin, Voltaire, Booth, the Barrymores, Duse, Shakespeare, Bernhardt and all the other legendary figures of the theatre and literature. The first night I went there, I found thirty-two fellows playing gin rummy with marked cards, five members shooting loaded dice on a suspiciously bumpy carpet and four members in separate phone booths calling women who were other members' wives.

A few nights later the club had a banquet. I don't clearly remember what the occasion was. I think it was to honor one of the members who had successfully managed to evade the police for over a year. The dining tables were long and narrow, and unless you arrived around three in the afternoon you had no control over who your dinner companion was going to be. That particular night I was sitting next to a barber who had cut me many times, both socially and with a razor. At one point he looked slowly around the room, then turned to me and said, "Groucho, we're certainly getting a lousy batch of new members!"

I chose to ignore this remark and tried talking to him about Chaucer, Ruskin and Shakespeare, but he had switched to denouncing electric razors as a death blow to the tonsorial arts, so I dried up and resumed drinking. The following morning I sent the club a wire stating, PLEASE ACCEPT MY RESIGNATION. I DON'T WANT TO BELONG TO ANY CLUB THAT WILL ACCEPT ME AS A MEMBER (pp. 320-321).

Allowances should certainly be made for a good deal of exaggeration in the account cited above. Much of it is tongue-in-cheek, and designed to entertain the reader. However, the basic picture, regarding Groucho's attitude toward the Friar's Club, can undoubtedly be taken at face value.

If the two accounts – the son's and the father's – are allowed to complete each other, we can conclude that the full sequence of events probably looked something like this:

1) Groucho allows himself to be talked into joining the Friar's Club, though he doesn't like clubs in general.

2) He quickly becomes fed up with this club in particular, because of what he sees as its low intellectual and ethical standards.

3) The last straw is the final offensive remark in a series of insults to which he is subjected by a member of the club.

4) Groucho notifies the club that he is quitting, inoffensively giving as his excuse that he just doesn't have time to participate in the club's activities.

5) Unhappy about Groucho's resignation and sensing that there may be more to it than the comedian is letting on, club members press him for the "real" reason.

6) Wanting to be done with this entanglement once and for all, Groucho pretends to disclose the real reason in the famous telegram, and is left alone from then on.

Seen in this light, it is clear that the "Resignation Joke" was invented to fulfill a *tactical* purpose: that of extricating Groucho from an unpleasant situation, by discouraging any further efforts on the part of club members to obtain a fuller explanation as to his reasons for resigning. But why did it work? To some degree, the apparent self-disparagement may have had a disarming effect. However, I suspect that two properties of the telegram played an even more important role in enabling it to fulfill its intended social function.

One of those properties is a defiance of logic of essentially the same type as that found in *impossible figures*, described on pp. 30-31 above. As the reader will recall, impossible figures induce cognitive confusion, by violating their own logic in so logically compelling a manner that we cannot grasp how they fit together.

When Groucho Marx couched his "explanation" in the form of an impossible figure, he confronted the club-members with a piece of reasoning that was as impregnable to logic as a "Penrose Triangle" or "three-stick clevis," and which undoubtedly mystified those who would otherwise have pressed him for the real reason for his resignation. There is simply no arguing with an impossible figure, or with a person who is capable of generating one, which in a game situation is like checkmate in the sense that it marks the end of the contest, allowing for no subsequent move.

The second property of the telegram which accounts for its effectiveness, is the fact that it was framed *as a joke*. In delivering his "explanation" in a form calculated to provoke laughter, Groucho made it difficult for the club-members to know how to react without looking foolish, especially since they were already implicated in the joke, as a collective butt. As one commentator put it--though not in connection with the famous telegram: "Groucho may be the most powerful clown ever. [...] because Groucho has the power to turn us nonfools into his private stock."[9]

Furthermore, the comedian's *toying* with shared ridicule may have functioned as a kind of negotiation on his part: signaling his preference for severing the relationship in a playful spirit, as well as his willingness to assume (or pretend to assume) the blame for its failure, thereby sparing the club-members' feelings in exchange for a clean break. It was also a means for telling them indirectly and unmistakably that they were no match for his wit.

In any event, the joke put an end to the club-members' requests for an explanation, thereby fulfilling a very specific social function. In the process, of course, Groucho launched a hilarious "one-liner" which (he must have sensed) would be retold countless times, and would become a lasting part of his own comic profile.

Paradoxically, one of the most striking examples of a self-disparaging joke turns out to have been motivated by a wish on the jokester's part to dissociate himself once and for all from a group of people to whom he felt superior.

Of all the jokes studied in this book, the "Resignation Joke" is the only one whose inventor is known; it is also the only one that may not come across as being a specifically Jewish joke. Yet its roots in the impossible figure of the "Cardplayer" story link it to Jewish humor as does its apparently self-disparaging nature. And just as the ethnic stereotypes evoked in "Ten Commandments" are actually undercut by the joke which pretends to endorse them, so is the personal self-

---

[9] Adriane L. Despot, "Some Principles of Clowning," *The Massachusetts Review* (Winter 1981), p. 671.

disparagement of Groucho's telegram a posture through which relationships are managed and a problem resolved.

QUOTATION RECORD

Curiously enough, this one-liner is never quoted in precisely the same way by any two people. However, its underlying concept is so strong that the wording of the punchline can be varied without in any way altering the impact of the joke. Here are twelve versions of the main sentence:

"I just don't want to belong to any club that will accept me as a member."	Arthur Marx, *Life with Groucho*. New York: Simon & Schuster, 1954; p. 45.
"I don't want to belong to any club that will accept me as a member."	Groucho Marx, *Groucho and Me*. New York: Bernard Geis, 1959; p. 321.
"I don't care to belong to any club that will have me as a member."	Arthur Sheekman in Groucho Marx, *The Groucho Letters*. New York: Simon & Schuster, 1967; p. 8.
I wouldn't belong to any organization that would have me for a member."	Joey Adams, *Encyclopedia of Humor*. Indianapolis and New York: Bobbs-Merrill, 1968; p. 359.
"I wouldn't join a club that would have me as a member."	Lore and Maurice Cowan, *The Wit of the Jews*. London: Leslie Frewin, 1970; p. 96.
"I wouldn't belong to an organization that would have me as a member."	Donald W. McCaffrey, *The Golden Age of Sound Comedy*. South Brunswick and New York: Barnes, 1973; p. 74.
"I would never want to belong to any club that would have someone like me for a member."	Woody Allen's film, *Annie Hall* (1977).
"I don't care to belong to any social organization that will accept me as a member."	Hector Arce in Groucho Marx, *The Groucho Phile*. London: W. H. Allen, 1978; p. xv.
"I don't wish to belong to any club that would accept me as a member."	Christopher P. Wilson, *Jokes: Form, Content, Use and Function*. London: Academic Press, 1978; p. 190.
"I wouldn't join any club that would have me as a member."	William Novak and Moshe Waldoks, *The Big Book of Jewish Humor*. New York: Harper & Row, 1981; p. 85.
"I do not care to belong to a club that accepts people like me as members."	Joseph Dorinson, "Jewish Humor. Mechanism for Defense, Weapon for Cultural Affirmation," *Journal of Psycho-History* 8, 4 (1981); p. 452.
I do not wish to belong to the kind of club that accepts people like me as member."	Leo Rosten, *Giant Book of Laughter*. New York: Crown, 1985; p. 227.

I have run into only one commentator who actually succeeded in butchering this joke:

"Another of the many stories about the Marx Brothers concerns Groucho, who is alleged to have applied for membership of an exclusive New York club. When he was told that his application was accepted he is said to have pointed out that no club with a good reputation could possibly accept Groucho Marx as a member – therefore he would rather stay away. And he did."	John Montgomery, *Comedy Films*. London: George Allen & Unwin, 1954; p. 251.

Chapter 6

The Meaning of Life

The beloved rabbi was dying, and lay motionless on his bed. On either side of him hovered his grieving disciples.

"Rabbi," pleaded the foremost of his followers, "please do not leave us without a final word of wisdom. Speak to us one last time!"

For a few moments, there was no response, and the weeping visitors feared their spiritual leader was no longer with them. But suddenly his lips began to move, ever so slightly. The disciples bent over him to hear his final words:

"Life is like a glass of tea," he managed to whisper with great difficulty.

The disciples looked at each other in perplexity. What did he mean? What great secret was hidden in that mystic statement? For nearly an hour, they exchanged opinions, analyzing the sentence from every conceivable standpoint, but they could not decipher its deeper meaning.

"We must ask him before it's too late," said the head disciple. Once again he leaned over the still figure of the revered rabbi.

"Rabbi, rabbi," he called out urgently, "we implore you to explain: why is life like a glass of tea?"

With his last spark of energy, the rabbi shrugged and whispered:

"All right, so life is *not* like a glass of tea."

Composite version inspired by Asimov (1972), Mindess (1972) and Spalding (1976).

The History and Variants of the Joke

The Suspension-Bridge Variant

Unlike any other joke studied in this book, this one seems to have begun its life in *two* forms – one laconic, the other elaborate – with the same punchline, circulated simultaneously, and both breaking into print in Berlin in 1907-1908.

We will begin with the shorter of the two forms, which was the one most widely circulated at the time. When first published in 1908, it looked like this:[1]

Deep

> Marcus: The whole of life strikes me as being like a suspension-bridge.
> Levy: Why is that? How should that be understood?
> Marcus: I should know!

Freud made no mention of this joke in the original 1905 edition of his *Jokes and Their Relation to the Unconscious*, but included it in a footnote added in 1912 to the second edition of his book. The joke had probably been invented in the interval. As cited by Freud, it is even more streamlined than in earlier anthologies:

"Life is like a suspension bridge," said one man. – "Why is that?" asked the other. – "How should I know?" was the reply.

There are essentially three ways in which this joke might be understood.

MISCONSTRUING THE QUESTION

In asking "Why?" or "Why is that?" ("Wieso?") of the person who has just made his philosophical pronouncement, the questioner is of course asking: "*In what way* is life a suspension-bridge?" The other person can be seen as answering as though the question were: "*Why has life turned out to be* a suspension-bridge?"

---

[1] Alexander Moszkowski, *Die unsterbliche Kiste* (Berlin: Lustige Blätter, 1908), p. 113.

Gags based on such misconstruing of questions have long been used in stage and film comedy. For example, in *Way Out West*, Stan Laurel is asked: "What did he die of?" and Stan replies: "He died of a Monday – or was it a Tuesday?" And the following dialogue occurs in one of the *Airplane* spoofs:

> Boy: Can I ask you a question?
> Pilot: What is it?
> Boy: It's an interrogative statement – used to test knowledge. But that's not important right now, Mister. Is my dog, Scraps, going to make it through this O.K.?

Not all versions of "Suspension-Bridge" are open to this reading. In the earliest one, for example, the question "How should that be understood?" ("Wie ist das zu verstehen?") is explicitly asked. However, in those versions in which the meaning of the question is left open – also in later variants of the joke, the ambiguity can provide one way of accounting for the answer.

POSE AND IRRESPONSIBILITY

Theodor Reik (1962) saw "Suspension-Bridge" as an expression of "self-caricature" which "mocks at alleged philosophical reflections."[2] What Reik seems to mean is that through this joke, Jews make fun of their own tendency to play at "being deep." In this respect, the joke might be seen as fulfilling a corrective function with regard to philosophical pretentiousness and role-playing.

It is in this spirit that Jewish jokesters have often placed pseudo-philosophical reflections in the mouths of comic figures, in order to make fun of the type of posing involved when one person tries to impress another – or himself – as being deep. Jokes of this kind usually contain pointless comparisons, as in the following example from 1920:[3]

---

[2] Theodor Reik, *Jewish Wit* (New York: Gamut Press, 1962), p. 117.

[3] "Schmil blickt tiefsinnig vor sich hin. Er philosophiert. Itzig Leib fragt ihn, warum so nachdenklich und erhält die lakonische Antwort: 'Der Mensch is geglechent zi a Schister.' 'Farwus in wiasoi geglechent zi a Schister?' fragt er erstaunt, worauf Schmil noch einmal verkündigt: 'Der Mensch is geglechent zi a Schister, hant lebt er, morgen starbt er."

Schmil looks thoughtfully into space. He is philosophizing. Itzig Leib asks him why he is so meditative and receives the laconic answer: "Man is like a shoemaker." "How and in what way like a shoemaker?" he asks in astonishment, whereupon Schmil once again proclaims "Man is like a shoemaker, now he lives, tomorrow he dies."

The same applies to the display of mock-profundity in this joke, dating from 1911:[4]

Deep

She: You are so meditative, my dear Joseph?
He: Yes, Rosa, I'm in such a philosophical mood. Do you know how all of human life strikes me? Like a shadow on the wall. Push down the wall, – gone is the shadow!

Though Joseph's simile was probably inspired by a passage in the Talmud,[5] it is not the Talmud that is being parodied, but rather a person trying to *sound* Talmudic.

Seen in this perspective, "Suspension-Bridge" would begin with a philosophical pose – possibly based on an old aphorism[6] – and end

---

Heinrich Loewe, *Schelme und Narren mit jüdischen Kappen* (Berlin: Welt-Verlag, 1920), p. 49. Another version of the same pseudo-epigram is found in P. J. Kohn's *Rabbinischer Humor* (Frankfurt: Kauffmann, 1930; orig. pub. 1915), p. 99: "'Der Mensch ist gegleichen zu einem Uhrmacher,' sagte ein polnischer Maggid. – So wie der Uhrmacher sterben muss, so muss auch der Mensch sterben." ("'Man can be likened to a watchmaker,' said a Polish maggid. – Just as the watchmaker must die, so must man also die.") Tevye the dairyman also utters such pseudo-epigrams. In "The Bubble Bursts," Tevye says at one point: "We must all die sometime. A man is compared to a carpenter. A carpenter lives and lives until he dies, and a man lives and lives until he dies." Sholom Aleichem, *Tevye's Daughters* (New York: Crown, 1949), p. 11.

[4] Alexander Moszkowski, *Die jüdische Kiste. 399 Juwelen* (Berlin: Lustige Blätter, 1911), p. 87. Another early example of this pseudo-proverb is found in Hans Ostwald, *Frisch, gesund und meschugge* (Berlin: Franke, 1928), p. 258.

[5] "Qu'est-ce que la vie d'un homme? Une ombre. Mais quelle ombre? Celle, immuable, d'un bâtiment? Ou celle d'un arbre qui survit aux saisons? Non, la vie d'un homme se compare à l'hombre d'un oiseau en plein vol: à peine aperçue, déjà elle est effacée." ("What is the life of a man? A shadow. But what shadow? The motionless shadow of a wall? Or that of a tree which survives the changing seasons? No, the life of a man is comparable to the shadow of a bird in flight: scarcely noticed, and it is already gone.") Cited as an epigraph by Elie Wiesel for his novel, *Le testament d'un poète juif assassiné* (Paris: Seuil, 1980).

[6] One possible source is "All creatures pass over a frail bridge, connecting life and death: life is its entrance, death its exit." *Bahya, Hobot HaLebabot*, 1040 *Tokeha*. Joseph L. Baron, *A Treasury of Jewish Quotations* (Aronson: 1985; orig. pub. 1956), p. 278. Another possibility is "The world resembles a collapsing bridge." 'Immanuel. Entry 5366 in Reuben Alcalay, *A Basic Encyclopedia of Jewish Proverbs, Quotations and Folk Wisdom* (Bridgeport: Hartmore House, 1973), p. 554.

with an outrageous shirking of the responsibility normally taken for the utterances one makes, since any statement which isn't framed as nonsense or in some other way disowned in an introductory comment, carries with it an implicit assurance that the speaker understands, endorses and would be ready to explain his utterance at the listener's request.

If the joke is understood in this way, then the speaker has no idea as to what he is talking about when he says, "Life is a suspension-bridge," and the joke ridicules philosophical posing as well as the flaunting of basic rules of accountability governing speech acts.

VIOLATING THE LAWS OF THE JOKE-TELLING EVENT

Freud characterized "Suspension-Bridge" not as a joke but as "idiocy masquerading as a joke" (p. 190), which he felt was also true of the following story:

A man at the dinner table who was being handed fish dipped his two hands twice in the mayonnaise and then ran them through his hair. When his neighbor looked at him in astonishment, he seemed to notice his mistake and apologized: "I'm so sorry, I thought it was spinach."

He wrote of both "non jokes":

These extreme examples have an effect because they rouse the expectation of a joke, so that one tries to find a concealed sense behind the nonsense. But one finds none: they really are nonsense. The pretense makes it possible for a moment to liberate the pleasure in nonsense. These jokes are not entirely without a purpose; they are a 'take-in', and give the person who tells them a certain amount of pleasure in misleading and annoying his hearer. The latter then damps down his annoyance by determining to tell them himself later on (p. 190).

Support for Freud's view can be found in a parallel development within the riddle-genre in Berlin at about the same time, as illustrated by the following example:[7]

---

[7] *Schlemiel. Illustriertes jüdisches Witzblatt* 2, 5 (1 May 1905), p. 44; my translation. The original text, entitled *Ein Rätsel*, reads as follows:

Berl: Ich vil dir frogen a Rätsel. Sog mir, wos is dos: a langer, a grüner, er hängt und pfeift. Schmerl: Nu??

Berl: I want to ask you a riddle. Tell me what this is: it's long, green, hangs on a wall and whistles.

Schmerl: So??

Berl: Fool, you don't know? It's a herring.

Schmerl: Alright, a herring is long but how is it green?

Berl: Someone painted it.

Schmerl: But why is it hanging?

Berl: Someone hung it up.

Schmerl: And it whistles? A herring can't whistle.

Berl: If I hadn't said "it whistles," it wouldn't have taken much cleverness to guess that it's a herring.

What is funny about this pseudo-riddle is the flagrancy with which it flaunts the rules of the genre, which include the requirement that the answer to a riddle must legitimately fulfill all of the constraints presented to the person trying to guess the solution.

Similarly, a "joke" can deliberately violate the rules of the joke-telling event, as did the following piece of nonsense that circulated in Brooklyn in the 1950's: "An elephant and a monkey are taking a bath. The elephant says, 'Please pass the soap,' to which the monkey replies: 'No soap, *radio!*'" As I recall, the idea when telling the joke was to try to trick the listener into laughing, even though the story made no sense at all as a joke. It was really a matter of putting one over on the listener.

Freud viewed "Suspension-Bridge" in a perspective of this kind, perhaps as a mini "shaggy dog story," baiting and teasing the listener by promising something it fails to deliver. In this respect, a tactical manoeuvre is involved – not within the fiction, but in the joke-teller's relationship to the listener.

I mentioned at the start that "Suspension-Bridge" has a more developed form as well as the very brief one discussed above. This

---

Berl: Narr, du weißt nicht? Dos is a Hering.

Schmerl: Gut, a Hering is a langer, aber wieso a grüner?

Berl: Man hot ihm angefärbt.

Schmerl: Aber far wos hängt er?

Berl: Man hot ihm ufgehangen.

Schmerl: Und er pfeift? A Hering kann doch nit pfeifen.

Berl: As ich wollt nit gesogt "er pfeift", wollt doch nit gewesen kein Chochme [Schlauheit] zu treffen, as dos is a Hering.

fuller version of the joke was first published in 1907, a year before the earliest example I have been able to collect of the shorter one:[8]

On another occasion, after the late services on a Sabbath afternoon, the pious men sit around their wise rabbi at the Sabbath meal. Again he sinks into a deep meditation. As the men become aware of this, they stop their debates and disputes and wait for the moment when the holy man will awaken from his meditation.

When this doesn't happen, the eldest member of the congregation touches the rabbi's shoulder, and as he gives a start, the rabbi is asked what thoughts had preoccupied him to such a degree.

The great man then raises his thoughtful gaze and speaks:

"Life... life is like a suspension bridge."

Then he falls silent once again.

"What did he say?... What did he say?" the men whisper, and after they have reverently murmured the statement to one another, they begin to discuss it eagerly and with passion. And so great is their eagerness in interpreting the statement that one after another their minds and finally also their fists intervene in the dispute. An agreement as to the meaning of the enigmatic statement cannot be reached, and they finally agree to ask the rabbi, still withdrawn in meditation, what he meant by it.

"Rabbi," they say, "you can see that we haven't understood you. Give us the meaning, tell us the significance. How is life like a suspension bridge?"

Once again the great rabbi raises his thoughtful gaze and speaks:

"How should I know?"

Here numerous elements strengthen our expectation of a rewarding solution to the riddle: the fact that the philosophical statement is drawn out of a "wise" and "holy" rabbi, from the depths of his meditative withdrawal, by a flock of pious followers who invest great effort in trying to decipher it, gives the statement a special status in our eyes, and such elements of staging as the rabbi's raising of his "thoughtful gaze" further contribute to the build-up.

Yet another element is added in the first English version of this rabbinic form of "Suspension-Bridge," dating from 1945: a differentiation within the group of followers into those who do not think of asking the rabbi to explain what he means, and the one disciple – in this case the youngest – who is identified for us as having the courage to ask.[9]

The great Rabbi meditates in the solitude of his study. Outside, the faithful disciples are waiting. What new revelation will emanate from the great man? They wait for three days. Then the door opens, and out comes the Rabbi in majestic silence. Slowly he opens his

---

8 Manuel Nuél, *Das Buch der jüdischen Witze* (Berlin: Gustav Rieckes Buchhandel, n.d. [1907]), pp. 16-17.

9 Harry Schnur, *Jewish Humor* (London: Allied Book Club, n.d. [1945]), pp. 17-18.

mouth and announces the result of his long meditation. In solemn, measured tones, he says: "The life of man is like a railway bridge."

The disciples ponder this deep saying whose solution each wishes to be the first to discover and announce. But it eludes them – until, many hours later, the youngest disciple summons courage and timidly asks: "Rabbi – why is man's life like a railway bridge?"

The Rabbi replies with simple dignity: "How do I know?"

The same three interpretive options described in relation to the short form of the joke, could be applied to this longer form as well, in which case:

a) The rabbi could be seen as misconstruing the question – as thinking he is being asked, not *what he means* by the statement, but why life *is* that way; even so, this would result in a deflation of the rabbi's status in our eyes.

b) The rabbi could be seen as a fraud – as having made a philosophical statement he himself did not understand, and then not even having enough sense to realize that in answering "How do I know?" when asked the meaning of his statement, he is exposing himself as a bluffer; if the 1945 version is viewed in this perspective, those disciples who do not question the rabbi would be seen as dupes, while the youngest one who musters the courage to ask is deserving of our admiration – like the child at the end of Hans Christian Andersen's tale about "The Emperor's New Clothes"; and the rabbi's behavior would begin as a tactical manoeuvre designed to impress those around him, and end as role-fiasco.

c) The joke could be seen as a kind of "shaggy dog story," arousing the reader's or listener's interest in a riddle that is simply dismissed.

A fourth possibility, not applicable to the shorter version, may also be in play here:

d) The joke can be understood as parodistically underfulfilling the positive stereotype of the rabbi as profound thinker.

This final interpretive option applies to a number of jokes in which a rabbi, from whom we are led to expect a revelation, turns out to be a dimwit, a charlatan or both, as illustrated by the following joke – yet another from the Berlin vintage of 1907:[10]

The Rabbi of Jaroslaw proclaimed on one Sabbath to his congregation that he had to withdraw from his teaching and other duties for a time, so that he might meditate undisturbed upon a thought that filled his spirit.

Everyone was proud to have in their midst such a "Light of Israel," and promised to provide for him and his family during those days when he was lost to the world and listened to his inner voice. Which also occurred in quite abundant measure.

Meanwhile week after week went by and the rabbi did not appear. He was still thinking. Finally the people began to worry and they sent off a man who was to probe what deep and meaningful thought the rabbi was turning around in his brain.

"Rabbi!" he asked, "have you finished contemplating your thought? And what have you contemplated?"

And the rabbi said:

"This is what I have contemplated: If all the men in the world became one man...

"...if all the trees in the world became one tree...

"...if all the axes in the world became one axe...

"...and if all the seas in the world became one sea..."

"What then...?" asked the man anxiously.

The rabbi continued:

"And if this man whom all men had become, took the axe which all axes had become... and chopped down the tree which all trees had become... and this tree fell into the sea that all the seas had become..."

He paused, overwhelmed by his thought and looked around.

"What then...?" asked the man once more.

"And then I contemplate and contemplate for myself," said the rabbi, "what a splash that would make..."

The punchline containing the long awaited revelation, can be understood both in terms of role-fiasco and the parodistic under-fulfillment of a positive stereotype. But rabbi's behavior can also be seen in terms of a tactical manoeuvre, in the sense that the weeks and months the rabbi spends in meditative withdrawal with everyone's consent, are periods during which he is released from all of his duties, while the congregation provides for his own and for his family's needs. Here we find the same combination of interpretive options already seen in relation to the "Dead Shames" joke discussed in Chapter 3.

---

[10] Nuél, op. cit., pp. 21-22; my translation. This joke subsequently appeared in the following anthologies: J. Ch. Rawnitzki, *Yidishe Witzn* (New York: Morris S. Sklarsky, 1959; orig. pub. 1923), vol. 2, pp. 62-63; Rufus Learsi, *The Book of Jewish Humor* (New York: Bloch, 1941), pp. 64-65; Solomon Simon, *The Wise Men of Helm and Their Merry Tales* (New York: Behrman, 1945), pp. 90-95; Henry D. Spalding, *Encyclopedia of Jewish Humor* (New York: Jonathan David, 1969), p. 118; and Bronislaw Aleksandrowicz, *Jødiske Anekdoter* (Copenhagen: Nordisk Bogforlag, 1975), p. 39.

The Jealous Brother-in-Law Variant

As a joke, this variant is a disaster. However, that doesn't make it any less interesting as a stage in the development of the meaning-of-life story.

Represented in only one anthology of Jewish jokes, published in 1935, the "Jealous Brother-in-Law" variant is entirely unambiguous in the sense that the character issuing the cryptic, philosophical statements is explicitly presented to us as a fraud. His utterances are part of a tactical manoeuvre designed to attract attention to himself and to win the admiration of a public, repeatedly impressed with the profundity of his thought. His philosophizing is nothing but a pose, and the statements he makes are meaningless:[11]

Samuel Kopman had the demeanor of a philosopher. When spoken to he would stare at the speaker, puff his cigar slowly, and say nothing. In company he would listen carefully to everything that was said and when the discussion reached a climax he would make some irrelevant, brief statement which convinced everyone that he was a deep thinker. Once when the unsatisfactory economic situation had been discussed from every angle for hours, Kopman interrupted the crowd, waited until he could get perfect attention, and then said: "Why do you all complain? Life is only electricity." Everybody present thought this was a profound saying befitting a thinker. Kopman's brother-in-law, Jake Mandel, was jealous.

On another occasion the subject of immortality was discussed at length. Here again Kopman waited for an opportunity to be heard and then said thoughtfully: "Why bother about immortality? Life is like a railroad train." Here again Kopman increased his reputation as a philosopher and Jake's jealousy intensified.

Once the subject of Zionism was being argued heatedly. When the discussion reached a high pitch Kopman managed to be heard saying deliberately: "What sort of problem is Zionism anyway? The Jewish people are like a tree." Again Kopman scored a victory and everybody remarked what a wise utterance this was–but Jake's jealousy had reached the limit.

"Just a minute," he burst forth. "Listen now, philosophic brother-in-law of mine. Will you please tell us why the Jewish people are like a tree?"

For a tense moment everybody's eyes were on Kopman.

"I really can't explain that," admitted Kopman flabbergasted, "but it took an ignoramus like you to ask such a fool question!"

The easy victories Kopman scores with his deep-sounding statements are not to the credit of his public, which is implicitly presented here as pretending to understand the meaning of utterly meaningless statements. In this respect, the public is not only taken in by Kopman but answers his pose with a pose of its own. The brother-in-law who sees through Kopman's imposture and publicly exposes him in the

---

[11] S. Felix Mendelsohn, *The Jew Laughs. Humorous Stories and Anecdotes* (Chicago: L. M. Stein, 1935), pp. 217-218.

end, is a positive character in that he is the only one who questions the nonsense everyone else seems to swallow. In fact, the exercise of a critical, questioning attitude toward cryptic statements is in itself the most positive factor within the implicit value system of the story. Curiously, however, the brother-in-law's motivation for cutting through the nonsense is not a disinterested concern for truth but a mounting jealousy over the admiration showered on Kopman – a jealousy which is understandable under the circumstances but not especially admirable. And even more odd is the fact that the "punch-line" seems more an opportunity for Kopman to have the last word than a comic act designed to trigger laughter at his expense.

Fortunately, this way of structuring the story will be bypassed in subsequent variants of the joke.

The Tea-Drinking Variant

First appearing in American anthologies of Jewish humor just after World War 2, the "Tea-Drinking" variant was probably designed to flesh out the short version of "Suspension-Bridge" by someone who didn't know the fuller, rabbinic form of that joke, in comparison to which this new variant is in some ways a regression:[12]

Philosophy

For a long time Levy and Bernstein sat over their teacups, saying nothing. At last Levy broke the silence. "You know, Bernstein," he said, "life is like a glass of tea."

"Life is like a glass of tea... why?" asked Bernstein.

"How should I know," said Levy, "am I a philosopher?"

Its improvements with respect to the short "Suspension-Bridge" version are still worth mentioning – such as the replacement of disembodied voices by people with names (eliminating the need for such clumsy constructions as "the first one" and "the other one," while establishing the speakers' ethnic background), and the embedding of the characters in the physical and social situation of tea-drinking, which – as a setting for discussing philosophical and other issues – was reportedly a vital part of Jewish culture in New York coffee

---

[12] Nathan Ausubel, *A Treasury of Jewish Folklore* (New York: Crown, 1948), p. 360.

houses.[13] The punchline is also expanded from "How should I know?" ("Weiss ich?" or "Ich soll wissen?") to "How should I know? Am I a philosopher?" Now a responsibility for knowing what one is talking about when philosophizing, is relegated to a particular role.

The most important change, however, is the replacement of the suspension-bridge analogy by a new one: "life is like a glass of tea." This is probably derived from the J. M. Barrie play, *The Admirable Chrichton* (1915), in which a character who is fond of making epigrams seizes on the chance to deliver one he has prepared, when he enters a drawing room filled with "a great array of tea things." He slyly manoeuvers his conversation with the butler around to the subject of teacups and finally announces: "Life, Chrichton, is like a cup of tea; the more heartily we drink, the sooner we reach the dregs." To which the servant obediently replies: "Thank you, sir."[14] In changing the Englishman's *cup* to the East European *glass* of tea, an extra charge of ethnicity was introduced into the joke.

The line "Life is like a glass of tea" is so well known today by fans of Jewish humor that it was the basis for an in-joke in the 1977 film, *Oh God*, starring George Burns in the title role. When asked in that film about the meaning of man's existence, God begins by saying, "Life is like a glass of tea," but then reconsiders, stating, "No, no... I'd better not go for laughs."

---

[13] The following account is found in Hutchins Hapgood, *The Spirit of the Ghetto. Studies of the Jewish Quarter of New York* (New York: Schocken, 1966), pp. 51-52: "Though called a coffee house, most of them were places where immigrant Jews drank tea and talked – and they talked as no other group has ever talked. They talked about Karl Marx and Bakunin, Henry George and Eugene Debs and Big Tim Sullivan. They talked about Ibsen and Dostoevsky and Shakespeare and Hegel. They talked about the performance of the prima donna at the Metropolitan Opera the night before. There were others whose whole day was a succession of tea and socialism. Still others denounced those who criticized the latest performance of the actor Jacob Adler, and wrote lengthy duel challenges to those who had traduced the playwright Jacob Gordin. All these topics were handled best over tea à la Russe, tea with a slice of lemon sipped between a sugar cube clenched in the teeth. / There were at least three hundred of these coffee houses on the Lower East Side, all of them daily populated."

[14] J. M. Barrie, *The Admirable Chrichton* (London: Hodder & Stoughton, 1951), p. 15. Barrie of course is best known today for his play, *Peter Pan*. The *Chrichton* epigram – "Life is like a cup of tea: the more heartily we drink, the sooner we reach the dregs"– represents an utterly *un*-Jewish outlook, since its resonances are pleasure-denying and it runs counter to the spirit of living life to the fullest, as exemplified by the often quoted statement from the *Ta'anit*: "Man will be held accountable in the coming world for every permitted pleasure abstained from in this one."

The Secluded Sage Variant

Although I can remember hearing this variant of the meaning-of-life joke in the 1960's, the earliest published record I have been able to find of it – in the form I recognize – is in a French anthology first printed in 1973:[15]

A millionaire had enjoyed all the pleasures money can buy. His riches had given him love, pleasures of the senses, travel, power... Now, at the threshold of old age, he wanted to withdraw into himself in order to find the meaning of life and nothing else interested him.

He began to visit philosophers, poets and sages in every country but it was in vain that he sought from them the answer to the crucial question.

Finally someone told him about a Hindu hermit who lived in a cave in the mountains of Tibet. Surely this old man would be able to ease his torment.

So the millionaire organized a great expedition. He hired guides and porters to lead him to the lost cave. After months of difficult travel, having overcome the pitfalls of the forest, the mountains and the cold, having beaten off the attacks of wild beasts, having been exposed to storms, cyclones and countless cataclysms, our man finally arrived, as the sole survivor of the caravan, at the end of his trials and at the threshold of the cave. He went inside.

There sat a white-haired and venerable old man, who seemed to have expected him. The millionaire bowed to him and said:

– I have come from very far in order to ask you what is the meaning of life...

The old man looked at his visitor in silence and then answered him very slowly:

– Life is a great river...

– What? said the other man.

– Life is a great river! repeated the old man blissfully.

– Come on, you can't be serious! shouted the millionaire. I have walked, suffered, and risked death a thousand times to come here. I have lost all my companions. I have almost lost my health. All that in order to reach the ultimate truth... And all you can tell me is that inanity?

Then old man, suddenly panic-stricken, began to stutter with trembling lips:

– Why? Life isn't a great river?

As in the earlier variants, a cryptic statement – in this case, "Life is a great river" (or "Life is a fountain," as I first heard it) – plays a central role in the joke, and there are two actors, one at the giving and the other at the receiving end of the statement. But there are a number of differences with respect to the short "Suspension-Bridge" and "Tea-Drinking" variants:

---

[15] Hervé Nègre, *Dictionnaire des histoires drôles* (Paris: Fayard, 1981; orig. pub. 1973), pp. 264-265; my translation.

a) Here, the person who issues the meaning-of-life statement enjoys a special philosophical status in our and the other actor's eyes: he is reputed to *know* the meaning of life, and his whole existence as a monk, living a life of seclusion and meditation, is apparently spent in contemplation of that meaning. His relation to the statement is not a casual one; the philosophical formula he generously shares is presumably the very foundation of his intense, spiritual life.

b) In the short "Suspension-Bridge" and "Tea-Drinking" variants, the initiative is taken by a person who issues the cryptic statement from out of the blue, without anyone's having asked for it. Here it is the other actor, seeking out the meaning of life, who elicits the statement from the reputed "knower".

c) Once the statement is spoken by the monk, the visitor does not merely ask a neutral "why". Instead, he demonstratively shouts his disappointment in it. And in place of the flippant "How should I know?" reply of the earlier variants, the punchline placed in the mouth of our secluded sage shows that his spiritual universe is caving in. It is he who suffers intimidation and loses faith in himself, while his counterpart in the other variants deals out a cheeky reply and maintains the upper hand.

d) The Jewish ethnicity is gone. In fact, this particular variant may not be a Jewish joke at all. It has, however, appeared in a French anthology of Jewish humor, in a slightly different form which peters out at the end:[16]

The Wednesday evening chess game between Avrom and the rabbi has been a tradition for years. But one Wednesday evening, Avrom does not show up for the game. Thinking he may be ill, the rabbi expects him to show up as usual on the following Wednesday and the ones after that. Avrom still doesn't come and leaves no word. Worried, the rabbi goes to Avrom's house and finds it empty.

Months and years go by. Avrom is practically forgotten.

One morning, thirty years later, the rabbi sees his old friend appear.

– Heaven be blessed! There you are at last! Where on earth have you been all these years?

– I withdrew into the mountains, alone, and there I thought.

– And what did you discover, my dear friend?

– I am going to tell you, Rabbi: I discovered that life is like a fountain.

---

[16] Adam, *L'humour juif* (Paris: Denoël, 1966), pp. 27-28; my translation.

– A fountain! the rabbi exclaims. He thinks for a moment and then he says: No, Avrom, no! Life is not like a fountain!

Avrom looks at him intently and says in a distressed voice:

– You're right... You're right. Life is not like a fountain.

The "Secluded Sage" variant, both in its general and its French-Jewish form, is unmistakably hostile toward withdrawal from the stream of active life. Indirectly, this variant of the joke suggests not only that a meditative quest for meaning is futile, but also that what is worthwhile in life is what is left behind when one withdraws from the world – such as sensual pleasures for the millionaire, and a weekly chess game with the rabbi for Avrom.

According to the premises of this variant, when a person cuts himself off from the social world, he loses his intellectual balance and may become enthralled with an abstraction which seems radiant to him in his cave or mountain retreat, but which turns out to be a piece of nonsense when exposed to the test of a social encounter.

In these respects, the variant includes a kind of warning against looking down upon the real world, the social world, and falling prey to the alienated notion that meaning necessarily resides in a higher sphere, remote from ordinary human activity. Because of this, the "Secluded Sage" variant is more likely to appeal to people who have made their peace with reality than to those poetic souls who are looking for something else.

The Dying Rabbi Variant

The full, rabbinic form of the old "Suspension-Bridge" joke was either not known or deliberately bypassed by those who devised the "Jealous Brother-in-Law," "Tea-Drinking" and "Secluded Sage" variants, all of which lack the ethnic and narrative richness of that original story. Fortunately, someone who knew it and appreciated its potential, gave it new life around 1970 by making two important changes.

First, he restaged as a death-bed scene the interaction that originally occurred in the rabbi's dining room or study, and placed grieving disciples around their dying rabbi. This introduced a sense of imminent loss into the narrative, deepening it and investing it with a solemnity against which the punchline could be played off with a greater "payload" of comic surprise.

It also gave a new sense of urgency to the story, since the rabbi is about to expire when he issues his cryptic statement. Here for the first time, an attempt to discover the meaning of the statement is linked to a race against time and the risk of never learning the answer because the one person who could disclose it died moments earlier. None of the previous variants of the story can match this one in purely dramatic terms.

Equally important was the invention of a new punchline. In place of the flippant "How should I know?" and the pathetic "You mean life *isn't* a fountain?", our jokester thought of having the rabbi respond to the question by making a concession: "All right, so life *isn't* like a glass of tea." This does for the meaningfulness of the story what the death-bed setting does for its narrative and dramatic appeal, the result being not only the best variant of the meaning-of-life joke, but quite possibly the richest of all Jewish jokes ever created.

Here are two versions of it published in 1972, the year it first broke into print. In one, life is like a cup of tea, in the other like a river. I would have preferred the glass of tea simile of Ausubel's 1948 version of the "Tea-Drinking" variant, and firmly believe that no other simile can match it because of its ethnic resonances.

Asimov[17]

Mindess[18]

The beloved rabbi on his deathbed, surrounded by his crowd of disciples, managed to say with great difficulty, "Life is like a cup of tea."

The words were repeated, with reverent whispers, from one to another of the disciples, until this final bit of wisdom had reached those farthest removed from the bedside. And at the very back of the crowd, a young disciple dared question the remark. Hesitantly, he whispered "But *why* is life like a cup of tea?"

Back through the crowd came the shocked comment, "He asks why life is like a cup of tea." "He asks why life is like a cup of tea."

Finally, the murmur reached the very bedside, and at a questioning glance from the dying rabbi, the foremost disciple leaned forward and said, "Someone has asked *why* life is like a cup of tea."

And the rabbi whispered, "All right, then. Life is *not* like a cup of tea."

A wise old rabbi lays dying, so his disciples line up next to his deathbed to catch his final words. They arrange themselves in order, from the most brilliant pupil to the most obtuse. The brilliant one bends over the prostrate form and whispers, "Rabbi, rabbi, what are your final words?" "My final words," murmurs the ancient, "are... life is a river." The disciple passes it on to the fellow next to him, and the phrase relays mouth to ear down the line. "The rabbi says life is a river." "The rabbi says life is a river."

When it reaches the oaf at the end, however, he scratches his head in perplexity. "What does the rabbi mean, life is a river?" he asks.

That question, of course, relays back up the line. "What does the rabbi mean, life is a river?" "What does the rabbi mean, life is a river?"

When the star pupil hears it, he leans over again. "Rabbi," he implores, for the old man is breathing his last, "what do you mean, life is a river?"

And the rabbi, shrugging, croaks, "So it's not a river!"

In aligning the Asimov and Mindess versions side by side, I wanted to make it as easy as possible for the reader to compare them with respect to three variables: a) the rabbi's statement may be solicited or unsolicited by the grieving disciples; b) the originator of the question may be framed positively – as "a young disciple" who is both courageous and respectful, since he "dares to question" yet does so "hesitantly" and in a whisper – or negatively, as "an oaf," though in both cases the questioner is farthest removed from the rabbi; and c) the other disciples may or may not be "shocked" by the question.

---

[17] Isaac Asimov, *Treasury of Humor* (New York: Vallentine-Mitchell, 1972), p. 227.
[18] Harvey Mindess, *The Chosen People* (Los Angeles: Nash, 1972), p. 42.

Probably the best retelling of the story is Spalding's (1976), though the simile he used is hardly an improvement:[19]

The venerable old rabbi, known throughout the land for his wisdom, lay in a coma, very near death. On either side of his bed, hovered his most worshipful disciples.

"Rebbenyu," pleaded the spokesman for the grieving congregants, "please do not leave us without a final word of wisdom. Speak to us for the last time, dear rabbi."

For a few moments there was no response, and the weeping visitors feared he had passed on to his well-earned reward. But suddenly the rabbi's lips moved, ever so slightly. They bent over him to hear his final words:

"The Jewish people are the twin stars of the night," he whispered in a faint voice.

The disciples looked at each other in perplexity. What did he mean? What great secret of life was hidden in that mystic statement? For the better part of an hour they exchanged opinions, analyzing the sentence from every conceivable standpoint, but they could not decipher the deeper meaning.

"We must ask him before it is too late," said the leader. Once again, he leaned over the still figure of the revered sage.

"Rabbi, rabbi," he called out urgently, "we implore you to explain: Why are Jewish people the twin stars of the night?"

With his last spark of energy, the rabbi lifted his palms and croaked:

"All right, so they're not the twin stars of the night!"

From that point on, I am sorry to say that the joke has gone down hill in anthologies. The great collective scene and dramatic tension is missing in the Novak and Waldoks version of 1981:[20]

A rabbinical student is about to leave Europe for a position in the New World. He goes to his rabbi for advice, and the rabbi, a great Talmud scholar, offers an adage which, he assures the younger man, will guide him throughout his life: "Life is a fountain."

The young rabbi is deeply impressed by the profundity of his teacher's remarks, and departs for a successful career in America. Thirty years later, hearing that his mentor is dying, the younger man returns for a final visit.

"Rabbi," he says to his old teacher, "I have one question. For thirty years, every time I have been sad or confused I have thought of the phrase you passed on to me before I left for America. It has helped me through the most difficult of times. But to be perfectly honest with you, rabbi, I have never fully understood the meaning of it. And now that you are about to enter the World of Truth, perhaps you would be so kind as to tell me what these words really mean. Rabbi, why *is* life like a fountain?"

Wearily, the old man replies, "All right, so it's *not* like a fountain!"

And in the most recent version, in the anthology edited by Lanigan in 1990, the concession punchline has been discarded in favor of the

[19] Henry D. Spalding, *A Treasure-Trove of American-Jewish Humor* (New York: Jonathan David, 1976), p. 336.

[20] William Novak and Moshe Waldoks, *The Big Book of Jewish Humor* (New York: Harper & Row, 1981), p. 17.

punchline used in the "Secluded Sage" variant – a regression that deprives the "Dying Rabbi" variant of the meanings specific to it, and which are about to be discussed:[21]

The old revered rabbi of the orthodox congregation in Brooklyn was on his death bed. Crowded around were at least a dozen rabbis, some almost as old as their wise leader, all of them straining to catch yet one more pearl of wisdom from the man who had led them for decades. The one closest to the ancient rabbi was bent over, his ear just inches from the prone leader's mouth.

"Rebbe," the younger rabbi whispered, "one last question. What is the secret of life?"

After a pause of some length the old man openend his eyes. "Hughhhhh," the ancient one gasped.

"What did he say? What did he say?" murmured those assembled in the room.

Once again the rabbi closest to the bed leaned over and repeated the question, "Most holy one, what is the secret of life?"

Again there was a barely audible, "Hughhhh."

Finally, after the question was repeated a third time, the old man roused himself. "Life," he said. "Life is a reever."

The younger rabbi turned to the man next to him and repeated the sentence, "Life is a river." And each rabbi turned and repeated the ancient leader's words down the line, "Life is a river. Life is a river," until it reached the last rabbi in the room.

"Life is a river?" he said, bemused.

The rabbi next to him looked at him, then turned to the next in line and repeated the statement. "Life is a river? Life is a river?" went back up the line till it reached the rabbi closest to the bed. He leaned over the old and beloved rabbi and repeated, "Life is a river?"

The old rabbi opened his eyes in astonishment. "It's not?!"

Interpreting the Dying Rabbi Variant

The Rabbi's Behavior

One important question which this joke leaves unanswered is whether or not the rabbi knows what he is talking about when he states: "Life is like a glass of tea." Both possibilities are open and each constitutes a starting point for developing an interpretation of the joke.

Let's assume for the moment that the rabbi's statement is meaningful and that he would be quite capable of explaining why life is like a glass of tea. We would then understand the concession he makes in the punchline – "All right, so life is *not* like a glass of tea" –

---

[21] Suds Lanigan, *A Minister, a Rabbi and a Priest* (New York: St. Martin's Press, 1990), pp. 6-7.

as resulting from a mistake on his part: a misconstruing of the disciples' request for an explanation as though it were a challenge. Thinking that his disciples disagree with him, he gives in for their sake, letting them win what he takes to be a contest. In the process, he unwittingly deprives them of the one thing they most desperately want. The paradox of making them lose by letting them win is an impossible figure somewhat reminiscent of the one seen in the "Rabbinic Judgment" joke in Chapter 1.

If we see the rabbi as a) fully capable of explaining why life is like a glass of tea; b) mistakenly believing that his disciples disagree with that statement; and c) yielding to their imagined challenge, rather than defending his own point of view, then we cannot help but marvel at a man who so incompetently misinterprets the situation at hand, while reacting so generously and with such suppleness to what he takes to be a challenge. Whatever else his faults may be, the rabbi is free from the tyranny of an inflated ego and from the arrogance of authority.

In addition to not taking *himself* too seriously, the rabbi – when seen in this light – is also free from taking any *idea* about the meaning of life too seriously. Unlike people who allow themselves to become entrapped in philosophical abstractions, the rabbi can easily let go of his statement without suffering any loss (as does the monk at the end of the "Secluded Sage" variant, whose universe crumbles when his confidence in a meaning-of-life formula is shaken). It is undoubtedly in this sense that Mindess described the rabbi in this joke as "a man who is man enough to shrug off the insufficiency of his ultimate wisdom," and who embodies "the deep-rooted self-esteem that enabled The Chosen People to weather many storms" (p. 42).

This first reading of the joke combines aspects of role-fiasco – in the rabbi's misunderstanding of the disciples' question – with exemplary deviance, in the freedom he embodies from ego and from over-investing in abstractions about the meaning of life.

A second and very different interpretation of the joke would flow from the assumption that the rabbi does *not* know what he is talking about when he says: "Life is like a glass of tea," in which case the making of that statement would be philosophical role-playing on the rabbi's part, in an effort to leave his disciples with an image of him as a deep thinker.

That initial pose would then require a second one when the rabbi is asked what the statement means. Unable to answer that question, and not wanting to lose face, he *pretends* to misconstrue their question as though it were a challenge – to which he promptly surrenders, thereby releasing himself from having to explain the meaningless statement. Seen in this perspective, the rabbi's behavior would be pure tactical manoeuvre, involving neither the role-fiasco nor the exemplary deviance aspects of the first interpretation outlined above.

Yet a third possibility is to see the joke as parodistically under-fulfilling the positive model found in Hasidic tales in which a great rabbi utters his last words of wisdom before dying, as a parting gift he leaves with his disciples and family. The most beautiful account of this type is the one about Rabbi Zusya of Hanipol, who said before dying:[22]

> In the coming world, they will not ask me: 'Why were you not Moses?' They will ask me: 'Why were you not Zusya?'"

Here is another type of story within the same tradition:[23]

> Before he died Rabbi Elimelekh [of Lizhensk] laid his hands on the heads of his four favorite disciples and divided what he owned among them. To the Seer of Lublin he gave his eyes' power to see; to Abraham Yehoshua his lips' power to pronounce judgment; to Isreal of Koznitz, his heart's power to pray; but to Mendel he gave his spirit's power to guide.

Given the existence of this tradition within Jewish folklore, it is quite possible to see the "Dying Rabbi" joke as evoking and playing with that positive image in the framework of an affectionate parody, just as "Dead Shames" parodistically underfulfills the image of the wonder-working rabbi, and "Splash" that of the rabbi lost in contemplation.

Schematically, these interpretive options might be represented as follows:

---

[22] Martin Buber, *Tales of the Hasidim. Early Masters* (New York: Schocken, 1961; orig. pub. 1948), p. 251. Zusya died in the year 1800.

[23] Martin Buber, *Tales of the Hasidim. Later Masters* (New York: Schocken, 1961; orig. pub. 1948), p. 126.

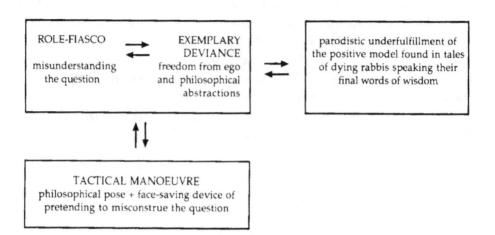

The Quest for Meaning

Nothing could be more Jewish than a fascination with attempts to grasp the deeper meaning of life – except perhaps an awareness that such attempts are futile, because the questions they involve are unanswerable, and in occupying the mind, those questions divert attention away from the here-and-now of family, social relationships, work and everything else that makes up the living fabric of daily life, which is where all meaning actually resides.

This is a point that was eloquently made in a Thirteenth Century fable by Shem-Tob Palquera:[24]

The Philosopher

There once lived a thoughtful man who sought solitude in order to probe into the problems of creation and being and to determine the purpose of all life. These thoughts preoccupied him all the time.

[24] Nathan Ausubel, *A Treasury of Jewish Humor* (Garden City: Doubleday, 1953), pp. 671-672. Shem-Tob Palquera (also spelled Shem Tov Falaquera) lived in Spain, and died about 1295.

One day he was walking as usual by the bank of the river, absorbed in contemplation. Suddenly, he lifted his eyes and saw a man standing near by. The man had dug a small hole on the bank and was pouring water from a jug into it.

Surprised, the philosopher asked the stranger, "What are you doing?"

"I am going to empty the river and pour all the water from it into this hole," the man answered.

"This is utter madness!" exclaimed the philosopher. "It's an impossible task!"

"Sillier and even more impossible are the questions you're trying to solve!" retorted the man.

Having spoken thus the stranger disappeared.

The meaning-of-life joke – in all its variants, but especially in its rabbinic forms – begins by appealing to that side of us which is fascinated by the deeper questions, and strings us along by dangling an answer in front of us; but it ends by pulling the rug out from under us in the punchline, as if to say: that's what you get for believing that insoluble questions can be answered. In that respect, the joke is on us and serves as a gentle warning against overinvesting in abstractions and overestimating the ability of the intellect to deal with ultimate questions.

That our ability to explain things has limits is beautifully expressed in *Hannah and Her Sisters* (1986), in the following dialogue between Mickey (played by Woody Allen) and his parents:

Mickey: ...But if there's a God, then why is there so much evil in the world? Just on a simplistic level, why were there Nazis?

Mickey's mother: Tell him, Max!

Mickey's father: How the hell do I know why there were Nazis? I don't know how a can-opener works!

The point of Palquera's fable, the meaning-of-life joke, the Woody Allen dialogue, is not that intellectual abdication is called for in the face of philosophical problems – that would hardly be a Jewish point of view – but rather that certain questions cannot be answered, and that a preoccupation with them is sterile and therefore fair game for parody.

Goldstein wrote of the "Tea-Drinking" variant that "laughter by Jews at jokes such as this [...] is an affirmation, a means of saying that, on the one level, the meaning of life and death are important issues, but that on another level, they are absurd."[25] This is even more true of the "Dying Rabbi" variant, in which life and death are literally a part of the story, and which implicitly suggests that real meaning is

---

[25] Jeffrey H. Goldstein, "Theoretical Notes on Humor," *Journal of Communication* 26, 3 (Summer 1976), p. 110.

found in the grieving presence of the disciples around their rabbi, not in the cryptic formula they will never understand.

PUBLICATION HISTORY

Suspension-Bridge Variant

Manuel Nuél,
DAS BUCH DER
JÜDISCHEN WITZE.
Berlin: Gustav Rieckes
Buchhandlung, n.d.
[1907]; pp. 16-17

Wieder einmal nach dem Vespergebet am Sabbat-nachmittag sitzen die Frommen um ihren weisen Rabbi beim Festmahl. Wieder versinkt er in tiefes Sinnen. Als die Männer [diesem] gewahr werden, hören sie mit ihren Debatten und Disputen auf und harren des Augenblicks, da der heilige Mann aus seinem Nachdenken erwachen werde.

Da dies aber nicht eintritt, berührt der Aelteste der Gemeinde die Schulter des Rabbi, und als dieser auffährt, fragt er ihn, was seine Gedanken so sehr beschäftigt habe.

Da hebt der große Mann seinen versonnenen Blick und spricht:

"Das Leben... das Leben ist wie eine Kettenbrücke'..."

Darauf verfällt er wiederum in Schweigen.

"Was hat er gesagt?... Was hat er gesagt?" flüstern die Männer, und nachdem sie sich das Wort ehrfurchtsvoll zugeraunt haben, beginnen sie, es eifrig und mit Leidenschaft zu besprechen. Und so groß ist ihr Eifer bei der Auslegung des seltsamen Ausspruchs, daß die Geister aufeinanderplatzen und schließlich auch die Fäuste in den Streit eingreifen. Eine Einigung über den Sinn des rätselhaften Wortes ist nicht zu erzielen, und sie einigen sich endlich dahin, den immer noch vor sich hinsinnenden Rabbi zu fragen, was er gemeint habe.

"Rabbi," sagen sie, "du siehst, wir haben dich nicht erfaßt. Gib du uns den Sinn, sag du uns die Bedeutung. Wieso ist das Leben wie eine Kettenbrücke?..."

Da hebt der große Rabbi wiederum den versonnenen Blick und spricht:

"Weiß ich?"

Alexander
Moszkowski, DIE
UNSTERBLICHE
KISTE. Berlin:
Verlag der "Lustigen
Blätter," 1908; p. 113.

Tiefsinnig

Marcus: Das ganze Leben kommt mir vor wie eine Kettenbrücke.

Levy: Wieso? wie ist das zu verstehen?

Marcus: Ich soll wissen!

Edmund Edel,
DER WITZ DER
JUDEN. Berlin: Louis
Lamm, 1909; pp. 10-11.

Ein Jude sagt zum Beispiel zum anderen: "Lange habe ich nachgedacht. Das Leben ist wie eine Kettenbrück'?"

"Was haißt? Wieso? Ausgerechnet eine Kettenbrück'?"

"Nu, weiß ich?"

Alexander Moszkowski, DIE JÜDISCHE KISTE. 399 JUWELEN. Berlin: "Lustigen Blätter," 1911; p. 88.	Schottländer: Das menschliche Leben kommt mer vor wie e Kettenbrücke.
	    Ascher: Wieso ausgerechnet wie e Kettenbrücke?
	    Schottländer: Ich soll wissen!

Sigmund Freud, DER WITZ UND SEINE BEZIEHUNG ZUM UNBEWUSSTEN [1905]. Frankfurt: Fischer, 1972. Cited in a footnote added in 1912.	"Das Leben ist eine Kettenbrück," sagt der eine. – "Wieso?" fragt der andere. – "Weiß ich?" lautet die Antwort.
Moritz Rund, PERLEN JÜDISCHEN HUMORS. Berlin: Mar Schildberger, 1914; p. 48.	Weißt Du, sagt jammernd Cohn zu Lewy: Das ganze Leben ist doch 'ne Kettenbrück'? Wieso ausgerechnet e Kettenbrück'? Worauf Cohn sagt: "Ich soll wissen"!

Tiefsinnig

Hans Ostwald, FRISCH, GESUND UND MESCHUGGE. Berlin: Franke, 1928; p. 48.	Markuse: "Das menschliche Lebe kommt mir vor wie e Karusell!"
	    Fabian: "Warum wie e Karusell?"
	    Markuse: "Wieß' mers?"

Harry Schnur, JEWISH HUMOR. London: Allied Book Club, n.d. [1945]; pp. 17-18.	The great Rabbi meditates in the solitude of his study. Outside, the faithful disciples are waiting. What new revelation will emanate from the great man? They wait for three days. Then the door opens, and out comes the Rabbi in majestic silence. Slowly he opens his mouth and announces the result of his long meditation. In solemn, measured tones, he says: "The life of man is like a railway bridge."

(cont.)

Schnur, *cont.*

The disciples ponder this deep saying whose solution each wishes to be the first to discover and announce. But it

eludes them – until, many hours later, the youngest disciple summons courage and timidly asks:

"Rabbi – why is man's life like a railway bridge?"

The Rabbi replies with simple dignity: "How do I know?"

The same Rabbi, walking out with his disciples, sees a poor road-mender sitting by the wayside. And again a pearl of wisdom drops from the Rabbi's lips: "Man is like a road-mender."

Again the disciples ponder for hours, again they fail to solve the riddle. Again they ask – and are answered: "Why is man like a road-mender? Here today, gone tomorrow."

Salcia Landmann, DER JÜDISCHE WITZ. Breisgau: Walter, 1960; p. 494.

"Das Leben kommt mir vor wie eine Kettenbrück!"

"Wieso: Kettenbrück?"

"Weiß ich?"

G. F. Lieberman, THE GREATEST LAUGHS OF ALL TIME. Garden City: Doubleday, 1961; p. 91.

"Life is like a suspension bridge."

"How is that?"

"How should I know?"

Theodor Reik, JEW-ISH WIT. New York: Gamut, 1962; p. 117.

"Life is like a suspension-bridge." "How?" asks someone. "How should I know?" is the answer.

Fritz Muliar, DAS BESTE AUS MEINER JÜDISCHEN WITZE-UND ANEKDOTEN-SAMMLUNG. Munich: Wilhelm Heyne Verlag, 1974; p. 91.

Scherpelz geht mit seinem Freund philosophierend durch die Straßen. Sogt er: "Sehste, das Leben is a tiefer Brunnen!" Nach langer Pause fragt der Freund: "Wieso?" Scherpelz gibt die Erklärung: "Siehst du, ich sag, das Leben is a tiefer Brunnen, weil es is unergriendlich, dunkel und ma seht ka End!"

Tief beeindruckt denkt der Freund nach. Nach einer halben Stunde des Klärens spricht er den bedeutenden Satz aus:

(cont.)

Muliar, *cont.*

"Das Leben is wie a Kettenbriecke!"
"Warum?"
"Waaß ich?"

Jealous Brother-in-Law Variant

S. Felix Mendelsohn,
THE JEW LAUGHS.
Chicago: L. M. Stein,
1935; pp. 217-218.

Samuel Kopman had the demeanor of a philosopher. When spoken to he would stare at the speaker, puff his cigar slowly, and say nothing. In company he would listen carefully to everything that was said and when the discussion reached a climax he would make some irrelevant, brief statement which convinced everyone that he was a deep thinker. Once when the unsatisfactory economic situation had been discussed from every angle for hours, Kopman interrupted the crowd, waited until he could get perfect attention, and then said: "Why do you all complain? Life is only electricity." Everybody present thought this was a profound saying befitting a thinker. Kopman's brother-in-law, Jake Mandel, was jealous.

On another occasion the subject of immortality was discussed at length. Here again Kopman waited for an opportunity to be heard and then said thoughtfully: "Why bother about immortality? Life is like a railroad train." Here again Kopman increased his reputation as a philosopher and Jake's jealousy intensified.

Once the subject of Zionism was being argued heatedly. When the discussion reached a high pitch Kopman managed to be heard saying deliberately: "What sort of problem is Zionism anyway? The Jewish people are like a tree." Again Kopman scored a victory and everybody remarked what a wise utterance this was–but Jake's jealousy had reached the limit.

"Just a minute," he burst forth. "Listen now, philosophic brother-in-law of mine. Will you please tell us why the Jewish people are like a tree?"

For a tense moment everybody's eyes were on Kopman.

"I really can't explain that," admitted Kopman flabbergasted, "but it took an ignoramus like you to ask such a fool question!"

Tea-Drinking Variant

Philosophy

Nathan Ausubel,
TREASURY OF
JEWISH FOLKLORE.
New York: Crown,
1948; p. 360.

For a long time Levy and Bernstein sat over their teacups, saying nothing. At last Levy broke the silence. "You know, Bernstein," he said, "life is like a glass of tea."

"Life is like a glass of tea. . . why?" asked Bernstein.

"How should I know," said Levy, "am I a philosopher?"

Gerry Blumenfeld,
SOME OF MY BEST
JOKES ARE JEWISH.
New York: Kanrom,
1965; p. 24.

Two elderly Jewish scholars sat drinking glass of tea after glass of tea without saying a word. After two hours of silence, Yankel said, "You know, Moishe, life is like a bowl of cherries!"

"Why?"

"Why," he's asking me. "What am I, a philosopher?"

Leo Rosten, THE
JOYS OF YIDDISH.
London: W.H.Allen,
1970; p. 188.

The men sat sipping their tea in silence. After a while the *klutz* [clod, bungler] said "Life is like a bowl of sour cream."

"Like a bowl of sour cream?" asked the other.

"How should I know. What am I, a philosopher?"

Isaac Asimov,
TREASURY OF
HUMOR. New York:
Vallentine-Mitchell,
1972; p. 227.

Moskowitz and Finkelstein were in a cafeteria, drinking tea. Moskowitz studied his cup and said with a sigh, "Ah, my friend, life is like a cup of tea."

Finkelstein considered that for a moment and then said, "But *why* is life like a cup of tea?"

And Moskowitz replied, "How should I know? Am I a philosopher?"

Henry B. Berman,
HAVE I GOT A JOKE
FOR YOU. New York:
Hart, 1975; p. 91.

Simon R. Pollack,
JEWISH WIT FOR ALL
OCCASIONS. New
York: A & W
Publishers, 1979; p. 91.

Sammy was sitting with his grandfather, having a glass of tea. The old man drank slowly, sipping the tea through the lump of sugar between his teeth. Then he put the glass down and heaved a deep sigh.

"You know, Sammy," he muttered. "Life is like a glass of tea." And he fell silent.

Sammy waited for him to continue, but he didn't. Finally Sammy prompted him, "Grandfather, why is life like a glass of tea?"

His grandfather shrugged, "And how should I know? What am I, a philosopher?"

Jeffrey H. Goldstein, "Theoretical Notes on Humor," JOURNAL OF COMMUNICA-TION 26, 3 (Summer 1976), p. 109.

Schwartz and Goldberg were in a cafeteria, drinking tea. Schwartz studied his cup and said with a sigh, "Ah, my friend, life is like a cup of tea."

Goldberg considered that for a moment and then said, "But *why* is life like a cup of tea?"

And Schwartz replied, "How should I know? Am I a philosopher?"

William Novak and Moshe Waldoks, THE BIG BOOK OF JEWISH HUMOR. New York: Harper & Row, 1981; p. 7.

Two Jews are sitting silently over a glass of tea.

"You know," says the first man, "life is like a glass of tea with sugar."

"A glass of tea with sugar?" asks his friend. "Why do you say that?"

"How should I know?" replies the first man. "What am I, a philosopher?"

Leo Rosten, GIANT BOOK OF LAUGHTER. New York: Crown, 1985; p. 344.

Two old men sat in rocking chairs on the front porch of the nursing home, rocking gently, back and forth, in silence. Finally, the first old man, Lupowitz, sighed, turned to the second old man, said, "Life." And with that, saying no more, he went back to his rocking.

Janovich, the second old man, coughed, then screwed up his eyelids. "'*Life*' you said?"

Lupowitz nodded. "Life..."

"So–what about Life?"

Lupowitz cleared his throat. "I have decided that life," he declaimed, "is like a bowl thick, cold sour cream!"

Janovich went "*Tchk-tchk-tchk!*" After taking thought, he quavered. "So why is Life like a bowl thick, cold sour cream?"

Lupowitz shrugged. "How should I know? Am I a philosopher?"

Secluded sage variant

Adam, L'HUMOUR JUIF. Paris: Denoël, 1966; pp. 27-28.

La partie d'échecs du mercredi soir est depuis plusieurs années une tradition entre Avrom et le rabbin. Pourtant, un certain mercredi, Avrom ne se rend pas au rendez-vous. Le croyant souffrant, le rabbin l'attend de nouveau le mercredi suivant et les autres mercredis. Avrom ne vient toujours pas et ne donne pas de nouvelles. Inquiet, le rabbin se rend chez Avrom: la maison est vide.

(cont.)

Adam, *cont.*

Les mois et les années s'écoulent. Avrom est presque oublié.

Trente ans plus tard, un matin, le rabbin voit paraître son vieil ami.

– Le Ciel soit loué! Te voici enfin! Où donc as-tu passé toutes ces années?

– Je me suis retiré dans la montagne, seul, et j'ai réfléchi.

– Et qu'as-tu découvert, ami très cher?

– Je vais te dire, rabbi: j'ai découvert que la vie, c'est comme un grand jet d'eau.

– Un grand jet d'eau! s'exclame le rabbin.

Il réfléchit, puis: Mais non, Avrom, mais non! La vie n'est pas comme un grand jet d'eau!

Alors Avrom le regarde intensément, et, d'un ton navré:

– Tu as raison... tu as raison. La vie n'st pas comme un grand jet d'eau.

Hervé Nègre,
DICTIONNAIRE DES
HISTOIRES DRÔLES.
Paris: Fayard, 1981;
pp. 264-265.
Orig. pub. 1973.

Un milliardaire avait tiré de l'argent tous les plaisirs possibles. L'argent lui avait donné l'amour, la volupté, les voyages, la puissance... Maintenant, au seuil de la vieillesse, il désirait se retirer en lui-même pour trouver un sens à la vie et plus rien d'autre ne l'intéressait.

Il se mit à rendre visite aux philosophes, aux poètes et aux sages de tous les pays, mais ce fut en vain qu'il chercha auprès d'eux une réponse à la question cruciale.

Enfin on finit par lui indiquer une ermite hindou qui vivait dans une grotte sur les contreforts du Tibet. Certainement ce vieillard saurait apaiser son inquiétude.

Alors le milliardaire mit sur pied une grande expédition. Il engagea des guides et des porteurs pour le conduire jusque dans la grotte perdue. Après des mois et des mois de difficle voyage, après avoir surmonté les embûches de la forêt, de la montagne et du froid, après avoir repoussé les attaques des grands fauves, après avoir subi des orages, des cyclones et des cataclysmes sans nombre, notre homme arriva enfin, seul survivant de sa caravane, au terme de ses épreuves et au seuil de la caverne. Il entra dedans.

Un patriarche chenu et vénérable était là, qui semblait l'attendre. Le milliardaire s'inclina devant lui et prit la parole:

– Je suis venu de très loin pour te demander quel est le sens da la vie...

(cont.)

Nègre, *cont.*

Alors le vieillard considéra son visiteur en silence et il lui répondit très lentement:

– La vie est un grand fleuve...

– Comment? dit l'autre.

– La vie est un grand fleuve! répéta le vieilard avec béatitude.

– Mais enfin, ce n'est pas possible! s'écria le milliardaire. J'ai marché, souffert et risqué mille fois la mort pour arriver jusqu'ici. J'ai perdu tous mes compagnons. J'ai presque perdu la santé. Tout cela pour atteindre à la vérité suprême... Et tout ce que tu trouves à me dire, c'est une ânerie pareille?

Alors le vieillard, soudain pris de panique, se mit à bégayer, les lèvres tremblantes:

– Pourquoi? La vie n'est pas un grand fleuve?

Dying Rabbi Variant

Isaac Asimov,
TREASURY OF
HUMOR. New
York: Vallentine-
Mitchell, 1972;
p. 227.

The beloved rabbi on his deathbed, surrounded by his crowd of disciples, managed to say with great difficulty, "Life is like a cup of tea."

The words were repeated, with reverent whispers, from one to another of the disciples, until this final bit of wisdom had reached those farthest removed from the bedside. And at the very back of the crowd, a young disciple dared question the remark. Hesitantly, he whispered "But *why* is life like a cup of tea?"

Back through the crowd came the shocked comment, "He asks why life is like a cup of tea." "He asks why life is like a cup of tea."

Finally, the murmur reached the very bedside, and at a questioning glance from the dying rabbi, the foremost disciple leaned forward and said, "Someone has asked *why* life is like a cup of tea."

And the rabbi whispered, "All right, then. Life is *not* like a cup of tea."

Harvey Mindess,
THE CHOSEN
PEOPLE. Los
Angeles: Nash,
1972; p. 42.

A wise old rabbi lays dying, so his disciples line up next to his deathbed to catch his final words. They arrange themselves in order, from the most brilliant pupil to the most obtuse. The brilliant one bends over the prostrate form

(cont.)

Mindess, *cont.*

and whispers, "Rabbi, rabbi, what are your final words?" "My final words," murmurs the ancient, "are... life is a river."

The disciple passes it on to the fellow next to him, and the phrase relays mouth to ear down the line. "The rabbi says life is a river." "The rabbi says life is a river."

When it reaches the oaf at the end, however, he scratches his head in perplexity. "What does the rabbi mean, life is a river?" he asks.

That question, of course, relays back up the line. "What does the rabbi mean, life is a river?" "What does the rabbi mean, life is a river?"

When the star pupil hears it, he leans over again. "Rabbi," he implores, for the old man is breathing his last, "what do you mean, life is a river?"

And the rabbi, shrugging, croaks, "So it's not a river!"

Henry D. Spalding, A TREASURE-TROVE OF AMERICAN JEWISH HUMOR. New York: Jonathan David, 1976; p. 336.

The venerable old rabbi, known throughout the land for his wisdom, lay in a coma, very near death. On either side of his bed, hovered his most worshipful disciples.

"Rebbenyu," pleaded the spokesman for the grieving congregants, "please do not leave us without a final word of wisdom. Speak to us for the last time, dear rabbi."

For a few moments there was no response, and the weeping visitors feared he had passed on to his well-earned reward. But suddenly the rabbi's lips moved, ever so slightly. They bent over him to hear his final words:

"The Jewish people are the twin stars of the night," he whispered in a faint voice.

The disciples looked at each other in perplexity. What did he mean? What great secret of life was hidden in that mystic statement? For the better part of an hour they exchanged opinions, analyzing the sentence from every conceivable standpoint, but they could not decipher the deeper meaning.

"We must ask him before it is too late," said the leader. Once again, he leaned over the still figure of the revered sage.

"Rabbi, rabbi," he called out urgently, "we implore you to explain: Why are Jewish people the twin stars of the night?"

With his last spark of energy, the rabbi lifted his palms and croaked:

"All right, so they're not the twin stars of the night!"

William Novak
and Moshe Waldoks,
THE BIG BOOK OF
JEWISH HUMOR.
New York: Harper &
Row, 1981; p. 17.

A rabbinical student is about to leave Europe for a position in the New World. He goes to his rabbi for advice, and the rabbi, a great Talmud scholar, offers an adage which, he assures the younger man, will guide him throughout his life: "Life is a fountain."

The young rabbi is deeply impressed by the profundity of his teacher's remarks, and departs for a successful career in America. Thirty years later, hearing that his mentor is dying, the younger man returns for a final visit..

"Rabbi," he says to his old teacher, "I have one question. For thirty years, every time I have been sad or confused I have thought of the phrase you passed on to me before I left for America. It has helped me through the most difficult of times. But to be perfectly honest with you, rabbi, I have never fully understood the meaning of it. And now that you are about to enter the World of Truth, perhaps you would be so kind as to tell me what these words really mean. Rabbi, why *is* life like a fountain?"

Wearily, the old man replies, "All right, so it's *not* like a fountain!"

Suds Lanigan,
A MINISTER, A
RABBI, AND A
PRIEST. New York:
St. Martin's Press, 1990;
pp. 6-7.

The old revered rabbi of the orthodox congregation in Brooklyn was on his death bed. Crowded around were at least a dozen rabbis, some almost as old as their wise leader, all of them straining to catch yet one more pearl of wisdom from the man who had led them for decades. The one closest to the ancient rabbi was bent over, his ear just inches from the prone leader's mouth.

"Rebbe," the younger rabbi whispered, "one last question. What is the secret of life?"

After a pause of some length the old man opened his eyes. "Hughhhh," the ancient one gasped.

"What did he say? What did he say?" murmured those assembled in the room.

Once again the rabbi closest to the bed leaned over and repeated the question, "Most holy one, what is the secret of life?"

Again there was a barely audible, "Hughhhh."

Finally, after the question was repeated a third time, the old man roused himself. "Life," he said. "Life is a reever."

The younger rabbi turned to the man next to him and repeated the sentence, "Life is a river." And each rabbi

(cont.)

Lanigan, *cont.*

turned and repeated the ancient leader's words down the line, "Life is a river. Life is a river," until it reached the last rabbi in the room.

"Life is a river?" he said, bemused.

The rabbi next to him looked at him, then turned to the next in line and repeated the statement. "Life is a river? Life is a river?" went back up the line till it reached the rabbi closest to the bed. He leaned over the old and beloved rabbi and repeated, "Life is a river?"

The old rabbi opened his eyes in astonishment. "It's not?!"

Der
Jüdische Humorist.

Auswahl

der geistreichsten Unterhaltungs-Gespräche

des weltberühmten Bonmotisten „Rajezer Maggid" und der
bedeutendsten Autoritäten des Judenthums aus alter und
neuer Zeit.

Motto: „Auch die profanen Gespräche der Gelehrten sind unterhaltend und belehrend."

Zweite

vielfach vermehrte u. vollständig umgearbeitete
Auflage.

Eigenthum u. Selbstverlag
von
— Julius Dessauer —
Budapest.

This anthology, published in Budapest c. 1879, contains the earliest
specimen I have been able to find of the "Rabbinic Judgment" joke
discussed in Chapter 1.

Chapter 7

On the Evolution of Jewish Jokes

Although every joke is unique and has its own history, certain patterns can nevertheless be discerned in the ways in which Jewish jokes tend to evolve. In the present chapter, I will try to describe some of those patterns or pathways.

Unlike the other chapters in this book, each of which dealt comprehensively with one major joke, the present discussion will require that a number of jokes be cited in order to illustrate developmental tendencies. This is an unavoidable departure from a principle proposed at the start of this book – a departure limited to this final section, attempting to make some general observations and to tie up loose threads.

From Non-Jewish to Jewish Joke

In our discussion of "Ten Commandments" and "He had a hat!", we have already seen that Jewish jokes can evolve from anti-Semitic stories which originate and circulate outside the Jewish community, before they are brought within the ethnic boundaries and are radically transformed by anonymous Jewish jokesters. That transformational process can occur in stages – with an intermediate form appearing in Jewish anthologies – before the really fundamental changes are made, changes which in one way or another:

a) embed the joke in Jewish culture – for example, by grafting the logic of the punchline onto an old Talmudic legend;

b) replace the role of the idealized Gentile with one allowing for a different kind of interaction – that role being attributed to none other than God in both jokes mentioned above;

c) invite us to hold a mixture of positive and negative attitudes toward the embodiment of Jewishness;

d) open the joke to at least two interpretive options, one of which involves seeing the story as playing with and parodying the stereotypes it evokes.

To whatever degree Gentiles are reintroduced into the story, for example in the form of "adulterous French" and "warlike Germans," they are no longer depicted as models of perfection when compared to the portrayal of Jewishness.

Anti-Semitic anecdotes are not the only stories of non-Jewish origin which can be transformed into Jewish jokes, one of which started out as the story of a "Highland shepherd," first published in London in 1924. It is presented as though it were an incident that actually occurred, which may well have been the case:[1]

One of my oldest friends, a famous Glasgow surgeon, told me that he was once conducting a party of students round the wards, stopping at each bed to explain to them the ailments of the occupants. He arrived at the couch of a Highland shepherd, who had been in the hospital for a considerable time suffering from an incurable disease. "Ah, Donald," said my famous friend, "I am afraid I can do nothing for you. Gentlemen, we will pass on." The students under his care were taken up the ward and while he was explaining to them the intricacies of an abdominal operation at a bed some distance away, Donald, who had time to think over the hopeless diagnosis of his condition, called out, "Doctor Macintyre, did you say that you could do nothing for me?" "I did, I am sorry to say," said the specialist with a wide-world reputation. "Well then," said Donald, "if *you* can't, for God's sake send along someone who can."

When the story is told in this manner, we are invited to enjoy the refreshing disrespect of the shepherd; but we are also led to consider the doctor's diagnosis as undoubtedly correct, since he is presented to us as "a famous Glasgow surgeon" and "a specialist with a world-wide reputation," suggesting that a better doctor could not be found. The fact that he himself told the story, at least according to the premises of the narrative, also implies that it is not intended to undercut his own

---

[1] Seymour Hicks, *Chestnuts Reroasted* (London: Hodder & Stroughton, 1924), p. 35.

authority in our eyes. Similarly, we are invited to see the patient as an uneducated man who misconstrues the statement, "I am afraid I can do nothing for you," as an admission of the doctor's personal limitations, while what the doctor obviously means is that nothing *can* be done for the patient – which we are intended to regard as true. The shepherd's no-nonsense manner is attractive, but embedded in a set of conditions that counteract any inclination on our part to see him as being in the right.

About forty years later, the story is transformed into a Jewish joke:[2]

> Three men lay dying on a hospital ward. Their doctor, making rounds, went up to the first and asked him his last wish. The patient was a Catholic. "My last wish," he murmured, "is to see a priest and make confession." The doctor assured him he would arrange it, and moved on.
>
> The second patient was a Protestant. When asked his last wish, he replied, "My last wish is to see my family and say goodbye." The doctor promised he would send for them and moved on.
>
> The third patient was, of course, a Jew. "And what is your last wish?" the doctor asked. "My last wish," came the feeble, hoarse reply, "is to see another doctor."

Here we have a classic, ethnic comparison structure of the type already seen in the "Learn to live under water" joke cited on pp. 89-90 above. A dramatic situation is confronted by representatives of three groups, the first two of which are Gentile, and embody the "normal" way of dealing with the circumstances – by facing "reality," which in this case means accepting that further treatment would be futile. The third point of view is Jewish, deviates radically from the Gentile norm, and is presented here as *exemplary* in its refusal to accept the definition of the situation as being hopeless. Contributing to the positive status of this Jewish point of view in the joke, is the absence of any cue suggesting that no better doctor could be found, or that the Jewish patient's remark is an endearingly ignorant misconstruing of the situation at hand. To the contrary, the joke plays on the image of the Jew as knowing *better* than to believe in anyone's infallibility. Consequently, once the punchline is sprung, the responses presented as Gentile, and which seemed so reasonable at first, appear in retrospect to be excessively resigned and gullible.

---

2 Jeffrey H. Goldstein, "Theoretical Notes on Humor," *Journal of Communication* 26, 3 (Summer 1976), p. 109. I prefer citing this version from 1976 to those appearing as early as 1963 because its language and structure are more logical. The publication history of the joke will be found on pp. 186-189 below.

   This is only one of a number of well-known Jewish jokes which evolved from a story that neither depicted nor was told by Jews. Another is the "Left-handed teacup" joke cited on p. 87 above, which can be traced back to an old English joke, found in an anthology first published in 1630. Here the butt of the humor is a wealthy French gentleman "hauing profound reuenues and a shallow braine":[3]

The said Monsieur commanded his man to buy him a great hat with a button in the brim to button it vp behind; his man bought him one, and brought him. He put it on his head with the button before, which when he looked in the glasse and saw, he was very angry saying: thou crosse vntoward knaue, did I not bid thee buy a hat with the button to hold it vp behind, and thou hast brought me one that turnes vp before? I command thee once more goe thy wayes, and buy mee such a one as I would have, whatsoever it cost me.

In the late 1930's, someone thought of using the basic logic of that story within a framework that cast Jewish astuteness in a positive light, even from the point of view of a leading Nazi. Note that in its first crystallization as a Jewish joke, published in Argentina in 1939, the story ends somewhat abruptly with the Jewish shopkeeper's clever manoeuvre:[4]

Schacht and Hitler are conversing more or less amiably. The former maintains that the persecution of the Jews should not be pushed too far.
   – In business – he states categorically – the Jew is very useful.
   Hitler stubbornly states the contrary. Schacht then proposes that they carry out a quick experiment.
   – Come with me.
   They enter a shop whose proprietor is one hundred percent Aryan.
   – We need teacups with the handles on the left side.
   – I don't have any, replies the merchant.
   They go into another shop, also run by a pure Aryan, and the same thing happens as at the first shop. They then decide to visit one run by a Jew. Schacht explains to him what they are looking for. And the Jew cheerfully replies:
   – What marvelous luck! Just today I received a shipment of cups of the kind you want.
   And he shows them the teacups, turned in such a way that their handles are on the left side.

---

[3] John Taylor, *Wit and Mirth*, 1630. Reprinted by W. Carew Hazlitt in *Shakespeare Jest-Books*, first published in 1864, and subsequently re-issued in New York by Burt Franklin in 1964; vol. 3, pp. 10-11.
[4] Lazaro Liacho, *Anecdotario Judío. Folklore, Humorismo y Chistes* (Buenos Aires: M. Gleizer, 1939), pp. 161-162. The publication history of the "Left-handed teacup" joke will be found on pp. 222-229 below.

Having become a Jewish joke in this way, it would soon be greatly improved by the addition of a final exchange between the Nazi leaders. A 1941 version of the joke includes these additional lines:[5]

> The two dignitaries told the proprietor that they would return a little later. Upon emerging from the store, Dr. Schacht said: "What did I tell you? The Jew is a cleverer businessman than his Aryan competitor."
> "Clever nothing," bellowed the *Fuehrer*. "The Jew was just lucky enough to have a cup for a left-handed person."

This final bit of dialogue vastly improves the joke by: a) manoeuvering Hitler into the role of butt, as the ultimate embodiment of stupidity; b) providing a punchline with real impact; and c) completing the framing of Schacht's "demonstration," thereby enhancing the sense of closure we experience as the joke concludes.

The examples cited above involve considerable restructuring of the original non-Jewish material within the new framework of the Jewish joke. In other cases, however, the original joke could simply be adopted as it was, with the substitution of a role or name in order to signal ethnicity. Consider the following joke, as it appeared in a Jewish anthology in 1948:[6]

The Mistake

The rabbi of Chelm and one of his Talmud students were spending the night at the inn. The student asked the servant to wake him at dawn because he was to take an early train. The servant did so. Not wishing to wake the rabbi, the student groped in the dark for his clothes and, in his haste, he put on the long rabbinical gabardine. He hurried to the station, and, as he entered the train, he was struck dumb with amazement as he looked at himself in the compartment mirror.

"What an idiot that servant is!" he cried angrily. "I asked him to wake me, instead he went and woke the rabbi!"

The forerunner of this story appeared in a Greek anthology, dating from somewhere between the 3rd and 10th centuries:[7]

---

[5] S. Felix Mendelsohn, *Let Laughter Ring* (New York: Jewish Publication Society, 1941), pp. 120-121.

[6] Nathan Ausubel, *Treasury of Jewish Folklore* (New York: Crown, 1948).

[7] *The Philogelos or Laughter-Lover*, translated with an introduction and commentary by Barry Baldwin (Amsterdam: J. C. Gieben, 1983), p. 11.

An egghead and a bald man and a barber were on a trip together. Having camped in a remote spot, they agreed that they would each keep watch over their belongings in shifts of four hours. The barber happened to draw the first watch. Wanting to have a bit of fun, he shaved the egghead's dome as he slept, then woke him up when his own shift was done. Rubbing his head as he came to, the egghead found that he was bald.

"What a big fool that barber is," he grumbled. "He's woken up baldy instead of me!"

The story would remain ethnically neutral through the 19th century, when it appeared in English collections published in 1821 and 1887 in a form nearly identical to the Greek version.[8]

In other cases, the mere substitution of a Jewish name for "a gentleman" or "a woman," would be enough to turn a joke which was ethnically non-specific in the 17th Century, into one which seemed perfectly at home in recent anthologies of Jewish jokes, as illustrated by the following stories:

[1639][9]

A Gentleman that bore a spleene to another meets him in the street, gives him a box on the eare; the other, not willing to stricke againe, puts it off with a jest, asking him whether it was in jest or in earnest? The other answers it was in earnest. I am glad of that, said he, for if it had been in jest, I should have been very angry, for I do not like such jesting; and so past away from him.

[1988][10]

Cohen, five foot nothing, is waiting in a bus queue, when a six foot four drunk kicks him to the ground and stands with one huge foot on Cohen's back.

Cohen: "Excuse me, you're standing on my back."

Drunk: "I know."

Cohen: "Tell me, did you do it on purpose or was it a joke?"

Drunk: "Purpose."

"Oh, good," said the relieved Cohen. "I don't like jokes."

---

[8] In both George Coleman's *The Circle of Anecdote and Wit* (London: Wilson, 1821) and W. Carew Hazlitt's *Jests, Old and New* (London: Jarvis, 1887), the same text is found, on pp. 88 and 118 respectively: "A scholar, a bald man, and a barber, travelling together, agreed each to watch four hours at night, in turn, for the sake of security. The barber's lot came first, who shaved the scholar's head while he was asleep, then waked him when his turn came. The scholar, scratching his head, and feeling it bald, exclaimed, 'You wretch of a barber, you have waked the bald man instead of me.'"

[9] *Conceits, Clinches, Flashes and Whimsies*, 1639, in *Shakespeare Jest Books*, op. cit., vol. 3, p. 16.

[10] Michael Dines, *Third Jewish Joke Book* (London: Futura, 1988), p. 44.

[1630][11]

A company of Neighbours that dwelt all in one rowe in one side of a street, one of them said: Let vs be merry, for it is reported that we are all Cuckolds that dwell on our side of the street (except one). One of the women sate musing, to whom her husband said: wife, what, all *amort*? Why art thou so sad? No, quoth she, I am not sad, but I am studying which of our neighbours it is that is not a Cuckold.

[1974][12]

Actor-Comedian Jesse White tells about the apartment house in the Bronx occupied entirely by Jewish tenants. McMurphy was the janitor.

"How do you like working here?" asked Wasserman, one of the building's occupants.

"Oh, I love working for the Jews!" said McMurphy. "In fact, I'll tell you a little secret. I've made love to every woman in this building – except one!"

Wasserman rushed upstairs. "You know what the janitor just told me," he exclaimed to Mrs. Wasserman. "He's made love to every woman in this building except one!"

"Well," said his wife, "it must be that stuck-up Mrs. Rudnick on the second floor!"

Improving the Joke

When the narrative framework of a joke is optimal from the start – as is the case with "Dying Merchant," whose publication history will be found on pp. 203-213 below – the joke will remain stable indefinitely, subject only to minor stylistic changes, even when transported from one country to another. Jokes which evolve do so because the people who tell them somehow hit upon a better way of fulfilling the stories' comic potential.

This is why the "Meaning of Life" joke underwent so many changes, until some jokester found what will probably turn out to be its definitive form in the "Dying Rabbi" variant, which combines the narrative fullness of the original rabbinic "Suspension-Bridge" story with a new situation and a new punchline, both of which enrich the joke to such a degree that the other variants seem shallow in comparison.

---

11 *Wit and Mirth*, 1630 in *Shakespeare Jest Books*, op. cit., vol. 3, pp. 75-76.
12 Larry Wilde, *Official Jewish Joke Book* (New York: Pinnacle, 1974), p. 84.

In some cases, the initial crystallization of a joke may be satisfactory as far as it goes, but may require an additional twist at the end. We saw this in the development of the "Left-handed teacup" joke from 1939 to 1941.

In other cases, what is needed is not an *additional* punchline but rather a *better* one, which plays out the possibilities of the joke in a more effective manner. Here is a joke which, in its initial form, as it appeared in a French anthology in 1925,[13] hardly lived up to its potential:

At the dinner table.
– Have another cake!
– Thank you, but I've already eaten three!
– Actually, you've eaten four, but you can still take some more.

Seven years later, in a book of Jewish jokes published in New York,[14] it still ended with a thud:

The coming-out party of Lucinda Freedman was in full swing. Her proud father kept making a tour of the house to see that the guests were enjoying themselves. Near the buffet stood Yascha Binder.
"Hava a sandwich, Mr. Binder," suggested the host.
"I had one," replied Yascha.
"You had three – but have another one, anyway," said Freedman.

Here again, the joke concludes with the host first contradicting the guest ("You had three") and then making a concession to him ("but have another one, anyway").

Nearly another decade elapsed and then something happened. Some jokester realized that the real potential of the story could be tapped if the second half of the punchline were changed. From 1941 on, the joke would be told with its new ending:[15]

Mrs. Finston (at a party): Have another sandwich, Mr. Cohen.
Mr. Cohen: I already had one, thank you.
Mrs. Finston: Never mind, you really had not one but five – but who's counting?

---

[13] Raymond Geiger, *Nouvelles histoires juives* (Paris: NRF, 1925), p. 203; my translation.

[14] Harry Hershfield, *Jewish Jokes* (New York: Simon & Schuster, 1932), joke number 138.

[15] S. Felix Mendelsohn, *Let Laughter Ring* (Philadelphia: Jewish Publication Society, 1946; orig. pub. 1941), p. 190. The publication history of this joke will be found on pp. 235-237 below.

In the original story, logic is not violated in any way; the host catches the guest in a fib and then politely renews the offer of another cake or sandwich. With the new "who's counting?" ending, the punchline doubles back upon itself, tracing an impossible figure that embodies just the kind of contradiction we poor humans constantly entangle ourselves in.

Another story which was improved in essentially the same way is the "Umbrella" joke, already discussed briefly on p. 32 and which fully embodies the insane logic of an impossible figure in this definitive form:[16]

Two sages of Chelm went out for a walk. One carried an umbrella, the other didn't. Suddenly, it began to rain.
"Open your umbrella, quick!" suggested the one without an umbrella.
"It won't help," answered the other.
"What do you mean, it won't help? It will protect us from the rain."
"It's no use, the umbrella is as full of holes as a sieve."
"Then why did you take it along in the first place?"
"I didn't think it would rain."

Here, bringing an umbrella because rain seemed unlikely, inscribes a full-blown contradiction at the heart of this joke. In its original form, no such contradiction existed in the comic figure's behavior:[17]

Kohn: "Sarah – it's raining – pull your skirt up higher – it's practically dragging in the mud!"
Sarah: "I can't do that – my stockings are torn!"
Kohn: "Why didn't you put a fresh pair of stockings on?"
Sarah: "Could I know it was going to rain?"

Yet another story which was improved by a jokester who found a way to make it more illogical, began in 1927 in the following form:[18]

A Jew who was travelling alone by train, found the trip long and boring; he was looking for an occasion to start a conversation with the gentleman sitting across from him. Since this man hardly seemed disposed to begin a conversation, our Jew finally decided to take the initiative:
    – Excuse me, sir, do I have the honor of speaking to Monsieur Weiss of Strasbourg?
    – No, you're mistaken, answered the gentleman gruffly.
    – That's amazing, I knew it right away because you don't look anything like him!

---

[16] Nathan Ausubel, *Treasury of Jewish Folklore* (New York: Bantam, 1980; orig. pub. by Crown in 1948), p. 338.

[17] H. Itler, *Jüdische Witze* (Dresden: Rudolph'sche Verlagsbuchhandlung, n.d. [1928]), p. 48; my translation. The publication history of this joke will be found on pp. 238-240 below.

[18] D. Acques, *Les contes du rabbin* (Paris: Quignon, 1927), p. 114; my translation.

While the Jew in this story makes a fiasco of the initiative he takes to start a conversation, we nevertheless know what he is up to and why. No such motivation is discernable in the joke that would evolve from this original story, some thirty years later. Here – and this is to the credit of the jokester who invented this new version – we cannot begin to account for the comic figure's behavior:[19]

A lady approaches a very dignified man on the subway and asks him, "Pardon me for asking, but are you Jewish?" He coldly replies, "No." She returns in a moment and apologetically asks again, "Are you sure you're not Jewish?" Yes, he is sure. Still not convinced, she asks a final time, "Are you absolutely sure you're not Jewish?" The man breaks down and admits it, "All right, all right, I am Jewish." To which she makes the rejoinder, "That's funny. You don't look Jewish."

In some versions of this joke (pp. 213-217 below), we are led to assume that the man admits to being Jewish even though he isn't, in order to stop the woman from pestering him further; in other cases, the man turns out to be Jewish – a fact he had initially been unwilling to admit. The whole question of "looking Jewish" is something of a mystery, especially when you consider that Leslie Howard, of Hungarian-Jewish background, was the screen's most perfect embodiment of the English gentleman, while the young Italian-American actor from the Bronx, Sal Mineo, won an Oscar nomination for his portrayal of a Jewish terrorist in *Exodus*.

The development of parallel variants

A number of Jewish jokes exist in two variants with approximately the same narrative structure and degree of detail, but a different designation of the roles in play. This is true of "Rabbinic Judgment," in which the visitors to the rabbi can either be two men with a business dispute, or a married couple seeking a divorce (pp. 13, 16-17 above). It is also the case with the "Ten Commandments" story, with either Middle Eastern peoples or nationalities from Western Europe involved in the refusal-sequences (pp. 75-77 above).

In some cases, the variation may occur both in the overall flavor of the joke and in the punchline itself, as illustrated by the "Job Announcement" story. The two earliest examples of this joke, published in Paris and New York, in 1923[20] and 1946[21] respectively, differ considerably in their tone and each ends with a punchline that would reappear in subsequent retellings:

---

[19] Bernard Rosenberg and Gilbert Shapiro, "Marginality and Jewish Humor," *Midstream* 4 (Spring 1958), pp. 70-71. The publication history of this joke will be found on pp. 213-217 below.

[20] Raymond Geiger, *Histoires juives* (Paris: NRF, 1923), p. 188; my translation. The publication history of this joke will be found on pp. 217-222 below.

In [Czarist] Russia, a nobleman places the following ad in a newspaper: "About to leave for travels in Western Europe, I am looking for a male secretary who must be young, elegant and able to speak French and English fluently."

Just hours after the paper is in print, an old Jew arrives at the nobleman's door and asks to speak with him about an urgent matter. The servant refuses to let him in.

"Tell your master that I have something very important to say to him."

The servant does as he is asked, and soon returns to get the old Jew, who is led in to see the master.

"Your Excellency, I have just read your advertisement... As you can see, I am neither young nor elegant. And I must add that I cannot speak a work of English or French."

"So?" asks the nobleman.

"So, I just came to tell you that I cannot accept the position you are offering."

Count Esterhazy was organizing an expedition to the Near East and beyond. He had engaged most of the helpers, but he needed a general factotum for the long journey. Knowing the position was hard to fill, he advertised for a seasoned traveler who spoke the languages of the Near East, a fearless swordsman, an intrepid rider, etcetera. The advertisement was worded to attract only the right man – and there were no applicants. After a week, the butler announced that a small and shabby looking fellow had come in response to the ad.

He doesn't sound very promising," said Count Esterhazy, "but show him up."

The man proved to be even less prepossessing than the butler's description. But clothes do not always make the man, and the Count began by asking, "You like to travel?"

"Me?" said the little man. "I hate traveling. Boats make me seasick. And trains are worse."

"But you are a linguist," continued the Count. "I presume you speak Arabian, Persian, Turkish, Hindustani – "

"Who? Me?" gasped the candidate. "I talk nothing but Yiddish."

"Your swordsmanship?" inquired the Count.

"What do you mean, swordsmanship? What should I do with a sword?"

"And as a horseman?"

"I hate horses. I wouldn't go near one."

"But," said the Count, "what did you come here for?"

"I saw your ad," said the man, "and I just came to tell you that on me you shouldn't depend."

The potential employer in this joke can be anyone from a Russian nobleman or Frankfurt Rothschild to NASA or even a Nazi police station (pp. 217-222 below). This joke is therefore one which varies not only in tone and punchline, but also in its designation of a major role. Especially in its earlier forms, it is also a story that responds to the

---

[21] Louis Untermeyer, *A Treasury of Laughter* (New York: Simon & Schuster, 1946), pp. 525-526.

exclusion of Jews from certain roles and sectors of the society at large by inventing a narrative construct – of the usual impossible figure variety – through which access is gained to forbidden social territory in order to manoeuvre into a losing position, a person who would never even recognize a Jew as a legitimate player in the social game.

Generally speaking, the alternate variants of a joke circulating at about the same time and *not* representing successive stages in its development, tend to be equally appealing and to differ in ways that reflect differing taste. There is, however, one unfortunate exception to this rule: the "Dachshund" joke, which is hilariously funny when told in accordance with the original German variant, as is usually done in American and English anthologies, and much less funny with the ending used in collections written in Spanish, French or Italian:

German variant [as told in the U.S.][22]

The great Russian landowner summoned his Jewish business-agent and said to him:

"Here are twenty-five rubles – I want you to buy me a dachshund!"

"May it please Your Excellency," urged the agent, "but how is it possible to buy a good dachshund for such a small sum? Take my advice, give me fifty rubles and I'll buy you a dachshund that *will be* a dachshund!"

"Good!" agreed the landowner. "Here are twenty-five more rubles – but make sure it's a first class dachshund!"

"You can rest on that, Your Excellency," the agent assured him.

And as he was about to leave he hesitated and asked apologetically: "A thousand pardons, Your Excellency, but what *is* a dachshund?"

Latin variant[23]

Jacob is summoned by the nobleman of the village.

– At your service!

– My dear Jacob, I would like you to find two dachshunds for me.

– Two dachshunds? Nothing could be simpler... What did you plan to spend on them?

– Two hundred rubles.

– Your Excellency, pardon me for saying this but you must be joking... Two hundred rubles... Do you realize [how inadequate that is]?

– All right, how much do you think they will cost?

– For two dachshunds... You did say two dachshunds? Right... Let's see now. All right, you'll have to spend three hundred rubles...

– Good gracious! But for that price, can you promise me that they will be superb?

– I guarantee it, Excellency! The most beautiful dachshunds in all the land...

– In that case, so be it!

And Jacob leaves. As soon as he is in the street, he runs into Yossel to whom he says:

– You know so many things... Can you tell me what dachshunds are?

---

[22] Nathan Ausubel, *Treasury of Jewish Folklore* (New York: Crown, 1980; orig. pub. 1948), p. 227. The publication history of this joke be will be found on pp. 190-200 below.

In the German variant, first published in Berlin in 1907 – a fertile period and location in the history of Jewish humor – the business agent commits a magnificently illogical and inexplicable act when he asks *the nobleman* what a dachshund is, after having pretended to be an expert on the matter. The well-meaning inventor of the Latin variant must have thought he was improving the story when he made the ending more plausible by having the business agent ask *someone else*! The result is the opposite of what happened when jokes like "Who's counting?," "Umbrella," and "Funny you don't look Jewish" were perfected by replacing a relatively logical punchline with one that defies explanation. I can't help wondering whether those master-pieces of Jewish humor which play on contradiction and lunatic logic, aren't primarily in the spirit of German and East European Jews – the Ashkenazim – rather than that of the Sephardim who settled around the Mediterranean.[24]

In any event, the Jewish business agent in the funnier of the two variants, embodies a unique combination of tactical manoeuvre and role-fiasco – the former residing in his putting one over on the nobleman, the latter coming into play when he innocently reveals to his employer that the purported expertise and being-in-the-know were all an act. In the Latin variant, only the tactical manoeuvre is retained, thereby limiting our interpretive options to a single position on the basic triad.

The nobleman, incidentally, is portrayed quite generously here, as in the "Job Announcement" joke. Although both stories evoke what we know to have been a precarious existence for Jews in Eastern Europe, and turn the tables on those in power, it is not the Russian nobleman who is made to behave comically in our eyes, but rather the Jewish character in the joke. The absence of bitterness in jokes of this kind, the utter harmlessness with which they deal with exclusion and

---

[23] *Popeck raconte les meilleures histoires de l'humour juif* (Paris: Mengès, 1978), p. 39; my translation.

[24] According to a study carried out at two Israeli universities, Jews of Asian or African descent find absurd humor to be less funny than Jews of European descent. How the definition of the two groups in this study relates to the distinction Ash-kenazic/Sephardic, is not at all clear to me. See Leonard Weller, Ella Amitsour and Ruth Pazzi, "Reactions to absurd humor by Jews of Eastern and Western descent," *The Journal of Social Psychology* 98 (1976), pp. 159-163.

the exploitation of Jewish know-how, are as much a part of their appeal as is their interpretive richness and impossible logic.

Conclusion

Several commentators have tried to define the term, "Jewish joke" – a risky enterprise, to say the least.

One of those attempts was made with tongue-in-cheek and states two criteria, the first of which I find both objectionable and untrue: "A Jewish story is one which no *goy* [Gentile] can understand and which a Jew says he has heard before."[1] This is reminiscent of an East European joke found in numerous anthologies, and which was told as follows in its first American appearance in 1935:[2]

When you tell a joke to a moujik [a peasant] he laughs three times. First, he laughs when you tell the joke; secondly, when you explain it to him; and thirdly, when he understands it.

A baron laughs twice. First, when you tell him the joke and secondly, when you explain it to him, since he never understands it anyway.

An army officer laughs only once – when you tell him the joke, since he will not allow you to explain it to him and he has no brains to understand it.

---

[1] Attributed by S. Felix Mendelsohn to Israel Zangwill in *The Jew Laughs* (Chicago: L. M. Stein, 1935), p. 15; no source given. In *Der jüdische Witz* (Breisgau: Walter-Verlag, 1960), p. 510, Salcia Landmann cites Alexander Moszkowski's verse, though without giving her source:

E jüdischer Witz	roughly	A Jewish joke
Mit e jüddisch Akzent:	translatable as:	With a Jewish accent
Was e Goi nischt versteht		Which a Goy doesn't understand
Und e Jüd immer schon kennt		And a Jew has already heard.

The verse is also cited by Theodor Reik in *Jewish Wit* (New York: Gamut Press, 1962), p. 182, in a somewhat more Germanic transcription:

Ein jüdischer Witz
Mit jüdischim Akzent:
Was ein Goy nicht versteht
Und ein Jud immer schon kennt.

[2] Mendelsohn, op. cit., p. 15. Versions of this joke appear in: Geiger (1925, p. 31), Löwit (1928, p. 3), Olsvanger (1935/1965, p. 3), Samard (1936, pp. 24-25), Cantor, (1943, p. 199), Ausubel (1948/1980, p. 15), Howe (1951, pp. 211-212), Howe & Greenberg (1955, pp. 26-27), Landmann (1960, p. 510), Katz & Katz (1971, p. 216), Mindess (1972, pp. 22-23), Asimov (1972, p. 281), Ben-Amos (1973, pp. 113-114), Koplev (1988, pp. 13-14), Novak & Waldoks (1981, pp. 4-5), Fölkel (1988, p. 215), Dundes (1987, p. 150).

But when you tell a joke to a Jew – *oi weh!* He says that the story is as old as the hills and besides, you don't know how to tell it.

In a more serious vein, Ed Cray (1964) suggested that a Jewish joke is "one which intrinsically deals with the Jew and one which would be pointless if the Jewishness of a character were removed."[3] This definition was challenged by Heda Jason (1967), on the grounds that it "does not take into account who tells the joke and in what society it is told."[4]

More recently, Christie Davies (1986) proposed that stories be classified as Jewish jokes if they: a) are "congruent with the Jewish cultural tradition, social experience and use of language"; b) exhibit a "very limited degree of switchability," a variable already described on p. 73 above; and c) imply an attitude toward Jews which is "generally favourable but with a very large range from highly positive to moderately negative."[5] With respect to the question of attitude, Davies' suggestion is consistent with Freud's view that Jewish jokes – as opposed to the vicious stories told about Jews by outsiders to the community – are expressive of what Jews take to be "their real faults as well as the connection between them and their good qualities."[6]

In the present book, I have called attention to other properties which are admittedly not found in all Jewish jokes, but which – I believe – are present in the very best of the classics, contributing to their special flavor and interpretive richness.

The most important of those properties is *reversibility*: the joke's openness to being understood in two or more radically different ways, those alternate interpretive options having nothing to do with "double entendre" or turnabouts within the fiction. I have argued that just as a "Necker's cube" or "Rubin's figure" changes its configuration before our eyes as we continue to look at it, so does a classic Jewish joke assume first one, and then another, and perhaps yet a third significance for us as we continue to to think about the comically deviant behavior enacted in the punchline. The "Rabbinic Judgment"

---

[3] Ed Cray, "The Rabbi Trickster," *Journal of American Folklore* 77, 306 (October-December 1964), p. 344.

[4] Heda Jason, "The Jewish Joke: The Problem of Definition," *Southern Folklore Quarterly* 31, 1 (March 1967), p. 49.

[5] Christie Davies, "Jewish Jokes, Anti-Semitic Jokes and Hebredonian Jokes," in *Jewish Humor*, edited by Avner Ziv (Tel Aviv: Papyrus, 1986), pp. 75-96.

[6] Sigmund Freud, *Jokes and Their Relation to the Unconscious* (Harmondsworth: Penguin, 1981), p. 157.

joke is a case in point, since the rabbi's violation of logic can be understood in three different ways: in terms of a) role-fiasco, b) tactical manoeuvre, and c) exemplary deviance – those three interpretive positions constituting what I have called the "basic triad."

I have also argued that a second set of interpretive options – the "parodistic triad" – raises to six the repertory of interpretive frameworks that can be applied to Jewish jokes. Though no one story can be understood in all six ways, jokes which can be understood in three or four different manners – such as "He had a hat!" and the "Dying Rabbi" story – are not uncommon.

In addition to exhibiting the property of reversibility, many of the best Jewish jokes contain an *impossible figure* – a verbal equivalent of such constructs as the "Penrose triangle" and "three-pronged clevis," which defy their own logic in so compelling a way that we cannot grasp how they fit together. Groucho Marx's "Resignation Joke" exemplifies a figure of that type, and I tried to demonstrate in Chapter Seven that several Jewish jokes, such as "Who's Counting?" and "Umbrella," are radically improved versions of forerunners that had been based on a relatively logical construct that was subsequently replaced by an impossible figure.

Jokes which are open to several interpretations and which violate their own logic in the manner of an impossible figure – as does "Rabbinic Judgment" – are quintessentially Jewish.

A third property of the very best classics is the fact that they are rooted, not in word-play or abstractions, but in the realities of human behavior, as illustrated most graphically by "He had a hat!" and its relation to the actual incident about the boy who had nearly been buried alive, his father and the missing boot. Each of these jokes is like a lesson on human nature, counteracting any tendency we might have to overestimate the degree to which people act in a manner consistent with logic. The humor they embody is the same improbable humor that is somehow at the heart of real events or circumstances – such as the ease with which R.A.F. pilots on a bombing raid could zero in on Gestapo headquarters in a Danish city, since those headquarters were the only building in town that the Germans had protected with camouflage paint.

Related to all three of the above-mentioned properties is a fourth one which might be described as an underlying mistrust of any mental construct in which the mind might become entrapped. The "Meaning of Life" joke, especially in its ultimate, "Dying Rabbi" variant, illustrates this principle most clearly. But it is present as well in any joke that depicts human behavior as subject to alternate interpretations or as embodying an impossible figure.

As I mentioned in connection with the exemplary deviance reading of "Rabbinic Judgment," according to which the rabbi in the joke embodies a higher and more enlightened conception of the truth than is accounted for by the common-sense norm he violates, Martin Buber suggested that when Adam and Eve ate of the forbidden fruit, they became aware of the opposites teeming in all creation. It was in order to protect them from this painful awareness of the contradictions inherent in all things, that God had prohibited their eating from the Tree of Knowledge. And once their eyes were opened to the true nature of reality, God drove Adam and Eve from the Garden, before they could eat from the Tree of Life and be forced to live forever in their painful awareness of contradiction.

What this reading of the myth suggests is that there are two modes of consciousness: one which filters out the contradictory nature of all things and helps to maintain the illusion that being – including our own – is essentially coherent and consistent with itself; and another, which fully registers the contradictions inherent in all things. The term "dialectical" might be used to refer to the mode of awareness attained when the fruit is eaten and the protective illusion dispelled.

By virtue of the four properties described above – in alternately assuming different interpretive configurations before our eyes, in confronting us with an impossible figure, in tapping the absurdities of our daily existence, and in counteracting any wish we might harbor for a formula into which the mind might all too comfortably settle – a classic Jewish joke is like a fruit on the Tree of Knowledge, its bitter-sweet taste serving as a gentle reminder that opposite perceptions of one and same thing may both be valid, and that human behavior is a patchwork of contradictions.

Supplementary Publication Histories

1. Another Doctor

Seymour Hicks,
CHESTNUTS
REROASTED.
London: Hodder
& Stroughton,
1924; p. 35.
One of my oldest friends, a famous Glasgow surgeon, told me that he was once conducting a party of students round the wards, stopping at each bed to explain to them the ailments of the occupants. He arrived at the couch of a Highland shepherd, who had been in the hospital for a considerable time suffering from an incurable disease. "Ah, Donald," said my famous friend, "I am afraid I can do nothing for you. Gentlemen, we will pass on." The students under his care were taken up the ward and while he was explaining to them the intricacies of an abdominal operation at a bed some distance away, Donald, who had time to think over the hopeless diagnosis of his condition, called out, "Doctor Macintyre, did you say that you could do nothing for me?" "I did, I am sorry to say," said the specialist with a wide-world reputation. "Well then," said Donald, "if *you* can't, for God's sake send along someone who can."

Edmund Fuller,
THESAURUS OF
ANECDOTES.
New York: Crown,
1942; p. 301.
Looking down at the sick man, the doctor decided to tell him the truth.

"I feel that I should tell you. You are a very sick man. I'm sure that you would want to know the facts. Now – is there anyone you would want to see?"

Bending down toward his patient, the doctor heard him feebly answer "Yes."

"Who is it?"

In a slightly stronger tone the sufferer said, "Another doctor."

Henny Youngman,
HOW DO YOU
LIKE ME SO FAR?
New York: Gramercy,
1963; p. 93.
Three scientists were given six months to live and told they could have anything they wanted. The first scientist was a Frenchman. He wanted a beautiful villa on the Riviera and a gorgeous woman. The second doctor was an Englishman. He wanted to have tea with the Queen. The third doctor was a Jewish doctor. He wanted the opionion of another doctor.

Ed Cray, "The
Rabbi Trickster,"
JOURNAL OF
AMERICAN
FOLKLORE 77
(1964); p. 337.
The rabbi, priest and minister were all ill. So they go to the doctor to get a diagnosis. They're sitting there in the waiting room of the doctor's office and the priest goes in. A half hour later, he comes out, white-faced, shaking, and the other two crowd around him. "What happened? What did he say?"

(cont.)

Cray, *cont.*

"I've got spinal meningitis, the doctor says, and I've got just six months to live," the priest whispers faintly.

Then the priest and the rabbi sit there while the minister goes in. And when he comes out, he too is white-faced and trembling.

"What's the matter?"

"I've got just three months to live," and he collapses in the chair.

Now it's the rabbi's turn, and he goes into the doctor's office. A half-hour later he comes out shaking his head. "What did he say to you?"

"He said I've got one month to live at most."

And the three of them sit there, commiserating with each other, discussing what to do in their last few months on earth. And the priest says, "Well, all my life I've wanted a woman. I've never been to bed with a woman and now I'm going to do it. And I'm going to keep on doing it until my six months are up."

And the minister says, "I've spent my whole life devoted to my little congregation. It's a small flock and hasn't been able to pay me much. Now I'm going to take the money in the building fund and I'm going to have one last three-month-long fling."

And they turn to the rabbi. "What are you going to do, Rabbi?"

"I'm going to see another doctor."

Isaac Asimov, TREASURY OF HUMOR. New York: Vallentine-Mitchell, 1972; p. 42.

Three men were engaged in one of those profitless conversations which involve all of us at one time or another. They were considering the problem of what each would do if the doctor told him he had only six months to live.

Said Robinson, "If my doctor said I had only six months to live, the first thing I would do would be to liquidate my business, withdraw my savings, and have the biggest fling on the French Riviera you ever saw. I'd play roulette, I'd eat like a king, and most of all, I'd have girls, girls, and more girls."

Said Johnson, "If my doctor said I had only six months to live, the first thing I would do would be to visit a travel agency and plot out an itinerary. There are a thousand places on earth I haven't seen, and I would like to see them before I die: the Grand Canyon, the Taj Mahal, Angkor Wat, all of them."

Said Goldberg, "If my doctor said I had only six months to live, the first thing I would do would be to consult another doctor."

Larry Wilde,
THE OFFICIAL
JEWISH JOKE
BOOK. New York:
Pinnacle, 1974;
pp. 92-93.

Doctor Kaplan approached his eighty-three-year-old patient in the hospital room. "Mr. Adler, you're the best patient we've ever had in this hospital, and because you've been so cooperative I'm going to tell you something we don't usually tell a patient. I'm sorry – but you're going to die. Is there anyone you'd like to see?"

"Yes," answered Adler. "I'd like to see another doctor!"

Henry B. Berman,
HAVE I GOT A JOKE
FOR YOU. New York:
Hart, 1975; p. 37.

Simon R. Pollack,
JEWISH WIT FOR ALL
OCCASIONS.
New York: A & W
Publishers, 1979;
p. 37.

Two Irishmen and a Jew were discussing what they would do if their doctor told them they had only six months to live.

O'Rourke said, "I know what I would do. I would sell everything and move to France. And for the next six months, I'd play with all the beautiful girls Paris and the Riviera had to offer!"

McLaughlin said, "If my doctor told me I had only six months, I too would sell everything. But I think I would like to travel. I would go all around the world from East to West, and then I'd go around again from North to South."

Then it was Levy's turn. "If my doctor said I had only six months to live," he said thoughtfully, "the first thing I would do would be to get another doctor!"

Jeffrey H. Goldstein,
"Theoretical Notes on
Humor," JOURNAL OF
COMMUNICATION
26, 3 (Summer 1976); p.
109.

Three men lay dying on a hospital ward. Their doctor, making rounds, went up to the first and asked him his last wish. The patient was a Catholic. "My last wish," he murmured, "is to see a priest and make confession." The doctor assured him he would arrange it, and moved on.

The second patient was a Protestant. When asked his last wish, he replied, "My last wish is to see my family and say goodbye." The doctor promised he would send for them and moved on.

The third patient was, of course, a Jew. "And what is your last wish?" the doctor asked. "My last wish," came the feeble, hoarse reply, "is to see another doctor."

Rabbi H. R. Rabinowitz, KOSHER HUMOR. Jerusalem: Rubin Mass, 1977; p. 195.

A Jew and a Frenchman worked in a radium plant operated by the government. They were infected with the rays of radium and a number of doctors pronounced them to be incurable. A government agent called on the Frenchman and told him that the government wishes to provide him with anything he wishes so he could end his life happily. "I would like a villa," he said, "and a dozen beautiful girls to entertain me." "Granted," said the agent. He then called on the Jew. "What is your wish?" asked the agent. "To see another doctor," said the Jew.

SMART COOKIE

Sanford Triverton, COMPLETE BOOK OF ETHNIC JOKES. New York: Galahad, 1981; p. 167.

"Tell me the truth," the sick man told his doctor. "I want to know just how ill I am."

"Well," said the doctor, "you are very sick – very low. In fact, I feel that I should ask you if there is anyone you would like to see."

"Yes," murmured the patient feebly.

"Who is it?"

"Another doctor."

Michael Dines, THE JEWISH JOKE BOOK. London: Futura, 1986; pp. 53-54.

Three television panelists were asked what they would do if they only had six months to live. One said he would spend time in riotous living, the second said he would travel and see the world. Cohen pondered the question and finally replied, "I'd want a second opinion."

2. Cardplayer

Zurechtweisung

Hans Ostwald, FRISCH, GESUND UND MESCHUGGE. SCHNURREN UND ANEKDOTEN. Berlin: Francke, 1928; p. 118.

Der junge Manasse, dessen Vater wegen sehr gewagter Geschäfte einen nicht besonders guten Ruf genießt, holt diesen aus dem Kaffeehaus und sagt auf dem Heimweg zu ihm:

"Daß du dich aber gar nicht schämst, öffentlich mit Leuten zu verkehren, die mit einem Menschen wie du Karten spielen!"

Salcia Landmann, DER JÜDISCHE WITZ. Breisgau: Walter-Verlag, 1960; p. 134.	Levy hat mit einem Bekannten im Caféhaus Karten gespielt. Es kommt zum Krach, Levy springt zornig auf und schreit: "Wieso spiele ich überhaupt mit dir? Ich verstehe selber nicht, wieso ich mich nicht schäme, mit einem Menschen Karten zu spielen, der sich nicht schämt, mit jemanden Karten zu spielen, der mit einem Kerl, wie er einer ist, Karten spielt!"
Theodor Reik, JEWISH WIT. New York: Gamut, 1962; pp. 57-58.	Every day, in a coffee house, two Jews sit and play cards. One day they quarrel and Moritz furiously shouts at his friend: "What kind of a guy can you be if you sit down every evening playing cards with a fellow who sits down to play cards with a guy like you!"
Christopher Wilson, JOKES: FORM, CONTENT, USES AND FUNCTION. London: Academic Press, 1978; p. 180.	...the famous Jewish joke – "What sort of a shmuck do you think I am? I'm not going to sit down and play cards with the sort of shmuck who'd sit down and play cards with me."
William Novak and Moshe Waldoks, THE BIG BOOK OF JEWISH HUMOR. New York: Harper & Row, 1981; p. 87.	Cohen and Katz used to play cards every day in a coffee-house. One day they quarreled, and Katz called out, "What kind of guy can you be if you sit down every day to play cards with a guy who sits down to play cards with a guy like you?"

3. Dachshund

Manuel Nuél, DAS BUCH DER JÜDSICHEN WITZE. Berlin: Gustav Riekes Buchhandlung, n.d. [1907]; pp. 85-86.	Graf Borinski kommt von seinem Gute nach Krakau und läßt seinen Faktor (das ist der Mann, der seine Geschäfte in der Stadt zu besorgen hat) zu sich ins Hotel kommen. Er gibt ihm verschiedene Aufträge, unter anderen auch den, für die Gräfin einen "Dackel" zu kaufen. Natan Chaimowitsch sagt: "Also schön, Herr Graf... ein Dackel... Was wollen Sie anlegen für den Dackel, Herr Graf?" "Ich denke, für zehn bis zwölf Gulden wirst du schon einen schönen Dackel bekommen, Natan . ." "Aber, Herr Graf!" ruft Chaimowitsch, "für zehn bis zwölf Gulden! Das ist nischt für einem wirklich schönem, gutem Dackel, wie ihn die Frau Gräfin brauchen kann. So

(cont.)

Nuél, *cont.*	ein Dackel muß doch aussehn nach was! Und es ist doch 'n Unterschied, ob man braucht ein Dackel für, sagen wir, für die Frau Oekonomin oder für die Frau Gräfin."
	"Gut, Natan! Du kannst meinetwegen zahlen fünfzehn Gulden für den Dackel... wenn er nur schön ist..."
	"Wie heißt, fünfzehn Gulden?" meint der Faktor. "Fünfzehn Gulden ist bei die heutigen Zeiten gar nischt für einem schönem, ausgezeichnetem Dackel erster Klass'... Sie werden schon zahlen müssen wenigstens zwanzig Gulden, Herr Graf! Unter dem wird nichts Brauchbares zu haben sein für die Frau Gräfin. Glauben Sie mir, Herr Graf!"
	"Meinetwegen!" stimmt der Graf zu, "also in Teufels Namen zwanzig Gulden. Aber mehr gebe ich auf keinen Fall für den Dackel, Natan."
	Chaimowitsch notiert sich den Auftrag, bliebt aber dann, anstatt loszuziehen, ruhig stehn.
	"Daß dich die Gans stoße, Natan!" flucht der Graf. "Das Geld hab ich dir gegeben, was willst du da noch?"
	"Entschuldigen Sie, Herr Graf," meint Natan Chaimowitsch verlegen, ...eine Frag... Was ist das ein Dackel...?"

Chaim Jossel, SHABBES SCHMUS. JÜDISCHE WITZE UND ANEKDOTEN. Berlin: Hermann Zeemann, 1907; p. 127.	Fürst Krapülinski laßt seinen Hausjuden kommen und gibt ihm den Auftrag, einen Dackel zu kaufen.
	"Und was darf er kosten Herr Fürst?"
	"Nun zwölf Gulden werden genügen?..."
	"Aber was denken Sie, bei die teire Zeiten!"
	"Also gut, da sind noch drei Gulden."
	"Was sind fünfzehn Gulden? Me kann doch nischt jeden Dackel kaufen? Es ist doch e Unterschied, ob der Dackel für den Herrn Fürsten oder für den Herrn Jäger bestimmt ist!"
	"Da sind noch fünf Gulden, aber nu is genug."
	Im Fortgehn fragt der Jude:
	"Entschuldigen Sie, Herr Fürst, aber sagen Sie mer noch, was is e Dackel??"

Schwierige Kommission

Alexander Moskowski, DIE UNSTERBLICHE KISTE. Berlin: Verlag der "Lustigen Blätter," 1908; p. 61.	Agent: Brauchen Sie sonst noch was, Herr Baron.
	Baron: Ja noch eins; ich will nächstens auf die Jagd; besorgen Sie mir doch einen guten Teckel.
	Agent: Wird besorgt; wieviel wollen der Herr Baron anlegen für den Teckel?
	Baron: Na, sagen wir 50 Mark.

(cont.)

Moskowski, *cont.*   Agent: Dafür kann ich ihn nicht verschaffen. Wenn's
                       wirklich ein guter Teckel sein soll, müssen Sie sich schon
                       wenigstens zu 70 Mark entschließen.
                       Baron: Also meinetwegen; wenn der Teckel nur was taugt.
                       Agent: Verlassen Sie sich ganz auf mich; für 70 Mark
                       verschaff' ich Ihnen e Teckel prima Qualité... sagen Sie
                       mir bloß noch eins, Herr Baron: was is das eigentlich, e
                       Teckel??

Alexander Moszkowsi,   Baron (zu seinem jüdischen Faktotum): "Hören Sie, für
DIE JÜDISCHE KISTE.   meine Jagd müssen Sie mir noch einen Teckel besorgen."
Berlin: Lustigen Blätter, – "Sollen Se haben bis morgen. Wieviel wollen Se
1911; pp. 130-131.   ausgeben vor dem Teckel?"
                       "Na, sagen wir: dreißig Gulden."
                       – "Das kann ich nischt übernehmen. Wo soll ich
                       beschaffen e Teckel, wie Sie ihn brauchen, vor so billig?"
                       "Also vierzig Gulden."
                       – "Herr Baron, es soll doch gewiß sein e guter Teckel, e
                       ausgezeichneter Teckel, unter fufzig Gulden is so e Teckel
                       überhaupt nischt zu haben."
                       "Meinetwegen fünfzig. Aber machen Sie schon, daß Sie
                       fortkommen."
                       Das Faktotum erklärt, daß er dafür einen Teckel prima
                       Qualität besorgen werde. An der Tür wendet er sich noch
                       einmal um: "Baronleben, sagen Sie mir bloß: wos is dos, e
                       Teckel?"

Teckel?

T. L. Hirsch,   Agent: "Brauchen der Herr Baron nicht sonst noch was?"
JÜDISCHES   Baron: "Ich will nächstens zur Jagd; Sie können mir noch
WITZBUCH.   einen guten Teckel besorgen."
Berlin: Reform-   Agent: "Wird gemacht, Herr Baron; wieviel wollen Sie
Verlagshus,   anlegen für den Teckel?"
1913; pp. 23-24.   Baron: "Ich denke fünfzig Mark."
                       Agent: "Dafür kann ich ihn nicht beschaffen; Sie müssen
                          wenigstens noch 20 Mark zulegen, wenn es ein wirklich
                          guter Teckel sein soll."
                       Baron: "Na, meinetwegen, wenn der Teckel nur was taugt."
                       Agent: "Sie können sich ganz auf mich verlassen; ich werde
                          Ihnen verschaffen für siebzig Mark e Teckel prima
                          Qualität. Aber noch eins, sagen Sie mir bloß, Herr
                          Baronleben, was ist eigentlich e Teckel?"

Moritz Rund,
PERLEN JÜDISCHEN
HUMORS. Berlin:
Mar Schildberger, 1914;
pp. 86-87.

Ein Graf hatte einer jungen Dame, die auf seinem Schloß zu Gast war, einen echten Teckel, also Geschenk, zugesagt. Er bestellt Cohn, der die Einkäufe für ihn besorgt, zu sich, und gibt ihm den Auftrag, schleunigst einen echten Teckel zu beschaffen. Mit der Uebergabe von zwanzig Mark macht der Graf Herrn Cohn aufmerksam, er möge aber darauf achten, daß der Teckel auch echt sei. "Hören Sie, Herr Graf, sagt Cohn, für zwanzig Mark gibt's keinen Teckel, besonders, wenn er echt sein soll. Darauf gibt ihm der Graf weitere dreißig Mark. Wo denken Sie hin, Herr Graf, für fünfzig Mark gibt's keinen Teckel, besonders keinen echten! Unter hundert Mark kann ich Ihnen keinen echten Teckel besorgen! Der Graf legt weitere fünfzig Mark zu, und ermahnt Cohn, beim Kauf ja sehr vorsichtig zu sein! Beim herausgehen aus dem Zimmer steckt Cohn von draußen den Kopf nochmal durch die Tür, und fragt: "Entschuldigen Sie, Herr Graf, ich hätte bald das Wichtigste zu fragen vergessen, was ist das eigentlich, ein Teckel?"

DER FACHMANN

Paul Nikolaus,
JÜDISCHE
MINIATUREN.
SCHNURREN
UND SCHWÄNKE.
Hannover and Leipzig:
Paul Steegemann
Verlag, 1924;
p. 24.

Zu Genendel Birnbaum kam eines Tages Silberstock und sagte: "Ich brauch zwa Teckel. Kannste se mir besorgen?"

"Nu nein nicht! Was legste an?"

"Zweihundert Kronen. Aber braune!"

"Für braune so 200 was zu wenig: sagen wir 250."

"Gemacht! Aber wirklich: braune Bein und lange Schwänz und hängende Ohren."

"Ojoi! So echt für 250 Kro... "

"Stammbaum will ich!"

"Dann leg 300 an, un De kriegst Teckel mit Stammbaum un braun, un lange Bein, un krumme Ohren, un hängende Schwänz."

"In Ordnung." – Und ging.

"Silberstock, Silberstock", rief Birnbaum. "Moment! Noch eine Frag: was sennen eigentlich Teckel?!"

Jacob Richman,
LAUGHS FROM
JEWISH LORE.
New York & London:
Funk & Wagnall's,
1926; pp. 147-148.

A Russian nobleman sent for a Jewish trader and asked him to get a dachshund for him.

"How much are you willing to spend for it?" asked the middleman.

"Thirty rubles was the reply.

"Thirty rubles won't do," declared the dealer. "I'm sure you want a nice, classy dachshund. Now, how do you expect to get a dachshund of that quality for thirty rubles? I'll have to pay more than that myself. It will cost you

(cont.)

Richman, *cont.*

forty rubles."

"All right, Moshke," yielded the wealthy sportsman. "But make sure it is a good one."

"Just leave it to me," assured the connoisseur of canines. "I'll select the very best dachshund there is in the market."

He said good-bye and turned to go. At the door he paused and hesitated.

"Well, Moshke," inquired the nobleman, "what is it?"

"Your excellency," quoth the dealer, humbly, "before I go, will you kindly tell me what a 'dachshund' is?"

IMMER GESCHÄFTSMANN

H. Itler,
JÜDISCHE WITZE.
Dresden: Rudolph'sche
Verlagsbuchhandlung,
n.d. [1928]; p. 17.

Der Baron (zu seinem Hausjuden): "Also, ich brauche unbedingt einen Teckel, den müssen Sie mir besorgen!"

–: "Sollen Se haben, Herr Baron! Aber wieviel wollen Se bezahlen für den Teckel?"

–: "Na, ich dachte etwa 50 Mark."

–: "O, o, das wird sich nicht machen lassen! Woher soll ich beschaffen e Teckel, wie Sie brauchen, so billig?"

–: "Na, sagen wir also 60 Mark!"

–: "Herr Baron, nix für ungut, es soll doch gewiß sein e guter Teckel; e Teckel, wo is zu brauchen für den Herrn Baron, is nicht unter 80 Mark zu haben!"

–: "Na also meinetwegen achtzig! Aber nun gehen Sie und besorgen Sie, was ich Ihnen auftrug!"

Der Jude (schon an der Tür): "Noch eine Frage, Herr Baronleben, sagen Se mir bloß, was is das, e Teckel?"

Harry Hershfield,
JEWISH JOKES.
Simon & Schuster,
1932; number 29.

They were partners and engaged in general merchandising.

"Go around, Sigmund, and get any kind of orders on anything."

Ten minutes later, Siggy was riding in a street car, listening to the conversation of two ladies opposite. One was expressing a desire to own a Pomeranian if it could be bought at a reasonable price. Sigmund saw his opportunity.

"Lady, pardon me for listening in. But if you want a high class Pomeranian, at a reasonable price, I can get it for you. I'm in the business."

The prospective purchaser was interested and gave the high pressure salesman her name and address. Sigmund got off at the next block, rushed to the phone and got his partner on the wire.

"Hey, Julius, I got an order from a woman for a Pomeranian–we can make a nice little commission."

"That's marvelous," answered Julius.

(cont.)

Hershfield, *cont.*

"You bet that's fine," answered the hustler. "Tell me, please, Julius, what's a Pomeranian?

YES, WHAT IS IT?

S. Felix Mendelsohn,
THE JEW LAUGHS.
Chicago: L. M. Stein,
1935; p. 56.

A Polish Count instructed his Jewish steward to obtain a dachshund for him not later than the following morning.

"Very good, your Excellency, but how much do you wish to spend on a dachshund?" inquired the Jew.

"Say, ten rubles," replied the Count.

"That's not enough."

"Make it twenty-five."

"Look here, now," insisted the Jew, "you will no doubt want a real dachshund, one of which you will never be ashamed. That kind of a dachshund will cost no less than fifty rubles."

"All right then, I'll make it fifty, but be sure to have it by tomorrow morning."

"Just leave it to me."

As he was about to depart the Jew stopped and asked: "By the way, your Excellency, will you please tell me what is a dachshund?"

A FOX-TERRIER

Rufus Learsi,
THE BOOK OF
JEWISH HUMOR. New
York: Bloch, 1941; p.
187.

The Polish squire summoned his Jewish purchasing agent.'

"Yankel," said he, "my wife has made me promise I would get her a fox-terrier. Will you please go out and buy me one? And remember, I want a good one!"

"Of course, Your Excellency! At once!" the agent replied. "And how much is Your Excellency willing to pay for a good fox-terrier?"

"Fifty crowns," said the squire.

"Impossible, Your Excellency," said Yankel.

"How much, then?"

"At least a hundred."

"A hundred crowns?"

"At least, Your Excellency."

"Well – all right. A hundred then. But hurry up!"

But Yankel stood still.

"Why don't you go?" the Pan demanded.

"Your Excellency... "

"Yes?"

"Tell me, I beg of you, what is a fox-terrier?"

E. M. S. Danero, NUEVOS CUENTOS JUDIOS. Buenos Aires: Editorial Tor, 1943; pp. 129-130.

Un propietario llama a su hombre de confianza, un judío, y le dice:

– He aquí 50 francos. Cómprame un buen *basset*.

– Pero, señor – responde éste –, no se puede comprar eso por 50 francos...

– Bien, en ese caso, aquí tienes cien. Pero, que el *basset* sea de primera.

– ¡Imposible, señor!

– ¡Vaya! Aquí van 150 y no hablemos más.

– Está bien, señor.

El judío se marcha.

Una vez fuera, ataja al primero que pasa por la calle y le pregunta:

– ¡Perdón, señor... Pero... podría decirme qué es un *basset*?

The Dachshund

Nathan Ausubel, A TREASURY OF JEWISH FOLKLORE. New York: Bantam, 1980; orig. pub. by Crown, 1948); 227.

The great Russian landowner summoned his Jewish business-agent and said to him:

"Here are twenty-five rubles – I want you to buy me a dachshund!"

"May it please Your Excellency," urged the agent, "but how is it possible to buy a good dachshund for such a small sum? Take my advice, give me fifty rubles and I'll buy you a dachshund that *will be* a dachshund!"

"Good!" agreed the landowner. "Here are twenty-five more rubles – but make sure it's a first class dachshund!"

"You can rest on that, Your Excellency," the agent assured him.

And as he was about to leave he hesitated and asked apologetically: "A thousand pardons, Your Excellency, but what *is* a dachshund?"

J. Klein-Haparash, KRUG UND STEIN. JÜDISCHE ANEKDOTEN. Munich: R. Piper, 1961.

Baron Warena sagt zu seinem Hausjuden: "Hier, Awrumko, zwanzig Gulden, kauf mir einen Dackel."

Den Zwanziger versenkt Awrumko in die Hosentasche und sagt: "Befehlen, Herr Baron, aber – "

"Was aber?"

"Ich mein', für zwanzig Gulden kann man schon einen ganz guten Dackel kaufen, einen Dackel für einen Gemeindesekretär – vielleicht."

"Na ja, hast recht, hier noch zehn Gulden." Das Goldstück gesellt sich zur Banknote, und Awrumko sagt: "Oh, für dreißig Gulden kauft man heute schon einen ganz guten Dackel. Ein Dackel für den Bürgermeister zum

(cont.)

Klein-Haparash,
cont.

Beispiel braucht nicht mehr zu kosten. Ein ganz feiner Dackel aber–"

"Noch zehn, Awrumko?"

"Das kann schon ein herrlicher Dackel sein, eine Pracht, jeder Gerichtsvorsteher kann stolz auf so einen Dackel sein." Das Goldstück klimpert bei der Begegnung mit seinem Vorgänger in Awrumkos Tasche, "aber – "

"Paß jetzt gut auf, Awrumko, hier noch ein Zehner, aber das ist der letzte! Und jetzt zieh ab und besorg den Dackel!"

"Jawohl, befehlen, gnädiger Herr Baron! Er wird sein *der* Dackel! Und was für ein Dackel! Seit Dackel sich dackeln, war noch so ein Dackel nicht. Ein Dackel eben für meinen gnädigen Herrn Baron, ein Herrschafts-, ein Luxusdackel, aber – "

"Awrumko!" grollt Herr von Warena drohend.

"Nein, nein, gnädiger Herr Baron, ich brauch kein Geld mehr, Gott bewahre, ich hab nur wollen fragen: Was ist das ein Dackel?"

Salcia Landmann,
JÜDISCHE WITZE.
Munich: Deutschen
Taschenbuch Verlag,
1982; pp. 200-201.
Orig. pub. 1962.

Herr von Pöllnitz zu seinem jüdischen Faktotum:

"Mordechai, verschaffen Sie mir bis morgen ein Paar hübscher Dackel. Hier haben Sie fünfzig Mark."

Mordechai, zögernd: "Fünfzig Mark – und Sie sagten, daß es erstklassige Dackel sein müssen?"

Pöllnitz: "Da haben Sie zwanzig Mark mehr."

Mordechai: "Glauben Sie, daß siebzig Mark genügen?"

Pöllnitz: "Ich geben Ihnen achtzig. Aber nach meiner Meinung ist das zuviel. Jetzt gehen Sie endlich!"

Mordechai steckt das Geld ein und geht. Bei der Türe dreht er sich noch einmal um und fragt:

"Verzeihung, gnädiger Herr, was sind das: Dackel?"

Gerald F. Lieberman,
THE GREATEST
LAUGHS OF ALL
TIME. Garden City:
Doubleday, 1961;
p. 298.

To "dynamite" is a procedure where a salesman sells anything he can find that anybody wants.

The dynamiter, in this case, was a man named Boris. "What's a good place to go?" Boris asked.

"Try Madison Square Garden. There's always something going on there in the way of commercial exhibits," he was told. "And remember, whenever you see a buyer going to buy something take him aside and tell him you can get it for him cheaper."

Boris took off for the Garden, where a kennel show was in progress. As he reached the lobby he heard a woman negotiating with a kennel operator. "I'm afraid fourteen hundred dollars for a pomeranian is too much," she said.

(cont.)

Lieberman, *cont.*

The kennel man told her he could do no better, then suggested she think it over and let him know. When the man was gone Boris saw his chance to dynamite and lit the fuse. "Pardon me, madam," he called. "Excuse me for listening in, but let me tell you I have a very classy pomeranian and the price is extra good. I can let you have it for eleven hundred dollars."

The woman was overjoyed. She gave Boris her name and address and asked him to please make delivery before the end of the week.

When she was gone he rushed to the phone and called the office. "How's things going?" Mr. Inside asked.

"Marvelous, I made a terrific sale," Boris shouted jubilantly. "But tell me, Seymour; what's a pomeranian?"

Adam, L'HUMOUR JUIF. Paris: Denoël, 1966; pp. 31-32.

Dans un village polonais, le vieux Moshé est réputé, il peut se procurer n'importe quoi dans des délais très rapides. Un jour, le seigneur du village va le trouver.

– Écoute, Moshé, il me faut une paire de teckels.

– Oui, seigneur, oui, oui.

– Mais ces teckels doivent être parfaits, sans défauts.

– Oui, oui, des très beaux teckels.

– Oui, mais il y a une chose à laquelle je tiens: je veux qu'ils soient absolument identiques.

– Oui, oui, des teckels, très beaux, et tout pareils l'un et l'autre.

– Oui; je suis très pressé. Il me faut ces teckels demain au plus tard; je payerai ce qu'il faut.

– Très bien, seigneur; demain matin, vous aurez deux beaux teckels identiques. C'est tout?

– Oui, répond le seigneur très étonné, et il s'en va.

Alors Moshé appelle:

– Sarah, Sarah, viens vite! Dis-moi: qu'est-ce que c'est des teckels?

Henry D. Spalding, ENCYCLOPEDIA OF JEWISH HUMOR. New York: Jonathan David, 1969; p. 17.

The immensely wealthy Russian landowner summoned Malbim, his Jewish business agent, and said to him, "Here are twenty-five rubles; I want you to buy me a dachshund."

"May it please Your Excellency," answered Malbim promptly, "but you cannot possibly obtain a first-class dachshund for so small a sum. I would have to pay twice as much as that. Take my advice; give me fifty rubles and I'll buy you a dachshund you can really be proud of."

(cont.)

Spalding, *cont.*

"Very well," agreed the nobleman. "Here are twenty-five more rubles. But remember, it must be the best in all the land, as befits my station in life."

"Your worries are over, Excellency," Malbim assured him confidently. "Just leave everything to me."

Malbim turned to leave, when a sudden thought occurred to him. He hesitated, and then asked apologetically:

"A thousand pardons, Your Excellency, but tell me, what is a dachshund?"

POPECK RACONTE
LES MEILLEURES
HISTOIRES DE
L'HUMOUR JUIF.
Paris: Mengès, 1978;
p. 39.

Jacob est demandé par le seigneur de son village.

– A votre disposition!

– Mon cher Jacob, je voudrais que tu me trouves deux teckels.

– Deux teckels? Rien de plus facile... Combien envisagez-vous de les payer?

– Deux cents roubles.

– Seigneur, pardonnez-moi de vous dire cela: mais c'est une plaisanterie... Deux cents roubles... Vous vous rendez compte?

– Eh bien, combien faudrait-il mettre selon toi?

– Pour deux teckels... Vous avez bien dit deux teckels? Oui... Bon! Eh bien, il faut compter trois cents roubles...

– Fichtre! Mais pour ce prix, tu me promets qu'ils seront superbes?

– Garanti, Seigneur! Les plus beaux teckels du pays...

– Alors, soit!

Et Jacob s'en va. Sitôt dans la rue, il rencontre Iossel à qui il demande:

– Toi qui sais tant de choses... Tu peux me dire ce que c'est que des teckels?"

Larry Wilde, THE
LAST OFFICIAL
JEWISH JOKE BOOK.
New York: Bantam,
1980; p. 111.

Antonovich, the rich Russian landowner, summoned Bleustein, his business agent, and said to him, "Here are twenty-five rubles. I want you to buy me a dachshund."

"Your Excellency," answered Bleustein. "It's not possible to obtain a first-class dachshund for so small a sum. I will have to pay twice that amount. For fifty rubles I'll buy you a dachshund you can really be proud of."

"Here are twenty-five more rubles," agreed the nobleman. "But remember, it must be the best in all the land, as befits my station in life."

"Don't worry!" Bleustein turned to leave and then said, "Your Excellency, tell me, what is a dachshund?"

William Novak and
Moshe Waldoks, THE
BIG BOOK OF JEWISH
HUMOR. New York:
Harper & Row,
1981; p. 188.

An emperor once called in his business advisor, who was a Jew. "Here are twenty gold pieces," said the emperor. "I want you to go out and buy me a dachshund."

"Your Excellency," replied the Jew, "where do you think I can get a good dachshund for twenty gold pieces? It will take at least forty gold pieces, and that way I can find you a really *good* dachshund."

"Very well," said the emperor, handing over twenty more coins. "But it must be a very fine dachshund."

"Have no fear, Your Excellency," replied the Jew. "I promise it will be the finest dachshund that money can buy. But there is just one small thing, if it please Your Excellency."

"And what is that?"

"A thousand pardons, Your Excellency, but what exactly *is* a dachshund?"

Ferruccio Fölkel,
STORIELLE
EBRAICHE.
Milan: Rizzoli,
1988; pp. 88-89.

Un feudatario polacco sollecita la visita di Yankel.

"Senti, Yankele, ti ho chiamato perché voglio fare con te un altro affare. Speriamo che sia buono come l'ultimo."

"Ai suoi ordini, eccellenza."

"Vorrei comperare due bassotti, poiché adesso vanno molto di moda."

"Benissimo, prendiamo i due bassotti. Ma quanto li vuol pagare?"

"Cento rubli."

"Scherza, eccellenza. Cento rubli sono una cifra da ridere, non ne facciamo niente."

"Un momento, Yankele, non te la prendere. Quanto vuoi?"

"Duecento rubli."

"D'accordo, però li voglio perfetti."

"Li avrà stupendi, eccellenza."

"Per quando me li fai avere?"

"Fra alcuni giorni. Diciamo la settimana prossima."

Yankele esce e incontra, appena voltato l'angolo, il suo amico Shlojmele.

"Senti," gli chiede "cosa sono i bassotti?"

4. Dead Shames

Raymond Geiger,
NOUVELLES
HISTOIRES JUIVES.
Paris: Gallimard, 1925;
pp. 36-37.

Dans une petite ville de Galicie, des Juifs viennent demander au rabbi de faire un miracle. Le schamès [bedeau] de la Schul [synagogue] vient de mourir: il faut le ressusciter.

- Bien, fait le rabbin. Allons chez le schamès.

Arrivé chez le mort, il demande un verre de bon vin rouge. Il le vide, puis, d'une voix tonnante, il ordonne au mort de se lever et de marcher. Le mort ne bouge pas.

- Apportez-moi un verre de bourgogne!

Il boit le bourgogne et ordonne au mort de revenir à la vie: le schamès ne bouge pas.

- Apportez-moi une bouteille de champagne!

Il en boit la moitié, puis il renouvelle sa tentative, mais toujours en vain.

- Eh bien, dit le rabbin, voilà ce que j'appelle être mort!

Harry Schnur,
JEWISH HUMOR.
London: Allied
Book Club, n.d.
[1945]; pp. 18-19.

The superstitious believe that the Holy Rabbi of Zhitomir is so powerful that he can even raise the dead.

One day a woman comes and begs him to revive her husband who has just died. The Rabbi accepts the commission and enters the room where the dead man is lying. He reads the Kabbalah, the sacred book of mysticism, from end to end and then commands: "Get up and be alive!"

But the dead man doesn't budge.

Again the Rabbi prays and reads the Kabbalah until he perspires. Again he commands the dead man: "Get up and be alive!" – but the dead man doesn't obey.

The Rabbi prays until all his clothes stick to him; again he recites the Kabbalah; again he commands the dead man to arise. But the corpse continues in its corpse-like passivity.

The Rabbi wipes his streaming brow. "Now that's what I call being dead."

Fritz Muliar,
DAS BESTE AUS
MEINER JÜDISCHEN
WITZE - UND
ANEKDOTEN-
SAMMLUNG.
Munich: Wilhelm
Heyne Verlag, 1974;
pp. 68-69.

Sure kommt angelofn zum Rebben: "Rebbe, mei Mann, mei giter Mann! Er is verstorbn! Aber, Rebbe, Ihr seid doch der greßte Mann, Ihr seid a Wundermann, ich bitt Euch eines, kemmt herieber und weckt mir auf meinem Mann!"

Der Rebbe zieht sich an den Kaftan, setzt sich auf dem Stramel, nimmt den Stock in die Hand und geht herieber. In der warmen Stube setzt er sich neben dem kalten Toiten. Er nehmt seine Hand, und er blickt ihm ins Antlitz. Und dann sogt er: "Sure, bring mir von dem Wodka, was du immer da gehabt hast!"

(cont.)

Muliar, *cont.*

Sure bringt ihm das Fläschchen, er schenkt sich ein a Glasl, schaut an dem Toiten und sogt: "Lechaim, leben sollst de!" Und trinkt. Der Toite riehrt sich nich. Sogt er: "Der Wodka is zu schwach! Du hast nich an stärkeren Wodka?"

Sure geht weg, bringt a zweite Flasche. Der Rebbe riecht, schenkt sich ein a Glasl, trinkt und sogt:

"Lechaim, leben sollst de!" Der Toite riehrt sich nich. Da kratzt sich der Rebbe die Nosn und sogt:

"Sure, ich erinner mich, ich erinner mich ganz genau, zu Pessach vor a poor Johr, da is gewesn da a ganz starker Brompfen, a Brompfen aus dem Jahr 1910, ein Wodka mit sechzig Prozent. Haste noch von dem?"

Still geht Sure heraus und kemmt mit der Wodka-flasche aus dem Jahre neunzehnhundertundzehn. Der Rebbe nimmt sich ein großes Wasserglas, schenkt es voll. Ernsten Blickes schaut er an dem Toiten, er riecht zu dem Wodka, und dann sogt er:

"Lechaim, leben sollst du!" Und er trinkt auf einem Zug herunter das ganze Wasserglas mit dem wunderbaren Wodka aus dem Jahre neunzehnhundertundzehn. Und dann kieckt er an dem Toiten, und as sich der nicht riehrt, steht er auf und schittelt dem Kopf und sogt:

"Das nenn ich toit!"

POPECK RACONTE LES MEILLEURES HISTOIRES DE L'HUMOUR JUIF.
Paris: Mengès, 1978; p. 216.

Le schamès [bedeau] de la schul [synagogue] de cette petite ville de Galicie vient de mourir. Cela attriste tout le monde, c'était un fort brave homme. Il faut le ressusciter. On lui doit bien ça... Dans ce but on va trouver le rabbin.

– Parfait! dit celui-ci, sûr de son fait... Allons chez lui.

Arrivé devant la dépouille du pauvre schamès, il demande un bon verre de vin rouge, le vide et d'une voix sépulcrale ordonne au mort de se lever. Mais le mort n'obtempère pas! Sans se démonter, le rabbin demande un verre de super-vin blanc, le boit et intime l'ordre au mort de se redresser... Aucun résultat!

Sans marquer de surprise, le rabbin demande une bouteille de Champagne millésimé, la liquide gaillardement et, impérativement, commande au bedeau de revenir à la vie. Peine perdue! Le rabbin quitte alors la maison en titubant et dit:

– On ne peut rien faire pour lui! Pour être mort, il est bien mort!

Ferruccio Fölkel,
NUOVE STORIELLE
EBRAICHE. Milan:
Rizzoli, 1990; p. 40.

È morto il vecchio Esaù, lo shames della sinagoga di Gorizia.

Alcuni vecchi ebrei pensano di andare dal rabbino Michelstädter, famoso per i suoi incantesimi e per i suoi miracoli, a chiedergli di resuscitare Esaù perché non sanno come sostituirlo.

"D'accordo," dice Michelstädter "però io ho bisogno di un presniz di Sesana e di un po' di vino rosso. Tutti alimenti non kasher, mi raccomando."

Il rabbino miracoloso giunge in casa dello shames, mangia una fetta di presniz e beve un bicchiere di vino rosso, poi, con voce autorevole, dice: "Alzati e cammina!"

L'ingiunzione rimane senza esito.

Allora il rabbino Michelstädter si fa portare del vino Terrano del Carso, mangia un'altra fetta di presniz, quindi con voce tonante ripete: "Alzati e cammina, Esaù!"

Ma neppure dopo questa ingiunzione, nonostante l'autorevolezza del rabbino miracoloso, succede qualcosa.

A questo punto rabbi Michelstädter si fa portare una bottiglia di vino frizzante del Collio, mangia un'altra fetta di presniz, poi dice solennemente: "Esaù, alzati e cammina!"

Lo shames non si muove.

Allora il rabbino conclude: "Temo che sia davvero morto."

5. Dying Merchant

Arthur Szyk,
LE JUIF QUI RIT.
Paris: Albin Michel,
1926; p. 109.

Kahn, sur son lit de mort:
– Tu es là, ma bonne Rébecca?
– Oui, mon cher époux.
– Et toi, Moïse, mon fils chéri?
– Oui, papa.
– Et toi, mon petit Abraham?
– Présent, papa.
– Et vous, Salomon, mon fidèle caissier?
– Oui, monsieur Kahn.
– Mais alors, nom d'un chien, qui donc garde le magasin?

BUSINESS FIRST

Charles N. Lurie,
MAKE 'EM LAUGH.
New York: Putnam's,
1927; p. 103.

A Hebrew storekeeper lay dying. The family was gathered around the bedside. His wife was trying to rouse him.

"Look, Isaac," she said, "ve're all here – me, you vife, and all der children, Jakey and Mosey and Benny and Rachel and Rebecca. Look, ve're all here!"

The dying man opened one eye. "Is dot so?" he asked. "And who is minding der store?"

Joe Hayman,
TWENTY DIFFERENT
ADVENTURES OF
COHEN ON THE
TELEPHONE. London:
Austin Rogers, 1928;
p. 71.

The old Hebrew lay at death's door. He was sinking fast: his breath was leaving his body and his eyesight was failing him. He was on the edge of the great beyond.

"Iss Becky here?" he gasped. "Yes, fadder, dear, I'm here," said Becky. "Iss Isadore here?" "Yes, fadder," said Izzy. "Iss Hyman here?" asked the old man. "Yes, fadder, I'm here," said Hymie. "Iss Yankil here?" "Yes, fadder," said Jakie. "Iss mein daughter Sarah here?" "Yes, fadder," said Sarah. "Iss everybody here den – all of you?" gasped the old man with what seemed his last breath. "Yes, fadder," they all chorused.

Then said the old man: "Who de h----'s lookin' after de shop?"

Cecil Hunt,
FUN WITH THE
FAMOUS. London:
Ernest Benn, n.d.
[1929]; p. 44.

There was a Scottish family gathered around the bedside of their father, who was sinking rapidly.

The old man said: "Is John here?"

"Yes, I am, father."

"And is Sandy here?"

"Yes, I'm here."

"And Jean, is she here, too?"

"Yes, dear, here I am."

"Oh," said the sinking man, "if you're all here, then who the de'el is looking after the shop?"

Harry Hershfield,
JEWISH JOKES.
New York:
Simon & Schuster,
1932; number 15.

Ginsberg, the owner of the model store, was on his death bed. He regained consciousness long enough to ask his family.

"Are you here, my darling wife," he asked.

"Yes," answered his better half.

"Is Milton here?"

"Yes, papa – here I am."

"Is Lena here?"

"Yes, dad – I'm here with you."

(cont.)

Hershfield, *cont.*

"Is Samuel here?"
"Yes, papa – right here. We're all here."
"My God!" moaned Ginsberg, "WHO'S MINDING THE STORE?"

HIS LAST WORDS

Lewis Copeland,
THE WORLD'S
BEST JOKES.
New York: Blue
Ribbon, 1936; p. 172.

The old pawn broker was on his death bed. His entire family had gathered in the little bedroom back of the pawn shop, and there were wails and tears aplenty. At last the old pawn broker roused himself as if to speak, and his wife and children pressed forward to hear his last words.

"Iz momma here?" he breathed painfully, when there was silence.

"Yez, poppa."
"Iz my daughter Rifka here?"
"Yez, poppa."
"Iz my daughter Rachel here?"
"Yez, poppa."
"Iz my son Isaac here?"
"Yez, poppa."
"Iz my son Max here?"
"Yez, poppa."
"Iz de whole family here?"
"Yez, poppa."
The father sprang up in bed and shouted –
"Den who iz out front teking care of de shop?"

BUSINESS BEFORE PLEASURE

S. Felix Mendelsohn,
LET LAUGHTER
RING. Philadelphia:
Jewish Publication
Society, 1941; p. 165.

Harry Solomon had been bed-ridden for many weeks and was not unaware of the seriousness of his condition. He knew that he was about to face his Maker and therefore told his wife Beckie to assemble the children for a final farewell. Before beginning his remarks, however, Solomon wanted to make sure that everybody was present.

"Are you here, Beckie?" he said feebly.
"Yes."
"And you, Sam?"
"Yes."
"And you, Morris?"
"Yes."
"And you, Benjamin?"
"Yes."
"And you, Rosie?"
"Yes."

(cont.)

| Mendelsohn, *cont.* | "And you, Sarah?"<br>"Yes."
"Well," said the sick man and sat up vigorously, "if you are all here, who is tending the store?" |

| Frederick Meier,
THE JOKE TELLER'S
JOKE BOOK.
Philadelphia: Blakiston,
1944;
p. 165. | Samuel Fein's small clothing store was a sad place. He was stretched out in bed in one of the back rooms, dying. His family of ten were around him bewailing their imminent loss. The old man spoke, "Momma, you here?"<br>"Yes, Poppa," she sobbed.
He rested a moment then continued, "Abelich, you here?"<br>"Yes, Poppa," said Abraham sadly.
Slowly and deliberately the old man called out the names of the rest of the family and all were present and accounted for.
Suddenly his eyes opened and he raised himself on one elbow. "Say," he said severely, "if everybody is in here yet, who de devil is minding de store?" |

| Harry Schnur,
JEWISH HUMOR.
London: Allied Book
Club, n.d. [1945]; p. 61. | Solomon, having reached the allotted span of years, is lying on his death bed. His sight is already beginning to fail, and in a feeble voice he calls out the names of his dear ones.
"Are you here, Rachel?"<br>"Yes, Solomon, I am here."
"Are you here, Isaac?"<br>"Yes, father."
"And you, Sarah, Betty, David?"<br>"We are all here, father," is the tearful reply.
The patriarch revives and exclaims in a thunderous voice:
"Then who's minding the shop?" |

BUSINESS TO THE END

| Elsa Teitelbaum,
ANTHOLOGY OF
JEWISH HUMOR AND
MAXIMS.
New York: Pardes,
1945; p. 318. | A Jewish storekeeper was lying on his deathbed. His entire family gathered near his bedside. His wife, a sorrowful sight, was crying painfully:
"Jacob, Jacob, have mercy on us, open your eyes. To whom are you going to leave us? Have pity, and look at us. We are all here around you. See – Morris, Harry, Rebecca, and Sarah!"
Jacob rose with a start: "If you are all here," he demanded, "then who is in the store to wait on customers?" |

Louis Untermeyer, A TREASURY OF LAUGHTER. New York: Simon & Schuster, 1946; p. 524.	The old shopkeeper was dying; his whole family was gathered about him. Just before he lost consciousness, he asked: "Is Momma here?" "Yes, poppa," answered his wife. "Is Jakey here?" "Yes, poppa." "Is Rifke here?" "Yes, poppa – right here." "Is my nephew Milton here?" "Yes, uncle – we're all here." "All of you!" cried the dying man. "Then who's minding the store?"

SO THEY SMOTHERED HIM

George Milburn, THE BEST JEWISH JOKES. Girard, Kansas: Haldeman-Julius, 1953; pp. 6-7.	The old pawn broker was on his death bed. His entire family had gathered in the little bedroom back of the pawn shop, and there were wails and tears aplenty. At last the old pawn broker roused himself as if to speak, and his wife and children pressed forward to hear his last words. "Is momma here?" he breathed painfully, when there was silence. "Yes, poppa." "Is my daughter Rifka here?" "Yes, poppa." "Is my daughter Rachel here?" "Yes, poppa." "Is my son Isaac here?" "Yes, poppa." "Is my son Max here?" "Yes, poppa." "Is de whole family here?" "Yes, poppa." The father sprang up in bed and shouted– "Den who is out in front taking care of de shop?"

Richard M. Dorson, "Jewish-American Dialect Stories on Tape," BIBLICAL AND JEWISH FORLKLORE (1960), pp. 152-153.	Jake's dying and he's in his last death throes, about to shuffle off the mortal coil, and, in some pain, he says, "Sam, are you here?" He can't even look around. "Yeah, I'm here, father." "And Becky, are you here?" "Yeah, Pop, I'm here." "Rose, Rose here?" [louder] "Yes, Jake, I'm here" [softly].

(cont.)

Dorson, *cont.*

"What about uncle Yitzok, you here?"
"Yes, Jake, I'm here, I'm here" [very soft].
"And, and Jake, you here?"
"Yeah, yeah, yeah, I'm here."
"Benny?"
"Yeah, yeah, I'm here."
"So who's watching the store?" [rising inflection]

Gerry Blumenfeld,
SOME OF MY BEST
JOKES ARE JEWISH.
New York: Kanrom,
1965; p. 88.

Old man Berkowitz lay dying and asked that the rabbi be called. His grief-stricken wife and children huddled about the bed. The old man took his wife's hand and with eyes half-closed said faintly, "Is our eldest son, Louie, here?"
"Yes, Papa, I'm here."
"And Avram, is he here?"
"Yes, Papa, I'm here too."
"And Benny, is he by the bed too?"
"Yes, Papa, I'm here."
"You're here too? So who's minding the store?"

Adam,
L'HUMOUR JUIF.
Paris: Denoël, 1966;
p. 64.

Le vieil Isaac est sur le point de mourir. Dans un souffle, et tendant les mains autour de lui, il appelle ses enfants.
– Rébecca, tu es là?
– Oui, fait Rébecca.
– Yankélé, mon petit, tu es là, toi aussi?
– Oui, mon père, je suis là.
– Et toi, Benjamin, mon enfant, tu es là?
– Oui, je suis là, répond le petit Benjamin.
– Mais alors, crie-t-il affolé, mais alors, qui garde le magasin!

Harry Golden,
THE GOLDEN BOOK
OF JEWISH HUMOR.
New York: Putnam,
1972; pp. 102-103.

Sidney Fedderman, called Reb Sidney, was on his deathbed. Around the aged and highly respected patriarch had gathered members of his family. His wife, Rachel, stood toward the head of the bed holding the old man's hand. "Rachel," breathed the venerable grand-father, "is Nathan here?" Nathan was the oldest son.
"Yes, Papa," she assured him. "Nathan is here. He came last night and hasn't left your side for eighteen hours."
The old man sighed. "Is Benjamin here?" Benjamin was the number two son.
"Yes, Papa," his wife replied. "Benjamin is here and has been weeping all afternoon."

(cont.)

Golden, *cont.*	Reb Sidney closed his eyes. "Is Gershon here?" he whispered. Gershon was his son-in-law. "Yes, Papa, Gershon was the first to arrive and he's standing at the foot of the bed." The old man folded his hands and said "Come close, Mama, I want to tell you something." Mrs Fedderman leaned close to the old man's face. "If Nathan is here, and Benjamin is here" – and now the Reb's voice grew angry – "and Gershon is here, THEN WHO THE HELL IS MINDING THE STORE?"
Isaac Asimov, TREASURY OF HUMOR. New York: Vallentine-Mitchell, 1972; pp. 249-250.	Mr. Levene was dying, and his sorrowing family was gathered around his bed. Mr. Levene, eyes closed, murmured weakly, "Are you there, Becky?" "I'm here, Jake," said Mrs. Levene weeping. "And Sammy, you're there?" "I'm here, Papa," said the oldest son. "And Toby?" "I'm here, Papa," said the oldest daughter. One by one, Mr. Levene went through the list of children down to the youngest, and each assured him of his or her presence. Whereupon Mr. Levene's eyes opened wide. He raised himself to his elbows and cried, "So who's minding the store?"
Hervé Nègre, DICTIONNAIRE DES HISTOIRES DRÔLES. Paris: Fayard, 1973; vol. 2, p. 65.	Le vieux Moshé agonise. Dans un dernier effort, il se dresse, il tâtonne des mains et il dit: – Toute la famille est là? Ma femme Rachel est là? – Oui, dit Rachel. – Et le jumeaux Ezéchiel et David sont là aussi? – Oui, on est là, disent les jumeaux. – Et Benjamin, le petit dernier, il est là? – Oui, papa, dit Benjamin. – Mais alors, nom de Dieu, si tout le monde est là, qui c'est qui garde le magasin?

HVEM PASSER SÅ FORRETNINGEN?

Bronislaw
Aleksandrowicz:
JØDISK HUMOR
FRA POLEN OG
RUSLAND.
Copenhagen:
Gyldendal,
1973; pp. 43-44.

En gammel jøde lå på dødslejet, og hans sørgende familie stod samlet omkring ham. Pludselig åbnede den syge sine øjne, så på de omkringstående og spurgte:
  – Er min kone Sorele her?
  – Ja, Isidor, jeg er her.
  – Er min søn Josele også her?
  – Ja, far, jeg er her.
  – Er min datter Chavele også her?
  – Ja, far.
  – Og er min søn Chaim også her?
  – Ja, far, jeg er her også.
Med opbydelsen af sine sidste kræfter spurgte den gamle fortørnet:
  – Hvem i alverden passer så forretningen?

Henry B. Berman,
HAVE I GOT A
JOKE FOR YOU.
New York: Hart,
1975; pp. 96-97.

Simon R. Pollack,
JEWISH WIT FOR ALL
OCCASIONS. New
York: A & W
Publishers, 1979;
pp. 96-97.

A grocer suffered a heart attack and was carried upstairs to his apartment. Now, pale and weak, he knew there was no hope. The doctor said it would be only a matter of minutes.
  "Are you there, Molly?" asked the man softly. His sorrowful wife pressed his hand.
  "And Bernard, are you there?" he went on faintly.
  "Yes, Father," came his son's reply.
  "And Marsha, you're there?"
  "Yes, Father," wept his daughter.
  Then the grocer's voice came out full force. "You're all here, so who's minding the store?" he growled.

HVEM PASSER BUTIKKEN?

Bronislaw
Aleksandrowicz,
JØDISKE
ANEKDOTER.
Copenhagen: Nordisk
Bogforlag, 1975;
pp. 8-9.

Den gamle jødeskrædder ligger for døden. Hans sørgende familie står omkring sengen. Med svag stemme spørger han:
  – Er min kone Sorele her?
  – Ja, Isidor, jeg er her.
  – Er min søn Josele her?
  – Ja, far, jeg er her.
  – Og min yngste søn Chaim – er han også her?
  – Ja far, jeg er også her.
Isidor rejser sig op i sengen med et sæt og udbryder harmdirrende:
  – Hvem i alverden passer så butikken?

| Alexander Drozdzynski, JIDDISCHE WITZE UND SCHMONZES. Düsseldorf: Droste Verlag, 1976; p. 34. | Rabbinowitsch liegt auf dem Sterbebett. Die ganze Familie versammelt sich um den Todkranken. Er fragt mit gebrochener Stimme: |

Rabbinowitsch liegt auf dem Sterbebett. Die ganze Familie versammelt sich um den Todkranken. Er fragt mit gebrochener Stimme:

"Feigele, mein liebe Frau, bist du bei mir?"

"Ja, mein Lieber, ich bin da."

"Chaim, mein ältester Sohn, mein Stolz und mein Nachfolger, bist du da?"

"Ja, Vater, ich bin da."

"Und meine Tochter Lea, bist du hier?"

"Ja, Papa, ich bin hier."

Da schreit der Kaufmann mit letzter Kraft:

"Und wer, zum Teufel, ist unten im Laden?"

POPECK RACONTE LES MEILLEURES HISTOIRES DE L'HUMOUR JUIF. Paris: Mengès, 1978; pp. 21-22.

Ephraïm va mourir. Sa famille toute entière l'entoure. Sur un signe qu'il fait, Sarah, sa chère femme, s'approche:

– Tout le monde est là? demande le mourant, dans un souffle. Même Samuel?

– Oui, mon bon mari.

– Et Aaron, aussi?

– Oui, mon cher Ephraïm!

– Et Jacob? Il est là?

– Oui, mon doux époux!

– Et ma petite Rachel?

– Elle est là! Elle est là! Tout le monde est là, te dis-je...

Alors se soulevant dans un effort surhumain, Ephraïm articule:

– Et le magasin? Hein? Qui est-ce qui garde le magasin?

William Novak and Moshe Waldoks, THE BIG BOOK OF JEWISH HUMOR. New York: Harper & Row, 1981; p. 301.

Dave was at death's door, and the family was gathered around him.

"Sarah, my wife, are you here at the bedside?"

"Yes, Dave, of course I'm here."

"And Bernie, my oldest son, are you here?"

"Yes, Dad."

"And Rachel, my daughter, are you here?"

"Yes, Father, at the foot of the bed."

"And Sam, my youngest, are you here too?"

"Right here, Pop."

"Well then," said the merchant, "if all of you are here, who's minding the store?"

Elizabeth Petuchowski,
DAS HERZ AUF
DER ZUNGE. AUS
DER WELT DER
JÜDISCHEN WITZES.
Freiburg: Herder, 1984;
pp. 118-119.

Die Familie des Kaufmanns hatte sich um sein Sterbebett versammelt.

"Recha, du wackeres Weib, bist du da?"

"Ja, ich bin bei dir, Samuel."

"Und du, David, mein Erstegeborener?"

"Ja, Vater, hier bin ich."

"Und Evchen Liebchen, meine Tochter?"

"Ich bin hier, Vater."

"Und Benjamin, mein Jüngster?"

"Ja, Vater, ich bin da."

"Und wer, um Himmels willen hütet den Laden?"

Ben Eliezer,
THE WORLD'S
BEST JEWISH JOKES.
London: Angus &
Robertson, 1984; p. 34.

Abie was on his death bed. "Sarah," he croaked, "are you there?"

"Yes, Abie, I'm here."

Silence... then: "Morrie, are you there?"

"Yes, Abie, beloved brother, I'm here."

Silence, but for Abie's agonised breathing... "Wilbur, are you there?"

"Yes, Dad, I'm here."

Silence... "Milton, are you there?"

"Yes, Pop, I'm here."

Abie jerked himself up, and shouted, "So who's minding the shop?"

Ferruccio Fölkel,
STORIELLE
EBRAICHE.
Milan: Rizzoli,
1988; pp. 158-159.

Odom Horowtiz, un piccolo bottegaio, è in fin di vita. Intorno a lui c'è tutta la sua numerosa famiglia. Improvvisamente Odom fa cenno alla moglie di avvicinarsi.

"Shmuel è qui," chiede con voce flebile.

"Certamente," risponde la moglie.

"E Moishe?"

"C'è anche lui."

"E dov'è Rochele?"

"È qui, dietro di te."

"E Avrom?"

"Non lo vedi, è qui."

"Gojim, imbecilli, chi bada alla bottega?"

Kjeld Koplev,
GUDS UDVALGTE.
Copenhagen: Haase,
1988; p. 22.

Gamle Mendelsson ligger for døden. Hans øjne er lukkede. Hovedet hviler blegt på puden. Hele familien er samlet omkring hans seng.

– Er min hustru Esther her? spørger han med en næppe hørlig stemme.

– Ja. Jeg er her.

– Og min datter Sara?

– Ja, din datter Sara er her, siger hans kone gennem et helt langt liv.

– Min søn Josep. Er han her?

– Ja, far, jeg er her også.

– Og min søn Herman?

– Ja, her ved din side.

– Og David, min svigersøn?

– Også jeg er her, siger svigersønnen ydmygt fra et hjørne af værelset.

Så rejser gamle Mendelsson sig med ét op i sengen.

– Hvem i himlens navn passer så forretningen?

6. Funny, You Don't Look Jewish

D. Acques,
LES CONTES DU
RABBIN. Paris:
Quignon, 1927; p. 114.

Un Juif, voyageant seul en chemin de fer, trouvait le temps long et ennuyeux; aussi chercha-t-il l'occasion de lier conversation avec un monsieur qui était assis en face de lui. Ce dernier ne semblant guère disposé à entamer une conversation, notre Juif se décida enfin à l'accoster:

– Pardon, monsieur, n'est-ce pas à Monsieur Weiss de Strasbourg que j'ai l'honneur de parler?

– Non, c'est une erreur, répond le monsieur, d'un ton bourru.

– C'est remarquable, je me le suis dit tout de suite, parce que vous ne lui ressemblez pas du tout!

Bernard Rosenberg and
Gilbert Shapiro,
"Marginality and
Jewish humor,"
MIDSTREAM 4 (Spring
1958), pp. 70-71.

A lady approaches a very dignified man on the subway and asks him, "Pardon me for asking, but are you Jewish?" He coldly replies, "No." She returns in a moment and apologetically asks again, "Are you sure you're not Jewish?" Yes, he is sure. Still not convinced, she asks a final time, "Are you absolutely sure you're not Jewish?" The man breaks down and admits it, "All right, all right, I am Jewish." To which she makes the rejoinder, "That's funny. You don't look Jewish."

Martin Grotjahn, "Jewish Jokes and Their Relation to Masochism" (1961), A CELEBRATION OF LAUGHTER. Los Angeles: Mara Books, 1970; p. 140.

A lady asked the driver of her bus, "Are you Jewish?" He said, "No."

After a while the lady asks again.

With slight irritation, the bus driver answers again, "No, I am not Jewish."

The lady does not give up. She can't let go of her question.

Finally, trying to finish this topic, the bus driver says, "Okay, lady, have it your way. I am Jewish." With an expression of deep satisfaction, the lady leans back, has one more good look at him and says, "You don't look it!"

Henry D. Spalding, ENCYCLOPEDIA OF JEWISH HUMOR. New York: Jonathan David, 1969; p. xiii.

...the old woman who approached a blonde, blue-eyed man. "Excuse me, Mister," she began tentatively, "but you're a Jewish boy?" He regarded her disdainfully for a moment and then replied, "No, madam, I am not." Still uncertain, she repeated her question. Irritated, he answered icily, "I told you, I am not a Jew!" But she was a persistent soul and she put the question to him for the third time: "You're sure you're not Jewish?" The old lady's determination finally broke down his defenses. "Yes," he confessed, "I'm Jewish." To which she replied, "That's funny, you don't *look* Jewish!"

Isaac Asimov, TREASURY OF HUMOR. New York: Vallentine-Mitchell, 1972; pp. 274-275.

Mrs. Moskowitz kept eyeing the very distinguished man who sat next to her in the subway.

Finally, unable to control her curiosity, she nudged him and said, "Pardon me, sir, but are you Jewish?"

The gentleman looked up from his *Wall Street Journal* and said, in cultured tones, "No, madam, as it happens, I am not."

Several moments passed, and Mrs. Moskowitz asked again, "Are you *sure* you're not Jewish?"

The gentleman, heaving a patient sigh, said, "Madam, I have nothing against the Jews and if I happened to be Jewish, I would be glad to admit it. It just happens that my ancestors are not Jewish. Please forgive me for that."

Mrs. Moskowitz shifted uneasily in her seat for another few moments, then nudged him again. "Listen," she said loudly, "are you absolutely *positive* you're not Jewish?"

Despairing of any chance of reading his paper while the inquisition continued, the gentleman lowered his paper and said calmly, "Well, madam, you have found me out. I *am* Jewish."

Whereupon Mrs. Moskowitz surveyed him critically and said, "Funny! You don't *look* Jewish!"

HE COULDN'T WIN

Henry B. Berman, HAVE I GOT A JOKE FOR YOU. New York: Hart, 1975; p. 146.

Simon R. Pollack, JEWISH WIT FOR ALL OCCASIONS. New York: A & W Publications, 1979; p. 146.

Sarah Finkel sat next to a handsome businessman on a flight to Miami, and finally could not resist asking, "Pardon me, sir, but are you Jewish?"

The man lifted his eyes from the newspaper in which he'd been buried and said, "No, madam, as it happens, I am not."

Mrs. Finkel thought about it for a while and when he'd become engrossed again in his article, she asked, "Are you *sure* you're not Jewish?"

The man kept his temper and explained, "Madam, I have nothing against the Jews, and if I happened to be Jewish, I would be glad to admit it. It just happens that my ancestors are not Jewish. Please forgive me for that." Then he noisily lifted his paper and began to read once more.

Mrs. Finkel hesitated another few minutes. Then she said, "Listen, are you absolutely *positive* you're not Jewish?"

The businessman, seeking quiet, decided there was only one way to get it. "Well, Madam, you're right. I *am* Jewish."

Then Mrs. Finkel looked at him quizzically and said, "Funny, you don't *look* Jewish."

William Novak and Moshe Waldoks, THE BIG BOOK OF JEWISH HUMOR. New York: Harper & Row, 1981; p. 7.

A woman on a train walked up to a distinguished-looking gentleman across the aisle. "Excuse me," she said, "but are you Jewish?"

"No," replied the man.

A few minutes later the woman returned. "Excuse me," she said again, "but are you sure you're not Jewish?"

"I'm sure," replied the man.

But the woman was not convinced, and a few minutes later she approached him a third time. "Are you absolutely sure you're not Jewish?" she asked.

"All right, all right," the man said. "You win. I'm Jewish."

"That's funny," said the woman. "You don't *look* Jewish."

Leo Rosten, HOORAY
FOR YIDDISH. New
York: Simon &
Schuster, 1982; p. 61.

Mr. Opshutz approached a young man on Collins Avenue.
"Excuse me, my boy. Are you Jewish?"
"No, I'm not."
"Are you sure?"
"Of course I'm sure!"
"You're not just teasing me?"
"No. Why should I tease you?"
Mr. Opshutz sighed. "I don't know. Stay well..."
"Wait." The young man glanced around and, lowering
his voice, said, "I'll tell you the truth. Not a soul in Miami
knows it. I am a Jew."
"That's funny," clucked Mr. Opshutz. "You don't *look*
Jewish."

Ben Eliezer, THE
WORLD'S BEST
JEWISH JOKES.
London: Angus &
Robertson, 1984; p. 20.

An old Jewish woman was sharing a compartment on a
train with a distinguished-looking young man who was
reading *The Times*.
"Excuse me, young man, can I ask you something? Tell
me, are you Jewish?"
"No. I'm not."
A little later: "Tell me, are you sure you're not Jewish?"
"Of course I'm not!" And he buried himself behind *The
Times* in a rage.
A little later: "Excuse me, young man, are you really sure
you're not Jewish?"
Utterly exasperated, he exploded. "All right, yes, I'm
Jewish!" he said, to keep her quiet.
"Hmm. Funny, you don't look Jewish."

Elizabeth Petu-
chowski, DAS HERZ
AUF DER ZUNGE.
AUS DER WELT DES
JÜDISCHEN WITZES.
Freiburg: Herder, 1984;
p. 92.

Eine Frau in der Untergrundbahn wendet sich dem fremden
Mann zu, der neben ihr sitzt.
"Entschuldigung: Sind Sie zufällig jüdisch?"
"Nein, ich bin nicht jüdisch."
"Bestimmt nicht?"
"Nein, bestimmt nicht."
"Merkwürdig, ich dachte Sie seien jüdisch."
"Also gut schon: Ich bin jüdisch."
"Komisch, Sie sehen gar nicht jüdisch aus."

Leo Rosten,
GIANT BOOK OF
LAUGHTER. New
York: Crown, 1985;
p. 307.

Mr. Lurie, a resident of Los Angeles for fifty years, approached a young man who was waiting for a bus on Wilshire Boulevard. "Young man, excuse me. Can I ask a personal question? Are you Jewish?"

"No, I'm not."

"Are you sure?"

"Of course I'm sure!" The young man laughed.

"You're not just teasing me?"

"No. Why should I tease you?"

Mr. Lurie sighed. "Well, excuse my question. I didn't mean to embarrass you."

"Wait, mister," the young man glanced around and, lowering his voice, said, "can you keep a secret?"

"Absolutely!"

"Well, not a soul in the world knows it – except you. The truth is: I am a Jew."

"My, my," clucked Mr. Lurie. "You don't *look* Jewish."

7. Job Announcement

Raymond Geiger,
HISTOIRES JUIVES.
Paris: NRF, 1923;
p. 188.

En Russie, un noble fait imprimer dans un journal une annonce ainsi rédigée: "Partant pour l'Occident, je cherche un homme jeune, élégant et sachant parler le français et l'anglais."

Le journal a à peine paru qu'un vieux Juif se présente à la maison du noble et demande à lui parler d'urgence. Le dvornik refuse de le laisser entrer.

– Dites à votre maître que j'ai à lui dire quelque chose d'important.

Le concierge va faire la commission et revient chercher le Juif. Il le met en présence de son maître.

– Seigneur, j'ai lu votre annonce, tout à l'heure... Comme vous le voyez, je ne suis ni jeune, ni élégant. Et je dois ajouter que j'ignore l'anglais et le français.

– Mais alors?

– Alors je suis venu vous dire que je ne puis accepter la situation que vous offrez.

Louis Untermeyer,
A TREASURY
OF LAUGHTER.
New York: Simon
& Schuster, 1946;
pp. 525-526.

The same version
appears as a contribu-
tion from a Rabbi
Montague Isaacs in
Henry D. Spalding's
ENCYCLOPEDIA OF
JEWISH HUMOR.
New York: Jonathan
David, 1969; p. 58.

Count Esterhazy was organizing an expedition to the Near East and beyond. He had engaged most of the helpers, but he needed a general factotum for the long journey. Knowing the position was hard to fill, he advertised for a seasoned traveler who spoke the languages of the Near East, a fearless swordsman, an intrepid ride, etcetera. The advertisement was worded to attract only the right man – and there were no applicants. After a week, the butler announced that a small and shabby looking fellow had come in response to the ad.

"He doesn't sound very promising," said Count Esterhazy, "but show him up."

The man proved to be even less prepossessing than the butler's description. But clothes do not always make the man, and the Count began by asking, "You like to travel?"

"Me?" said the little man. "I hate traveling. Boats make me seasick. And trains are worse."

"But you are a linguist," continued the Count. "I presume you speak Arabian, Persian, Turkish, Hindustani--"

"Who? Me?" gasped the candidate. "I talk nothing but Yiddish."

"Your swordsmanship?" inquired the Count.

"What do you mean, swordsmanship? What should I do with a sword?"

"And as a horseman?"

"I hate horses. I wouldn't go near one."

"But," said the Count, "what did you come here for?"

"I saw your ad," said the man, "and I just came to tell you that on me you shouldn't depend."

THOU ART FORGIVEN

S. Felix Mendelsohn,
HERE'S A GOOD
ONE. New York: Bloch,
1947; pp. 194-195.

A Frankfurt Rothschild advertised for a personal secretary. The announcement stated that the candidate must be versed in Jewish and secular subjects, master European languages, and possess sufficient polish to be able to handle the many callers at Rothschild's private office.

Among those who applied for the position was a bearded young man who wore a steimel and a long kaftan with a black girdle – the typical garb of the Galician hasidim. This young man refused to be interviewed by anyone other than the Baron himself since, he said, he had a message of extreme importance. When the young man was in Rothschild's private office he said:

"Herr Baron, I came to offer my humble apologies. I know how badly you need a private secretary but I am utterly unfit for the position. I am extremely sorry I cannot accommodate you."

Henry Bulakow, QUAND ISRAEL RIT. Paris: Presses du Temps, 1963; pp. 28-29.

Dans la rubrique matrimoniale d'une publication juive très répandue, paraît cette annonce:

"Industriel cherche pour sa fille 28 ans, belle dot, monsieur 30 à 45 ans, abonne présentation, situation en rapport, de préférence profession libérale. S'adresser: M. Fridlander, fourreur." (suit l'adresse).

Le lendemain de la parution, un vieux Juif, portant barbe et papillotes, aux vêtements râpés, un petit ballot de vagabond à la main, se présente.

A M. Fridlander qui le regarde avec surprise, il déclare:

– C'est vous qui cherchez pour votre fille un monsieur bien, ayant une bonne situation et moins de 45 ans?

– Oui, mais vous semblez avoir largement dépassé cet âge.

– Précisément, je suis venu vous prévenir qu'il ne fallait pas compter sur moi.

Lillian Miriam Feinsilver, THE TASTE OF YIDDISH. New York: Thomas Yoseloff, 1970; p. 316.

My husband tells the story of a newspaper ad asking for a physicist who is unmarried and free to travel. A little Jewish man answers the ad and is asked, "Are you a physicist?" "No. I'm a tailor." The interviewer proceeds, "Are you single?" "No. I have a wife and seven children." "Are you free to travel?" "Of course not. How could I be, with a wife and family?" "Then what," the interviewer explodes, "are you doing here?" "I just came to tell you," the applicant replies, "on me you shouldn't count."

Leo Rosten, THE JOYS OF YIDDISH. London: W. H. Allen, 1970; p. 435.

Old Hirshbein, in a *yarmulkah*, appeared at Nazi police headquarters carrying a newspaper, in which he had circled an advertisement.

Exclaimed the sergeant: "*You* came about this ad?"

"That's right."

"But it reads: 'Wanted: young man, well-built, over 6 feet tall!' You're at least seventy, thin as a match, and not over 5 feet 2. The ad says: 'Must have excellent eyesight.' Your glasses are so thick you can barely see! The ad says, 'Must be Aryan,' and you are obviously a Jew! Why did you come here?"

"I just want to tell you," said Hirshbein, "that on *me*, you shouldn't depend."

Sig Altman,
THE COMIC IMAGE
OF THE JEW.
Cranbury, N. J.:
Farleigh Dickensen
University Press, 1971;
p. 167.

A man appears in a business office. "Herr Tietz? I saw your ad in which you look for a young, educated, experienced man. I am 58, speak a little German but mostly through the nose, and have been a *shnorrer* all my life!" "Well, what are you doing *here*?" "I just wanted to tell you that the job is *not for me.*"

Larry Wilde,
THE OFFICIAL IRISH
JOKE BOOK. New
York: Pinnacle Books,
1974; p. 64.

McCracken saw an ad in the papers for a man who didn't drink, could drive a car, and was reliable. The next day he showed up at the prospective employer's house.
"Do you drive a car?"
"No!" said McCracken.
"Do you drink?"
"Yes!"
"If you can't drive and you drink, why did you answer the ad?"
"I just wanted to tell you that I'm not reliable!"

POPECK RACONTE
LES MEILLEURES
HISTOIRES DE
L'HUMOUR JUIF.
Paris: Mengès, 1978;
p. 112.

Un homme très riche fait passer la petite annonce suivante: "Cherche homme, jeune, connaissant parfaitement l'anglais et l'allemand et possédant de solides notions de comptabilité."
Le lendemain, parmi le courrier envoyé par les postulants, il trouve cette lettre.
"Monsieur, je m'appelle Jacob Lewinsky. Je suis âgé de 65 ans, n'y connais rien en comptabilité. Aussi, j'ai le regret de vous faire savoir que je ne peux accepter la situation que vous me proposez"...

Henry B. Berman,
HAVE I GOT A JOKE
FOR YOU. New York:
Hart, 1975; p. 173.

Simon R. Pollack,
JEWISH WIT FOR ALL
OCCASIONS.
New York: A & W
Publications, 1979;
p. 173.

A professor was about to set out on an expedition to Africa and the Near East and he needed an assistant. So he put an advertisement in the newspaper requesting a man who spoke foreign languages, loved to travel, was able to use a gun, and so forth through a long list of qualifications. It was a pretty rare man who could fit his demanding specifications, and there were no responses to the advertisement.
But at the end of the week, one fellow did appear. He was short, unmuscular, unimpressive, but the professor interviewed him anyway.
– "Do you like to travel?" asked the professor.
– "Me?" said the man. "I hate traveling. Boats make me sick, planes I wouldn't get on and trains the worst of all."

(cont.)

Berman/Pollack, *cont.*

– "But you are a linguist," continued the professor. "I presume you speak Urdu, Arabic, Turkish–"

– "Who me?" interrupted the little man. "I know nothing but Yiddish."

– "Well, can you use a gun?" the professor persisted.

– "Me? I'm afraid of firearms."

– "Well," the exasperated professor exploded, "then what did you come here for?"

– "I saw your ad. And I just came to tell you that on me you shouldn't rely."

William Novak and Moshe Waldoks, THE BIG BOOK OF JEWISH HUMOR. New York: Harper & Row, 1981; p. 181.

During the Nazi period, Lefkowitz walks into a German police station, carrying a newspaper with a job advertisement circled in red.

"You've come about this job?" asks the desk sergeant. "You must be kidding. Can't you read? We need a young man, strong and hardy, a man who doesn't wear glasses. And look--the ad specifically mentions that we want an Aryan. You're obviously a Jew. So what are you doing here?"

"I've just come to tell you," says Lefkowitz, "that on me you shouldn't count."

Leo Rosten, HOORAY FOR YIDDISH. New York: Simon & Schuster, 1982; p. 244.

Into an office of NASA came an old man in a yarmulke, hunched over a cane. To the receptionist, he handed a newspaper clipping: "Who should I see about this ad?" The clipping read:

WANTED

For training as Astronaut. Age: 21-26. Should have degree in science or engineering. Must be in perfect health. Write National Aeronautics and Space Agency.

The receptionist said, "Our Mr. Fleming is in charge of recruiting..."

"Tell him I'm here. The name is Gittelman. Sol Gittelman."

"Excuse me, sir, but – for whom are you here?"

"For mineself."

"Your*self*?! Mr. Gittelman, do you – have a degree in science – "

"No. Also no for engineer. Plus, I am over seventy-four years old."

"Then why do you want to see Mr. Fleming?"

"I want to tell him," said Mr. Gittelman, "that on *me*, he shouldn't depend!"

ONE-UPSMANSHIP

Leo Rosten,
GIANT BOOK OF
LAUGHTER. New
York: Crown, 1985;
p. 397.

At the height of the Nazi terror in Berlin, an elderly Jew, Heinrich Schlosser, appeared at S.S. headquarters. He went up to the Storm Troop lieutenant at the desk, respectfully removed his hat – revealing a neat, embroidered *yarmulka* (skullcap) – and said, "I am answering your advertisement in this morning's *Beobachter.*" He handed the officer a page from the newspaper, on which an advertisement was boldly circled.

The lieutenant glanced at the ad. His jaw fell. "*You* are answering *this*?"

"*Ja wohl,*" beamed Schlosser.

"But it reads: 'Wanted: Young, strong Aryan, for special service to the *Führer...*'"

"*Ja wohl,*" nodded Schlosser.

The lieutenant could scarcely contain himself. "You? '*Young*?' You must be seventy years old!"

"Seventy-two," said Schlosser.

"'Strong'? Why you're as skinny as a rail!"

"Skinnier," said Schlosser.

"'*Aryan*'?! You are obviously a Jew!"

"Absolutely," Schlosser nodded.

"Then why the *hell*," the lieutenant fumed, "did you come here?!"

Schlosser spread his arms pacifically. "I just want you to know that on *me*, you shouldn't depend."

---

8. Left-Handed Teacup

John Taylor, WIT
AND MIRTH, 1630.
In SHAKESPEARE
JEST BOOKS, first
edited by W. Carew
Hazlitt in 1864.
New York: Burt
Franklin, 1964;
vol. 3, pp. 10-11.

...The said Monsieur commanded his man to buy him a great Hat with a button in the brim to button it vp behind; his man bought him one, and brought him. He put it on his head with the button before, which when he looked in the glasse and saw, he was very angry, saying: thou crosse vntoward knaue, did I not bid thee buy a hat with the button to hold it vp behind, and thou hast brought me one that turnes vp before? I command thee once more goe thy wayes, and buy mee such a one as I would have, what-soever it cost me.

Lazaro Liacho, ANECDOTARIO JUDIO. FOLKLORE, HUMORISMO Y CHISTES. Buenos Aires: M. Gleizer, 1939; pp. 161-162.

Schacht y Hitler conversan más o menos amigablemente. El primero sostiene que no deben extremarse las persecuciones contra los judíos.

– En el comercio – sentencia – el judío es muy útil.

Hitler se empecina en lo contrario. Schacht lo invita, entonces, a realizar una rápida experiencia.

– Acompáñeme.

Y entran en un bazar, cuyo dueño es ario al cien por ciento.

– Necesitamos tazas de té con las asas a la izquierda.

– No hay – responde el comerciante.

Penetran en otro bazar, también de propiedad de un ario puro, y vuelve a sucederles lo que en el primero. Se resuelven, entonces, a visitar el de un judío. Le expone Schacht a éste lo que quieren. Y el judío le contesta, alegre:

– ¡Qué suerte la mía! Precisamente hoy recibí una partida de tazas en las condiciones que ustedes desean. Y les muestra tazas de té colocadas de modo que las asas aparecen del lado izquierdo.

BUSINESS ACUMEN

S. Felix Mendelsohn, LET LAUGHTER RING. Philadelphia: Jewish Publication Society, 1941; pp. 120-121.

After months of persuasion the *Fuehrer* finally permitted Dr. Schacht to demonstrate his pet theory about the Jews. The Nazi party was bent on going through with the program of Aryanization at a rapid pace, but Dr. Schacht pleaded caution. "The Jews are excellent businessmen and the Reich still needs them," maintained Dr. Schacht, and in order to prove his point he took Hitler on a brief shopping tour on Leipzigerstrasse.

They stopped at a store run by an Aryan and asked for a teacup for a left-handed person. The proprietor said that he did not have any. They went to another Aryan store and received the same reply.

The *Fuehrer* and Dr. Schacht then entered a Jewish store and repeated their request. The Jew went to the back of the store and returned in a few minutes.

"I have only one such cup left," said the Jew, "and it will cost fifty percent more than the ordinary cup."

The two dignitaries told the proprietor that they would return a little later. Upon emerging from the store, Dr. Schacht said: "What did I tell you? The Jew is a cleverer businessman than his Aryan competitor."

"Clever nothing," bellowed the *Fuehrer*. "The Jew was just lucky enough to have a cup for a left-handed person."

Bennet Cerf,
THE POCKET BOOK
OF WAR HUMOR.
New York: Pocket
Books, 1943;
pp. 166-167.

Hitler and Goebbels were immersed, one day, in a long conversation concerning the Jewish population. "One thing you've got to admit," said Goebbels, "and that is that the Jews are a very resourceful and quick-witted people. If you will come with me incognito and visit a couple of tobacco shops on Unter den Linden, I will show you just what I mean."

Thereupon Mr. H. and Mr. G. sallied forth. The first visit was to a respected Nazi tobacconist's shop. The tobacconist did not recognize either of them. "We want to buy about 10,000 boxes of matches," said Goebbels. "Let's see what you've got in stock."

"Well," said the tobacconist, "we've just got the regular matches. Here's what they look like."

"But these won't do at all," said Goebbels quickly. "These matches have the sulphur on the right-hand side of the stick. We need matches with the sulphur on the left-hand side of the stick."

The tobacconist regarded the two prospective customers with blank amazement. "I am very sorry," he said in a small voice, "these are the only matches we've got."

"Now," said Goebbels to Hitler as they crossed the street to the Jewish merchant's shop, "I will show you how old Mr. Klein here will handle the same situation."

Mr. Klein produced a box of matches identical with the ones that the fellow across the street had shown. When Goebbels told him, however, that he wanted his matches with the sulphur on the left-hand side of the stick, Mr. Klein had a very different response for him. "Just wait a minute, gentlemen," he begged, "and let me see what I have in my stockroom." A moment later he reappeared before them with a contented smile. "By sheerest good fortune," he said, "I found that we've just received a shipment of exactly 10,000 boxes of left-handed matches and I can deliver them to you at once."

"We'll let you know," said Goebbels.

As they returned to the Chancellery, he turned to the Fuehrer and said, "Now do you see what I mean?"

Hitler was lost in thought. "Well, I have to admit," he said finally, "that Klein seemed to have a much more complete stock than his competitor."

Edvard Andersen and Edward Clausen, UNDERJORDISK HUMOR. Copenhagen: Waterman, 1945; pp. 137-139.

Føreren kunde ikke begribe, at Jøderne var dygtigere Handelsfolk end Tyskerne, men lille Goebbels lovede at demonstrere Forskellen.

De gik saa ind i en tysk Butik og bad om en Æske Tændstikker. Købmanden lagde Tændstikkerne op paa disken og forlangte 3 Pfennig.

– Jeg vil helst have en Æske med Svovlet i den anden Ende, sagde Goebbels.

Købmanden saa forvirret ud og indrømmede saa, at det havde han ikke.

Saa spørger vi efter det samme hos en Jøde, foreslog Goebbels.

Den jødiske Købmand reagerede hurtigere. Han vendte Æsken i Laaget, saaledes at Svovlet kom i den anden Ende og forlangte saa 5 Pfennig.

– Der kan du se, sagde Goebbels. De er hurtigere i Opfattelsen.

– Sikke noget Sludder, svarede Hitler indigneret. Den ariske Købmand *havde* maaske ikke de andre.

Bent Andersen, VINTERGÆKKER. Aarhus: Aros, 1963; pp. 37-38. Orig. pub. 1945.

Goering var ved at tro, at jøderne var klogere end tyskerne. Men Hitler protesterede – og så gik de ud for at se. I en forretning forlangte Goering et par kopper, "men det skal være kopper med hanken i venstre side." Man beklagede meget, men det førte man ikke.

Og sådan gik det i den ene forretning efter den anden.

Endelig kom de ind til en jøde. "Hvad koster det par kopper," spurgte Hitler. "En mark." "Men har De ikke nogen med hanken i den anden side?" "Et øjeblik, så skal jeg se." Jøden kom virkelig tilbage med et par. "Jo, vi havde et enkelt par af den slags, men de koster 1,35."

Da de kom ud, sagde Gøring: "Der kan du selv se!" "Ja, det er godt nok," svarede Hitler. "Men det er da ikke sikkert, at de andre havde sådan et par."

BUSINESS ACUMEN

S. Felix Mendelsohn, HERE'S A GOOD ONE. New York: Bloch, 1947; pp. 80-81.

Hitler and Goering were discussing the criticalness of the war.

"It's all the fault of your inefficient air force," said Hitler.

"No, sir," replied Goering. "Don't blame me for a situation which you have created. You have destroyed German morale by ruining the Jews, our best business people."

(cont.)

Mendelsohn, *cont.*

"You will have to prove that," shouted Hitler. "I am tired of hearing your panegyrics about the business ability of the Jews."

"I am taking up your challenge," said Goering. "Come with me and see what happens."

The two walked out into the street and stopped an Aryan. "We are ready to sell the smoke of Berlin," said Goering.

"Awfully sorry I can't buy it," said the Aryan. "I hate to say that but it seems to me you are only joking."

A little farther the two made the same offer to a Jew.

"If you will give me a contract that the smoke of Berlin is mine I'll pay you a million marks," said the Jew. The agreement was executed.

Fortified with this document the Jew went to a dozen German hotels and charged them 100,000 marks each for permission to run their heating plants. Within a week the Jew paid his contracted obligations to Goering.

"Are you satisfied with the deal?" asked Goering?

"I certainly am," replied the Jew. "Now I am ready to buy the smoke of Hamburg."

Jacob Richman,
JEWISH WIT
AND WISDOM.
New York: Pardes,
1952; pp. 366-367.

Hjalmar Schacht, who was Minister of Finance and Economics under the Hitler regime, had a high opinion of Jewish business acumen.

To prove his contention that the Jew was a better business man than the German, he once invited a high Nazi official to accompany him on a shopping tour.

They first entered the emporium of a blue-blooded Aryan and asked for a pitcher that has its handle on the left side, so that a left-handed waiter might use it conveniently. The proprietor apologized and said that he had no such pitcher. They got the same reply at a dozen other Aryan stores.

At last they went into a Jewish store and stated the nature of their quest. For a moment the Israelite was puzzled, but instantly regained his composure. "Certainly," he said suavely. "I have just what you want. It's the only one I have in stock, and you are lucky to have come in time."

He withdrew for a moment and returned with a pitcher, which he carried with his left hand.

Bernard Rosenberg and Gilbert Shapiro, "Marginality and Jewish Humor," MIDSTREAM 4 (Spring 1958), p. 75.

A Jew is discussing the Jewish problem with a Gentile in the Old Country. The Gentile contends that Jews cheat and lie. The Jew replies that they really are smarter than Goyim and sets out to prove it. He brings his companion to a Gentile store and asks for some matches, but refuses them when they are offered saying, "These matches light at the wrong end. I want the kind that light at the other end." Proprietor: "I'm sorry these are the only kind we have." They then proceed to a Jewish establishment, where the same transaction takes place. This time however, the Jewish businessman shouts to his helper, "Moishe, bring me those matches from the new consignment." He hands over the matches, turning them around. Outside the store, the Jew triumphantly faces the Gentile, exclaiming, "See!" The latter protests, "But maybe the first store didn't get that new consignment."

Henry D. Spaulding, ENCYCLOPEDIA OF JEWISH HUMOR. New York: Jonathan David, 1969; p. 188.

Hjalmar Schacht, finance minister of the Third Reich, was ushered into Hitler's office, where *Der Fuehrer,* more stone-faced than usual, awaited him.

"I hear that you have expressed some disapproval about the final solution to the Jewish problem," said Hitler coldly.

"Not at all, my *Fuehrer,*" said Schacht. "I only meant that a few of the Jewish businessmen should be spared. The Reich still needs them. As a whole, they are more clever than their Aryan counterparts."

"Nonsense! No Jew ever lived who could outsmart a pure Aryan."

"Allow me to prove it, my *Fuehrer.* Come with me on a shopping tour of Berlin tomorrow."

On the following day, Hitler and Schacht stopped first at an Aryan store. "We would like to buy a left-handed teacup," said the finance minister.

"Sorry, I don't have any," replied the proprietor.

They stopped at another Aryan store and again asked for a left-handed teacup. As before, the store-owner answered, "Sorry, gentlemen, I don't have any."

Hitler and Schacht then entered a Jewish-owned shop. "We would like to buy a left-handed teacup," they said.

"What color?" asked the Jew instantly.

"Any color. It makes no difference."

(cont.)

Spaulding, *cont.*

The merchant withdrew one of the dozens of cups on the shelf and placed it on the counter with the handle facing the left side. "This is the only left-handed teacup in all of Germany," he announced. "I'll have to charge you fifty percent more because of its value."

"We'll consider it," said Schacht as he followed the outraged *Fuehrer* into the street.

"I told you those Jews were good businessmen," said the finance minister, smiling. "Who else but a Jew would have thought of such a clever way to sell goods?"

"Clever!" screamed Hitler. "What was so clever about it? That damned Jew was just lucky enough to have a left-handed teacup, that's all!"

Hervé Nègre,
DICTIONNAIRE DES
HISTOIRES DRÔLES.
Paris: Fayard, 1973;
vol. 2, pp. 73-74.

On ne peut pas dire qu'on adore les Juifs dans les milieux dirigeants de l'Union soviétique. Pourtant une controverse s'est développée entre Brejnev et Kossyguine au sujet des marchands juifs. Le premier soutient qu'ils ne sont pas plus malins que les marchands russes. Et l'autre dit le contraire.

Pour en avoir le coeur net, les deux hommes se rendent dans un quartier commerçant de Moscou. Ils s'arrêtent d'abord chez un marchand de faïence ukrainien, et Kossyguine lui demande:

– Est-ce que vous avez des tasses à café pour gauchers?

– Ah! Je regrette, balbutie le marchand. C'est la première fois qu'on me demande cela! J'ai bien des tasses à café, mais ce sont des tasses à café normales.

– C'est-à-dire qu'elles n'ont pas l'anse à gauche? demande Brejnev.

– Euh... non!

La même scène se reproduit chez un second, puis un troisième marchand russe qui avouent tristement ne pas avoir l'article.

Alors, Brejnev et Kossyguine entrent dans une boutique de faïence à l'enseigne d'Igor Kaganovitch, et ils posent la même question. Un petit Juif sort de derrière son comptoir et il s'exclame aussitôt:

– Mais bien sûr, chers messieurs, que j'ai des tasses à café spéciales pour gauchers, avec l'anse à gauche. Je vais vous chercher ça tout de suite...

Il disparaît dans son arrière-boutique et il revient avec les mêmes modèles de tasses à café qu'avaient présentés les autres marchands. Mais il a pris la précaution de tourner les anses vers la gauche.

Les deux hommes paient, emportent leur paquet et sortent. Alors Kossyguine dit à Brejnev:

(cont.)

Nègre, *cont.*

– Vous voyez bien que ce Kaganovitch est beaucoup plus habile que nos marchands russes!

– Par exemple? dit Brejnev. Et pourquoi? Les autres n'avaient pas l'article. Et lui, oui. Voilà tout...

Larry Wilde,
THE OFFICIAL
JEWISH JOKE
BOOK. New York:
Pinnacle, 1974; p. 28.

A German politician pleaded with Hitler not to mistreat the Jews. "If for no other reason," he said, "than just because they're so smart!"

"What makes you think the Jews are so smart?" asked the dictator.

"Come and I'll show you!"

He took the Nazi leader to Guttman's Gift Shop and said, "Ask him for a *left*-handed teapot."

The Führer did. Guttman went to the back of the store, picked up a teapot, turned it around, and returned.

"You're in luck," said Guttman, handing the teapot to Hitler. "I just happened to have one left!"

Back out in the street, the politician said, "You see, that's what I mean about the Jews being so smart!"

"What's so smart about that?" exclaimed Hitler. "He just happened to have one left!"

Ben Eliezer,
MORE OF THE
WORLD'S BEST
JEWISH JOKES.
London: Angus &
Robertson, 1985;
p. 26.

A German priest is pleading with Hitler to spare the Jews. "I'll tell you why you shouldn't harm them – because they're so smart."

"Smart?" says our Adolf. "Who says they're smart?"

"Come with me. I'll show you." So the priest took Hitler to a little shop run by Mr. Isaacson.

"Mr. Isaacson," says the preist, "we're looking for a left-handed beer mug. Do you have one?"

"Sure," says Isaacson, and fetches one from the back of the store.

The priest turns to Hitler. "See what I mean?"

"What's so smart about that?" Hitler says. "He happened to have one in stock."

9. Live Under Water

PERFECT ADAPTATION

S. Felix Mendelsohn,
HERE'S A GOOD
ONE. New York: Bloch,
1947; p. 4

A Spanish and an Italian tourist in Palestine were discussing with their Jewish guide the political outlook of the late thirties. Both the Spaniard and Italian agreed that since war was imminent no one was able to plan for the future. The Jew, however, was more optimistic.

"One has to be prepared for everything," commented the Jew. "You must remember that man is called on to fight also against the evil forces of nature, such as floods, earthquakes, and hailstorms." Turning to the Spaniard the Jew continued, "Your country, for example, might sink into the ocean. What would you do then?"

"We would not be around to do anything," replied the Spaniard.

"And your country," said the Jew to the Italian, "might be destroyed by earthquake. What would you do then?"

"We would do nothing," replied the Italian. "We are Catholics and we always accept stoically the will of God."

"And supposing Palestine is inundated by the Mediterranean," inquired the Spaniard, "what would you Jews do?"

"Our answer is a foregone conclusion," replied the Jew. "We Jews would learn to live under water."

Ed Cray, "The Rabbi
Trickster," JOURNAL
OF AMERICAN
FOLKLORE 77 (1964),
p. 335; attributed to
"Miss Rita Weill, a
professional signer
[who] told this story in
Los Angeles in 1959."

A great tidal wave was rushing towards the land. In two days this huge wave was going to inundate all the continents. Evacuation was futile, since the wave was higher than all the mountains. Earth was doomed.

So with the end of the world imminent, the big TV networks decided to donate their time to the clergy to calm the populace. Perhaps a panic might be averted.

So Pope John gets on and he makes the sign of the cross and says a couple of Hail Marys, and all the cardinals are praying and there's this guy swinging the incense around under the golden canopy and the Pope is standing there in all the glory of St. Peter's and he says, "Your duty as sons and daughters of Rome is to confess your sins and meet your maker with clean souls. We have stationed priests at every street corner where they will stay on duty for the next two days so that you may confess and take the last Sacrament. *Pax vobiscum.*"

(cont.)

Cray, *cont.*

From New York comes the Protestant in his business suit and buttoned-down collar. He gets up and takes off his horn-rimmed glasses and says, "It's really up to you as individuals to meet this great crisis with dignity and peace of mind. I would stress also that you think positively that this tidal wave is not the end, but a beginning of a new life."

Finally, the little reb gets on and he shrugs, "Nu. Ve got two days to learn how to live under water."

Lillian Mermin Feinsilver, THE TASTE OF YIDDISH. New York: Thomas Yoseloff, 1970; p. 68.

A story that was going the rounds of Christian clergymen several years ago concerns a second worldwide flood; it has engulfed Europe and Asia and is heading toward the United States. The Protestant and Catholic clergy all call their people together for Communion, baptism and the last rites. The rabbis and Jewish lay leaders, on the other hand, call a conference on How to Live Under Water.

Isaac Asimov, TREASURY OF HUMOR. New York: Vallentine-Mitchell, 1972; p. 282.

A Dean of a school of comparative theology, a dean of a school of law, and a dean of a school of general studies were engaged in scholarly studies on a low-lying coral island far off in the South Pacific. A radio message reached them to the effect that a tidal wave was advancing on the island and would sweep it completely in six hours. Because of storms at sea, moreover, it was doubtful if rescue could reach them in time.

At once, the dean of the school of comparative theology began a series of prayers, in appropriate form, to the gods of all the major religions on earth, and to those of such minor religions as he had time for.

At the same time, the dean of the school of law began to write an elaborate will hedged in with all the clauses that lawyers had ever dreamed up.

And at the same time, the dean of the school of general studies began an intensive six-hour rehearsal of the art of breathing under water.

Larry Wilde, THE OFFICIAL JEWISH JOKE BOOK. New York: Pinnacle, 1974; p. 103.

Scientists concluded that the icecap was going to melt and the whole world would be flooded within six months. When the news broke, religious leaders went into deep conference.

The Protestant hierarchy released a statement: "Because of the impending disaster Protestants will go to church and pray for two hours every day."

(cont.)

Wilde, *cont.*

Then the Catholics made an announcement: "Because of the coming deluge, Catholics will make every other day–all day–a day of prayer for the next six months!"

Rabbis from all over the land convened, then they too issued a message to the world: "Because the whole world will be flooded in six months, Jews will learn how to live underwater!"

Rabbi H. R.
Rabinowitz:
KOSHER HUMOR.
Jerusalem: Rubin Mass,
1977; p. 90.

An Italian and a Jew once met. It so happened that a tidal wave struck a certain city in Italy and the Italians deserted the city. "We Israelis wouldn't have deserted the city," said the Israeli to the Italian, "we would have done business under water."

Kurt Schlesinger:
"Jewish Humor as
Jewish Identity,"
INTERNATIONAL
REVIEW OF PSYCHO-
ANALYSIS 6
(1979), p. 322.

An Englishman, a Frenchman, an American and a Jew are in the midst of philosophic discussion. The problem is posed how each would act when it became unmistakably clear that they had only a few hours to live. They hypothesize the situation in which a flood inundates the land, there are no means of escape, and they are awaiting the inevitable end. The Englishman speaks first: "I would open my best bottle of port. Sit and enjoy every sip. Think of the life I've lived, the experiences I've had and let the waters come and take me."

The Frenchman says, "I would drink a great Bordeaux, prepare a *coq au vin*, make love and let the waters overwhelm me thus."

The American is next: He would eat, drink, make love, try to improvise a raft and finally swim until his strength gave out, and he drowned, "fighting to the end."

The Jew says: "I would do all you have described, and when the water got over my head, I guess I would have to learn *how to live underwater.*"

William Novak
and Moshe Waldoks,
THE BIG BOOK OF
JEWISH HUMOR.
New York: Harper
& Row, 1981; p. 304.

A new flood is foretold and nothing can be done to prevent it; in three days, the waters will wipe out the world.

The leader of Buddhism appears on television and pleads with everybody to become a Buddhist; that way, they will at least find salvation in heaven.

The Pope goes on television with a similar message: "It is still not too late to accept Jesus," he says.

The Chief Rabbi of Israel takes a slightly different approach: "We have three days to learn how to live under water."

10. Mother's manoeuvre

Martin Grotjahn, "Jewish Jokes and Their Relation to Masochism" (1961) in A CELEBRATION OF LAUGHTER, ed. Werner W. Mendel. Los Angeles: Mara Books, 1970; pp. 139-140.	A mother gave her son two neckties as a present. The son wants to show his appreciation and wears one. Says the mother, "What's the matter? Don't you like the other one?"
Theodor Reik, JEWISH WIT. New York: Gamut Press, 1962; p. 84.	A mother gave her son two neckties as a present. The son, who wants to show his appreciation, wears one at their next meeting. Noticing it, the mother says, "What's the matter? Don't you like the other one?"
Henny Youngman, HOW DO YOU LIKE ME SO FAR? New York: Gramercy, 1963; p. 88.	To give you an idea how difficult a wife can be, she bought me too ties for my birthday. To please her I wore one. She hollered, "What's the matter, don't you like the other one?"
Dan Greenberg, HOW TO BE A JEWISH MOTHER. Los Angeles: Price, Stern & Sloan, 1975 (orig. pub. 1964); p. 16.	Practice Drill 1. Give your son Marvin two sportshirts as a present. The first time he wears one of them, look at him sadly and say in your Basic Tone of Voice: "The other one you didn't like?"
Henry D. Spalding, ENCYCLOPEDIA OF JEWISH HUMOR. New York: Jonathan David, 1969; p. 382.	A mother gave her son two neckties as a going-away present when he left to attend the university. When he returned home for his vacation he wore one of the ties to demonstrate his appreciation for the gift. The mother took one look at the necktie and asked anxiously, "What's the matter, the other one you didn't like?"
Harvey Mindess, THE CHOSEN PEOPLE? Los Angeles: Nash, 1972; p. 80.	A mother gives her son two neckties for his birthday. Anxious to show his appreciation, he wears one of them at their very next meeting. When she sees it, she whines: "What's the matter? You don't like the other one?"

Harry Golden, THE GOLDEN BOOK OF JEWISH HUMOR. New York: Putnam, 1972; p. 107.	A mother gave her son two neckties as a present. The son, who wanted to show his appreciation, wore one at their next meeting. Noticing it, the mother said, "What's the matter? Don't you like the other one?"
Henry B. Berman, HAVE I GOT A JOKE FOR YOU. New York: Hart, 1975; p. 187. Simon R Pollack, JEWISH WIT FOR ALL OCCASIONS. New York: A & W Publications, 1979; p. 187.	For his birthday, Mrs. Finkelstein gave her grown-up son Charlie two Dior ties. One was red and the other blue. On his next visit to his mother, Charlie put on the red tie and strode into the apartment. His mother took one look at him and sighed, "Ah! The blue one you didn't like."

TIE ONE ON

Sanford Triverton, COMPLETE BOOK OF ETHNIC JOKES. New York: Galahad Books, 1981; p. 261.	For his birthday, Mrs. Finkelstein gave her grown-up son Charlie two Dior ties. One was red and the other blue. On his next visit to his mother, Charlie put on the red tie and strode into the apartment. His mother took one look at him and sighed, "Ah! The blue one you didn't like."
Leo Rosten, HOORAY FOR YIDDISH. New York: Simon & Schuster, 1982; p. 82.	One of my favorite jokes, a telling commentary on Jewish mothers' capacity to lay on guilt, involves the mother who gave her son two neckties on Chanuka. The boy hurried into his bedroom, ripped off the tie he was wearing, put on one of ties his mother had brought him, and hurried back. "Look, Mama! Isn't it gorgeous?" Mama asked, "What's the matter? You don't like the other one?"
Ben Eliezer, THE WORLD'S BEST JEWISH JOKES. London: Angus & Robertson, 1984; p. 25.	A mother gave her son two ties for his birthday, a striped one and a spotted one. The next day he wore the spotted one. "So what's the matter with the striped one? You don't like it?"

Alan Dundes, "The Jewish American Princess and the Jewish American Mother in American Jokelore" (1985) in CRACKING JOKES. Berkeley: 10 Speed Press, 1987; p. 63.

A mother gave her son two neckties as a present for his birthday, a red one and a green one. The son, to show his appreciation for the gift, puts on the red one and is wearing it when he picks her up to take her out for dinner. Says the mother, "What's the matter? You didn't like the green one?"

11. Who's counting?

Raymond Geiger, NOUVELLES HISTOIRES JUIVES. Paris: NRF, 1925; p. 203.

A table.
– Mais prenez donc encore un gâteau!
– Oh! merci, j'en ai déjà mangé trois!
– A dire vrai, vous en avez mangé quatre, mais vous pouvez encore en manger.

Harry Hirschfield, JEWISH JOKES. New York: Simon & Schuster, 1932; number 138.

The coming-out party of Lucinda Freedman was in full swing. Her proud father kept making a tour of the house to see that the guests were enjoying themselves. Near the buffet stood Yascha Binder.

"Have a sandwich, Mr. Binder," suggested the host.

"I had one," replied Yascha.

"You had three – but have another one, anyway," said Freedman.

S. Felix Mendelsohn, LET LAUGHTER RING. Philadelphia: Jewish Publication Society, 1946; p. 190. Orig. pub. 1941.

Mrs. Finston (at a party): Have another sandwich, Mr. Cohen.

Mr. Cohen: I already had one, thank you.

Mrs. Finston: Never mind, you really had not one but five – but who's counting?

Louis Untermeyer, A TREASURY OF LAUGHTER. New York: Simon & Schuster, 1946; pp. 524-525.

After T. Whitney Nadelson had entered the upper income tax bracket, Mrs. Nadelson entertained heavily. Her proudest moment came when she gave an afternoon tea for the literary lion of the day. "Do have another of those delicious little cakes," she urged.

"Thank you," said the lion. "But I've already had two."

"You've had five," Mrs. Nadelson corrected him. "But *who's counting?*"

Nathan Ausubel, A TREASURY OF JEWISH FOLKLORE. New York: Crown, 1948; p. 378.	The guests were bidding their hosts farewell. "And I want to tell you, Mrs. Liebowitz," Mrs. Ginsberg concluded, "your cookies were so *tasty*, I ate four." "You ate five," Mrs. Liebowitz corrected, "but who counts?"

Philip Goodman, REJOICE IN THY FESTIVAL. New York: Bloch, 1956; p. 239.	After the Shavuos morning services in the synagogue, a kind householder invited a stranger to his home for the festival meal. As was traditional, the hostess served cheese *Blintzes*.

The host, proud of his wife's cooking and especially of the tasty *Blintzes* she made, urged the stranger:

"I see that you too enjoy my wife's *Blintzes*. Help yourself to more."

"Yes, I certainly do love the *Blintzes*," the stranger readily admitted. "However, I don't want to deprive you of any more as I've already had six."

"So you've already eaten eight," the host reminded his guest, "but who's counting?" |

Gerry Blumenfeld, SOME OF MY BEST JOKES ARE JEWISH. New York: Kamron, 1965; p. 77.	The ladies were playing gin rummy at the home of one of the members of the sisterhood. Rebecca was leaving and told her hostess she had enjoyed her hospitality.

"And your home-made cookies were so delicious that, believe it or not, I ate four!"

"You ate six – but who's counting?" |

Henry D. Spalding, ENCYCLOPEDIA OF JEWISH HUMOR. New York: Jonathan David, 1969; p. 321.	Mrs Ginsberg: "Thank you for a lovely party, Mrs. Leibowitz. I want you to know your brownies were so tasty I ate four!"

Mrs. Leibowitz: "Five, but who counts?" |

Leo Rosten, THE JOYS OF YIDDISH. London: W. H. Allen, 1970; p. 452.	The ladies were having tea. As the hostess passed the cookies around, she said, "So take a cookie."

"I already had five," sighed Mrs. Bogen.

"You had, excuse me, six, but take another: Who's counting?" |

Henry B. Berman, HAVE I GOT A JOKE FOR YOU. New York: Hart, 1975; p. 66.	At a dinner party, the hostess served the appetizers herself, carrying the tray around to each guest. One man, however, declined. "But you must!" insisted the lady. "Really, they're delicious," replied the guest, "but I've had six already." "Actually, you had seven," advised the hostess, "but who's counting?"
POPECK RACONTE LES MEILLEURES HISTOIRES DE L'HUMOUR JUIF. Paris: Mengès, 1978; p. 120.	Madame Lévy prend le thé chez Madame Salomon. – Prenez donc un gâteau, Mme Lévy! – J'en ai déjà pris trois... – Non! Vous en avez pris cinq... Mais prenez-en encore un quand même... Est-ce que vous croyez que je compte?
Sanford Triverton, COMPLETE BOOK OF ETHNIC JOKES. New York: Galahad, 1981; p. 286.	At a dinner party, the hostess served the appetizers herself, carrying the tray around to each guest. One man, however, declined. "But you must!" insisted the lady. "Really, they're delicious," replied the guest, "but I've had six already." "Actually, you had seven," advised the hostess, "but who's counting?"
William Novak and Moshe Waldoks, THE BIG BOOK OF JEWISH HUMOR. New York: Harper & Row, 1981; p. 142.	The afternoon was drawing to a close, and the guests were getting ready to leave. "Mrs. Goldberg," said one of the ladies, "I just wanted to tell you that your cookies were so delicious I ate four of them." "You ate five," replied the hostess. "But who's counting?"
Leo Rosten, GIANT BOOK OF LAUGHTER. New York: Crown, 1981; p. 299.	The hostess was making the rounds, at her tea for the ladies, with a platter of freshly baked, home-made cookies. "So, Mrs. Pearlstein," she smiled, "have some cookies." "No, thank you," said Mrs. Pearlstein. "They're absolutely delicious – but I already had four." "You already have *five*," said the hostess. "But who's counting?"

12. Umbrella

KANN MAN'S WISSEN?

H. Itler,
JÜDISCHE WITZE.
Dresden: Rudolph'sche
Verlagsbuchhandlung,
n.d. [1928]; p. 48

Kohn: "Sarah – es regnet – nimm den Rock höher – er schleift im Schlamme nach!"
Sarah: "Das geht nicht – meine Strümpf' sind zerrissen!"
Kohn: "Warum haste nicht angezogen e Paar frische?"
Sarah: "Hab' ich denn gewußt, daß es regnen wird?"

Nathan Ausubel,
TREASURY OF
JEWISH FOLKLORE .
New York: Crown,
1948; p. 338.

Two sages of Chelm went out for a walk. One carried an umbrella, the other didn't. Suddenly, it began to rain.
"Open your umbrella, quick!" suggested the one without an umbrella.
"It won't help," answered the other.
"What do you mean, it won't help? It will protect us from the rain."
"It's no use, the umbrella is as full of holes as a sieve."
"Then why did you take it along in the first place?"
"I didn't think it would rain."

AESTHETIC VALUE

Martin Rywell,
LAUGHING WITH
TEARS. Harriman:
Pioneer Press, 1960;
p. 99.

Two Chelmer sages met. One carried an umbrella. Suddenly it began to rain. "Open your umbrella," said the one without the umbrella. "It won't help us with such a heavy rain," replied the one with the umbrella. "Open the umbrella quickly! I'm getting drenched," commanded the other. "It won't help us. The umbrella has more holes than a sieve," said the one with the umbrella. "Then why did you carry the umbrella with you?" "I didn't think it would rain," replied the umbrella bearer.

Henry D. Spalding,
ENCYCLOPEDIA OF
JEWISH HUMOR.
New York: Jonathan
David, 1969; p. 122.

There are many kinds of status symbols in the world. In America it may be a fancy new car, a pastel mink stole, or maybe a swimming pool. In India it is a white elephant or a sacred cow. In England it is a whole side of beef in the freezer. Not so in Chelm.

Two Chelmites were taking a walk, one carrying with him his status symbol – an umbrella. Suddenly it started to rain.

"Quick, open your umbrella!" cried the man who had none.

"It's no use," answered the other. "My umbrella is full of holes."

"Then what in the world did you take it for in the first place?"

The answer was perfectly logical – or a Chelmite: "I didn't think it would rain!"

DER REGENSCHIRM

Hermann Hakel, WENN DER REBBE LACHT. Munich: Kindler, 1970; p. 66.	Ein Warschauer kam einmal nach Chelm und ging mit einem Chelmer spazieren. Der Warschauer bemützte einem feinem Stock, der Chelmer zum gleichen Zweck einem Regenschirm.
	
	    Plötzlich begann es zu regnen.
	    "Wie gut, dass du einem Schirm hast! Öffne ihm," sagte der Warschauer zum Chelmer.
	    "Das hat keinen Sinn, er ist ja zerrissen!" antwortete der Chelmer dem Warschauer.
	    "Ja warum hast du ihn dann mitgenommen?"
	    "Ich war überzeugt, es wird nicht regnen."

Sig Altman, THE COMIC IMAGE OF THE JEW. Cranbury, N. J.: Fairleigh Dickinson University Press, 1971; p. 132.	A Chelmer walked in the rain with an umbrella that he didn't open.
	    "Why don't you open the umbrella?"
	    "It's full of holes."
	    "Then why did you bring it?"
	    "I didn't think it would rain."

Alexander Drozdzynski, JIDDISCHE WITZE UND SCHMONZES. Düsseldorf: Droste Verlag, 1976; pp. 200-201.	Ein Chelmer Jude geht mit einem Schirm unter dem Arm durch den Regen. Ein Bekannter fragt ihn:
	    "Warum machst du deinen Schirm nicht auf?"
	    "Es nützt nichts, er hat zu viel Löcher."
	    "Warum hast du ihn denn mitgenommen?"
	    "Weil ich wußte, daß es regnen wird."

Larry Wilde: THE LAST OFFICIAL JEWISH JOKE BOOK. New York: Bantam, 1980; p. 128.	Littner and Klemer, two Chelmites were taking a walk. Littner carried an umbrella with him. Suddenly it started to rain.
	    "Quick, open your umbrella!" said Klemer.
	    "It's no use," answered Littner. "My umbrella is full of holes."
	    "Then what the hell did you take it for in the first place?"
	    "I didn't think it would rain!"

William Novak and Moshe Waldoks, THE BIG BOOK OF JEWISH HUMOR. New York: Harper & Row, 1981; p. 23.	Two wise men of Chelm went out for a walk, when suddenly it began to rain.
	    "Quick," said one man. "Open your umbrella."
	    "It won't help," said his friend. "My umbrella is full of holes."
	    "Then why did you bring it in the first place?"
	    "I didn't think it would rain."

Ben Eliezer, MORE OF THE WORLD'S BEST JEWISH JOKES. London: Angus & Robertson, 1985; p. 31.	Two men from Chelm were going to see the rabbi when it started raining.
	    "Shmulik, put up your umbrella, it's raining."
	    "I can't, Mendel, it's got holes in it."
	    "Holes in it? Then why did you bring it with you?"
	"I didn't think it would rain."

Leo Rosten, GIANT BOOK OF LAUGHTER. New York: Crown, 1985; p. 257.	Jeb and Lem were walking down dusty Skunk Hole Road, when suddenly the heavens opened up and the rain came down in buckets. "Lem," said Jeb, "open that goldurn umbrelly!"
	    "This umbrelly?" Lem snorted. "Shucks, Jeb, it's chuck full o' holes."
	    Jeb stopped short. "Then why in tarnation'd you bring it along?"
	    "How'd I know't was goin' t' rain?"

Salcia Landmann, DIE KLASSISCHEN WITZE DER JUDEN Frankfurt, Berlin: Ullstein, 1989; p. 80.	Chelm. "Jossel, es regnet! Öffne doch deinen Schirm!" "Das ist zwecklos, er ist voller Löcher." "Wozu hast du ihn dann mitgenommen?" "Ich konnte ja nicht wissen, dass es regnen wird!"

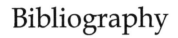

Bibliography

Acques, D. *Les contes du rabbin. Les meilleures histoires juives.* Paris: Quignon, 1927.

Adam. *L'humour juif.* Paris: Denoël, 1966.

Adams, Joey. *Joey Adams' Joke Book. A Mad, Merry Mixture.* New York: Fell, 1952.

Adams, Joey. *Encyclopedia of Humor.* Indianapolis and New York: Fell, 1952.

Adamson, Joe. *Groucho, Harpo, Chico and Sometimes Zeppo. A Celebration of the Marx Brothers.* New York: W. H. Allen, 1973.

Adler, Bill. *Jewish Wit and Wisdom.* New York: Dell, 1969.

Adorno, T. W. et al. *The Authoritarian Personality.* 2 vols. New York: Harper, 1950.

Afek, Yishai. *Israeli Humor and Satire.* Tel Aviv: Sadan, 1974.

Agnon, S. J. and Ahron Eliasberg. *Das Buch von den polnischen Juden.* Berlin: Jüdischer Verlag, 1916.

Alcalay, Reuben. *A Basic Encyclopedia of Jewish Proverbs, Anecdotes and Folk Wisdom.* New York: Hartmore House, 1973.

Aleksandrowicz, Bronislaw. *Jødisk Humor fra Polen og Rusland.* Copenhagen: Gyldendal, 1973.

Aleksandrowicz, Bronislaw. *Jødiske Anekdoter. Gamle og Nye.* Copenhagen and Oslo: Nordisk Bogforlag, 1975.

Algazi, Léon. "Aspects psychologiques des 'histoires juives'," *Revue de la pensée juive* II, 6 (January 1961), pp. 76-83.

Allen, Jay. *500 Great Jewish Jokes.* New York: Signet, 1990.

Allen, Steve. *The Funny Men.* New York: Simon & Schuster, 1956.

Allen, Woody. *Four Films of Woody Allen.* New York: Faber & Faber, 1983.

Allport, G. W. *The Nature of Prejudice.* Cambridge: Addison-Wesley, 1954.

Alter, Robert. "Jewish Humor and the Domestication of Myth," in *Veins of Laughter,* ed. Harry Levin. Cambridge: Harvard University Press, 1972; pp. 255-267.

Altman, Sig. *The Comic Image of the Jew. Explorations of a Pop Culture Phenomenon.* Cranbury, N.J.: Farleigh Dickensen University Press, 1971.

Andersen, Bent. *Vintergækker.* Aarhus: Aros, 1963; orig. pub. 1945.

Andersen, Edvard and Edward Clausen. *Underjordisk Humor.* Copenhagen: Westerman, 1945.

Anecdote Library, Being the Largest Collection of Anecdotes Ever Assembled in One Volume. London: Whittaker, 1822.

Anobile, Richard J. (ed.). *Why a Duck? Visual and Verbal Gems from the Marx Brothers Movies.* London: Studio Vista, 1972.

Arnau, Frank [Heinrich Schmitt]. *Jüdische Anekdoten und Witze.* Freiburg: Hyperion-Verlag, 1965.

Asimov, Isaac. *Treasury of Humor. A Lifetime Collection of Favorite Jokes, Anecdotes, and Limericks with Copious Notes on How to Tell Them and Why.* New York: Vallentine Mitchell, 1972.

Atlan, Henri. *A tort et à raison. Intercritique de la science et du mythe.* Paris: Seuil, 1986.

Ausubel, Nathan. *A Treasury of Jewish Folklore, Stories, Traditions, Legends, Humor, Wisdom and Folk Songs of the Jewish People.* New York: Crown, 1948; abridged edition, 1980.

Ausubel, Nathan. *A Treasury of Jewish Humor.* Garden City: Doubleday, 1953.

Ayalti, Hanan. *Yiddish Proverbs.* New York: Schocken, 1971; orig. pub. 1949.

Baba Mezi'a, a volume of *The Babylonian Talmud,* ed. Rabbi Dr. I. Epstein. London: Soncino Press, 1935.

Baldwin, Barry. *The Philogelos or Laughter-Lover.* Amsterdam: J. C. Gieben, 1983.

Baron, Salo W. *A Social and Religious History of the Jews.* 3 vols. New York: Columbia University Press, 1937.

Baron, Salo W., Ernest Nagel and Koppel S. Pinson (eds.). *Freedom and Reason. Studies in Jewish Philosophy and Culture.* Glencoe: The Free Press, 1951.

Baudelaire, Charles. "De l'essence du rire" (1855), pp. 710-728 in *Oeuvres complètes.* Paris: Pléiade, 1954.

Bava Mezi'a, a volume of *The Talmud,* ed. Rabbi Dr. A. Zvi Ehrman. Tel Aviv: El-'Am–Hoza'a Leor Israel, 1969.

Beda. *Israeliten und andere Anti-semiten.* Vienna: Huber & Lahme, 1909.

Ben-Amos, Dan. "The 'Myth' of Jewish Humor," *Western Folklore* 32, 2 (April 1973), pp. 112-131.

Benayoun, Robert. *Anthologie du nonsens.* Paris: Pauvert, 1957.

Bennett, D. J. "The Psychological Meaning of Anti-Negro Jokes," *Fact* (March-April 1964), pp. 53-59.

Bergler, Edmund. "Contribution to the Psychogenesis of Humor," *Psychoanalytic Review* 24 (1937), pp. 34-53.

Bergler, Edmund. *Laughter and the Sense of Humor.* New York: International Book Corporation, 1956.

Bergson, Henri. *Le rire. Essai sur la signification du comique.* Paris: Presses Universitaires de France, 1958; orig. pub. 1899.

Berkovitz, Eliezer. *Faith After the Holocaust.* New York: Ktav, 1973.

Berkovitz, Eliezer. *With God in Hell. Judaism in the Ghettos and Death Camps.* New York and London: Sanhedrin Press, 1979.

Berl, Emmanuel. "L'humour et le judaisme," *Revue de la pensée juive* 2, 6 (January 1951), pp. 20-23.

Berle, Milton. *Milton Berle's Fabulous Fantasy. Out of My Trunk.* New York: Grayson, 1945.

Berman, Henry B. *Have I Got a Joke for You.* New York: Hart, 1975. [Same as Pollack 1979.]

Bermant, Chaim. *What's the Joke? A Study of Jewish Humor through the Ages.* London: Weidenfeld & Nicolson, 1986.

Best Jewish Stories, The. London: Grant Richards, 1925.

Bienstock, Beverly Gray. "The Changing Image of the American Jewish Mother," pp. 173-190 in *Changing Image of the Family,* ed. Virginia Tufts and Barbara Myerhoff. New Haven and London: Yale University Press, 1979.

Bier, Jesse. *The Rise and Fall of American Humor.* New York: Holt, Rinehart & Winston, 1968.

Blau, Joseph L. et al. (eds.). *Essays on Jewish Life and Thought.* New York: Columbia University Press, 1959.

Blau, Zena Smith. "In Defense of the Jewish Mother," *Midstream* 13, 2 (February 1967), pp. 42-49.

Bloch, Chajim. *Ostjüdische Humor.* Berlin: Benjamin Harz, 1920.

Bloch, Chajim. *Hersch Ostropolier. Ein jüdischer Till-Eulenspiegel des 18. Jahrhunderts. Seine Geschichte und Streiche.* Berlin and Vienna: Benjamin Harz, 1921.

Bloch, Chajim. *Das jüdische Folk in seiner Anekdote. Ernest und heiteres von Gottsuchen, Gelehrten, Künstlern, Narren, Schelmen, Aufschniedern, Schnorrern, Reichen, Frommen, Freidenkern, Täuflingen, Antisemiten.* Berlin: Verlag für Kulturpolitik, 1931.

Block, Jack and Jeanne Block. "An Investigation of the Relationship between Intolerance of Ambiguity and Ethnocentrism," *Journal of Personality* 19 (1951), pp. 303-311.

Blumenfeld, Gerry. *Some of My Best Jokes Are Jewish.* New York: Kanrom, 1965.

Blumenfeld, Gerry. *Tales from the Bagel Lancers. Everyman's Book of Jewish Humor.* Cleveland: World, 1967.

Blumenthal, Hermann. *Die besten jüdischen Anekdoten. Perlen des Humors.* Vienna: Rudolf Lechner, n.d. [c. 1924].

Bock, Orla. *Trolden i æsken. En god vits til hver dag i aaret.* Copenhagen: E. Jespersens Forlag, 1908.

Bourdoiseau, Yannick. "Le rire juif," *Crapouillot* 80 (February-March 1985), pp. 31-34.

Brandes, Stanley. "Jewish-American Dialect Jokes and Jewish Identity," *Jewish Social Studies* 45 (1983), pp. 233-240.

Bruce, Lenny. *The Essential Lenny Bruce,* ed. John Cohen. Frogmore: Panther, 1975.

Buber, Martin. *Good and Evil.* New York: Scribner, 1952.

Buber, Martin. *Tales of the Hasidim.* 2 vols. New York: Schocken, 1961; orig. pub. 1947.

Budner, Stanley. "Intolerance of Ambiguity and Need for Closure," *Psychological Reports* 43 (1978), p. 638.

Bulawko, Henry. *Quand Israel rit. De l'humour juif à l'humour israélien.* Paris: Presses du Temps, 1963.

Bulawko, Henry. *Anthologie de l'humour juif et israélien.* Paris: Éditions Bibliophane, 1988.

Burdette, R. *Gems of Modern Wit and Humor*. Chicago: L. W. Walter, 1903.

Burg, J. G. *Jüdische Anekdotiade*. Munich: Ederer Verlag, 1970.

Burstein, Abraham. *An Anthology of Jewish Humor and Maxims*. Compiled by Elsa Teitelbaum. New York: Pardes, 1945.

Büschenthall, L. M. *Sammlung witziger Einfälle von Juden, als Beiträge zur Characteristik der jüdischen Nation*. Elberfeld: B. Büschles, 1812.

Cantor, Eddie. *World's Book of Best Jokes*. Cleveland: World, 1943.

Carey, Thomas Joseph. *Hebrew Yarns and Dialect Humor. Comprising Original and Selected Laughable Dialect Stories, Comic Situations, with Sayings and Rare Anecdotes, with Many Humorous Illustrations*. New York: Popular Publication Company, 1900.

Castel, Robert. *Robert Castel raconte... Les meilleures histoires de Kaouito le pied-noir*. Paris: Mengès, 1978.

Cerf, Bennet. *Pocket Book of War Humor*. New York: Pocket Books, 1943.

Chambers, F. W. *Ever Heard This One? Over 390 Good Stories*. London: Methuen, 1922.

Chaplin, Charles. "What People Laugh At" (1918), pp. 48-54 in *Focus on Chaplin*, ed. Donald W. McCaffrey. Englewood Cliffs: Prentice-Hall, 1971.

Chapman, Anthony J. and Hugh C. Foot (eds.). *Humour and Laughter: Theory, Research and Applications*. London: Wiley, 1976.

Chapman, Anthony J. and Hugh C. Foot (eds.). *It's a Funny Thing, Humour*. Exeter: Pergamon Press, 1977.

Charles, Lucile Hoerr. "The Clown's Function," *Journal of American Folklore* 58, 227 (January-March 1945), pp. 23-34.

Choice Dialect and Vaudeville Stage Jokes. Chicago: Drake, 1902.

Chotzner, J. *Hebrew Humour and Other Essays*. London: Luzac, 1905.

Chotzner, J. *Hebrew Satire*. London: Kegan Paul, Trench and Trübner, 1911.

Clément, André. *Les 100 meilleures histoires de l'Occupation*. Paris: Lesourd, 1945.

Cohan, Sam. *Jewish Joke Book*. Reading: United Sales Co., n.d. [c. 1966].

Cohen, Israel. *Jewish Life in Modern Times*. London: Methuen, 1914.

Cohen, Morris. *Reason and Nature. An Essay on the Meaning of Scientific Method*. Glencoe: The Free Press, 1953; orig. pub. 1931.

Cohen, Morris. "The Principle of Polarity," pp. 11-16 in *Studies in the Philosophy of Science*. New York: Holt, 1949.

Cohen, Myron. *Laughing Out Loud*. New York: Citadel, 1958.

Cohen, Myron. *More Laughing Out Loud*. New York: Gramercy, 1960.

Cohen, Sarah Blacher (ed.). *Jewish Wry. Essays on Jewish Humor*. Bloomington and Indianapolis: Indiana University Press, 1987.

Coleman, George. *The Circle of Anecdote and Wit*. London: Wilson, 1821.

Cooper, Goerge. *Yankee, Italian and Hebrew Dialect Readings and Recitations*. New York: Wehman, 1911.

Copeland, Lewis. *The World's Best Jokes*. New York: Blue Ribbon, 1936.

Coser, Ruth Laub. "Laughter Among Colleagues. A Study of the Social Functions of Humor Among the Staff of a Mental Hospital," *Psychiatry* 23, 1 (February 1960), pp. 81-95.

Cowan, Lore and Maurice. *The Wit of the Jews*. London: Leslie Freewin, 1970.

Cray, Ed. "The Rabbi Trickster," *Journal of American Folklore* 77 (1964), pp. 331-345.

Danero, E. M. S. *Nuevos Cuentos Judíos*. Buenos Aires: Editorial Tor, 1943.

Davidson, Adolph. *Here's a New One. A Book of After-Dinner Stories*. New York: Caldwell, 1913.

Davies, Christie. "Jewish Jokes, Anti-Semitic Jokes and Hebredonian Jokes," pp. 75-98 in *Jewish Humor*, ed. Avner Ziv. Tel Aviv: Papyrus, 1986.

Debré, S. *L'humour judéo-alsacien*. Paris: Reider, 1933.

Dershowitz, Alan. *Chutzpah*. Boston: Little, Brown & Co., 1991.

Despot, Adriane L. "Some Principles of Clowning," *Massachusetts Review* 22 (Winter 1981), pp. 661-678.

Dessauer, Julius. *Der jüdische Humorist: Auswahl des geistreichsten Unterhaltungs-Gespräche des weltberühmten Bonmotisten "Rajezer Maggid" und der bedeutendsten Autoritäten des Judenthums aus alter und neuer Zeit.* Budapest, Hungary: Selbstverlag, n.d. [c. 1879].

Dick, Isaac Meir. *Witzen un Spitzen oder Anecdoten.* Wilna: Widow & Bros. Romm, 1873.

Dines, Michael. *The Jewish Joke Book.* London: Futura, 1986.

Dines, Michael. *The Second Jewish Joke Book.* London: Futura, 1987.

Dines, Michael. *The Third Jewish Joke Book.* London: Futura, 1988.

Dini, Massimo and Rachele Enriquez. "E Dio scoppiò a ridere. Umorismo Ebraico. Perché ha conquistato il mondo," *Panorama* (11 June 1984), pp. 184-189.

Dooley, Lucile. "The Relation of Humor to Masochism," *Psychoanalytic Review* 28 (1941), pp. 37-46.

Dorinson, Joseph. "Jewish Humor: Mechanism for Defense, Weapon for Cultural Affirmation," *Journal of Psycho-History* 8, 4 (Spring 1981), pp. 447-464.

Dorson, Richard M. "Jewish-American Dialect Stories on Tape," pp. 111-174 in *Biblical and Jewish Folklore,* ed. Raphael Patai, Francis Lee Utley and Dov Noy. Bloomington: Indiana University Press, 1960.

Dorson, Richard M. "More Jewish Dialect Stories," *Midwest Folklore* 10 (1960), pp. 133-146.

Drozdzynski, Alexander. *Jiddische Witze und Schmonzes.* Düsseldorf: Droste Verlag, 1976.

Dubnow, S. M. *History of the Jews in Russia and Poland from the Earliest Times until the Present Day.* Philadelphia: Jewish Publication Society of America, 1946. Translated from the Russian; orig. pub. 1916.

Dundes, Alan. *Cracking Jokes. Studies of Sick Humor Cycles and Stereotypes.* Berkeley: Ten Speed Press, 1987.

Eastman, Max. *Enjoyment of Laughter.* New York: Simon & Schuster, 1936.

Edel, Edmund. *Der Witz der Juden.* Berlin: Louis Lamm, 1909.

Eidelberg, Ludwig. "A Contribution to the Study of Wit," *Psychoanalytic Review* 23 (1945), pp. 33-61.

Eliezer, Ben. *The World's Best Jewish Jokes.* London: Angus & Robertson, 1984.

Eliezer, Ben. *More of the World's Best Jewish Jokes.* London: Angus & Robertson, 1985.

Ellinger, Werner. "Studie über den jüdischen Witz," *Der Morgen* 11, 12 (March 1936), pp. 545-553.

Emerson, Joan P. "Negotiating the Serious Import of Humor," *Sociometry* 32 (1969), pp. 169-181.

Epshteyn, N. "Vi azoy tsu klasifitsieren dem yidishe witz," *Yivobleter* 12 (1937), pp. 484-493.

Eyles, Allen. *The Marx Brothers. Their World of Comedy.* South Brunswick: Barnes, 1969; orig. pub. 1966.

Farb, Peter. *Word Play. What Happens When People Talk.* New York: Bantam, 1976.

Feder, Mark. *It's a Living. A Personalized Collection of Jewish Humor.* New York: Bloch, 1948.

Feinsilver, Lillian Mermin. *The Taste of Yiddish.* New York and London: Thomas Yoseloff, 1970.

Finkelstein, Louis. *The Jews. Their History, Culture and Religion.* 2 vols. New York: Harper, 1949.

Finkelstein, Louis. *Akiba. Scholar, Saint and Martyr.* New York: Atheneum, 1970.

Fölkel, Ferruccio. *Storielle ebraiche.* Milan: Rizzoli, 1988.

Fölkel, Ferruccio. *Nuove storielle ebraiche.* Milan: Rizzoli, 1990.

Frank, Helena. *Yiddish Tales.* Philadelphia: Jewish Publication Society of America, 1912.

Franklin, Max. *Anthology of Wit and Humor.* New York: the author, 1923.

Frenkel-Brunswick, Else. "Tolerance Toward Ambiguity as a Personality Variable," *The American Psychologist* 3, 7 (July 1948), p. 268.

Frenkel-Brunswick, Else. "Intolerance of Ambiguity as an Emotional and Perceptual Personality Variable,"

Journal of Personality 18 (1949), pp. 108-143.

Freud, Sigmund. *Der Witz und seine Beziehung zum Unbewussten* [1905]. Frankfurt: Fischer, 1972.

Freud, Sigmund. *Jokes and Their Relation to the Unconscious* [1905]. London: Penguin, 1981.

Freud, Sigmund. *Aus den Anfängen der Psychoanalyse. Brief an Wilhelm Fliess, Abhandlungen und Notizen aus den Jahren 1887-1902.* London: Imago, 1950.

Freud, Sigmund. "Humour" [1927], pp. 160-166 in *The Standard Edition of the Complete Psychological Works of Sigmund Freud,* vol. 21. London: Hogarth Press, 1968-1974.

Fromm, Erich. *You Shall Be as Gods. A Radical Interpretation of the Old Testament and Its Traditions.* New York: Holt, Rinehart & Winston, 1966.

Fuller, Edmund. *Thesaurus of Anecdotes.* New York: Crown, 1942.

Für Schnorrer und Kitzinim. Sammlung gediegener jüdischer Witze und Anekdoten. Berlin: Cassirer & Danziger, 1889.

Gary, Romain. *La promesse de l'aube.* Paris: Gallimard, 1960.

Gary, Romain. *La nuit sera calme.* Paris: Gallimard, 1974.

Geiger, Raymond. *Histoires juives.* Paris: NRF, 1923.

Geiger, Raymond. *Nouvelles histoires juives.* Paris: Gallimard, 1925.

Gilman, Sandor. *Jewish Self-Hatred. Anti-Semitism and the Hidden Language of the Jews.* Baltimore: Johns Hopkins University Press, 1986.

Giniewski, Paul. *Les complices de Dieu.* Neuchâtel: Editions de la Baconnière, 1963.

Ginzberg, Louis. *The Legends of the Jews.* 7 vols. Philadelphia: Jewish Publication Society, 1946-1947; orig. pub. 1911-1928.

Goffman, Erving. *Frame Analysis. An Essay on the Organization of Experience.* New York: Harper & Row, 1974.

Goldberg, Isaac. *What We Laugh at and Why.* Girard, Kansas: Haldeman-Julius, n.d. [1938].

Golden, Harry. *The Golden Book of Jewish Humor.* New York: Putnam, 1972.

Goldman, Albert. "Boy-man, schlemiel: the Jewish element in American humour," pp. 3-17 in *Explorations,* ed. Murray Mindlin and Chaim Bermant. London: Barry and Rockliff, 1967.

Goldstein, Jeffrey H. and Paul E. McGhee (eds.). *The Psychology of Humor. Theoretical Perspectives and Empirical Issues.* New York and London: Academic Press, 1972.

Goldstein, Jeffrey H. "Theoretical Notes on Humor," *Journal of Communication* 26, 3 (Summer 1976), pp. 104-112.

Goodman, Philip. *Rejoice in Thy Festival. A Treasury of Wisdom, Wit and Humor for the Sabbath and Jewish Holidays.* New York: Bloch, 1956.

Goodrich, Anne T. "Laughter in Psychiatric Staff Conferences: A Socio-psychiatric Analysis," *American Journal of Ortho-psychiatry* 24 (1954), pp. 175-184.

Graf, Kurt. *Jüdisches und anderer Schmonzes.* Leipzig: Wilhelm Goldman Verlag, [1928?].

Greenburg, Dan. *How to Be a Jewish Mother: A Very Lovely Training Manual.* Los Angeles: Price, Stern & Sloan, 1975; orig. pub. 1964.

Greenburg, Dan with Marcia Jacobs. *How to Make Yourself Miserable for the Rest of the Century. A Vital Training Manual.* New York: Vintage, 1987.

Grossman, William. *Jewish Humor in the Home and Synagogue.* Passaic: Columbia, 1940.

Grotjahn, Martin. *Beyond Laughter.* New York: McGraw-Hill, 1957.

Grotjahn, Martin. "Jewish Jokes and Their Relation to Masochism" (1961), pp. 135-144 in *A Celebration of Laughter,* ed. Werner W. Mendel. Los Angeles: Mara Books, 1970.

Gutman, Jonathan and Robert F. Priest. "When is Aggression Funny?" *Journal of Personality and Social Psychology* 12, 1 (1969), pp. 60-65.

Guttman, Allen. "Jewish Humor," pp. 329-338 in *The Comic Imagination in American Literature,* ed. Louis D. Rubin. New Brunswick: Rutgers University Press, 1973.

Hakel, Hermann. *Oi, bin ich gescheit!* Munich: Südwest Verlag, n.d. [1965].

Hakel, Hermann. *Jiddische Geschichten aus aller Welt.* Tübingen and Basel: Horst Erdmann Verlag, 1967.

Hakel, Hermann. *Wenn der Rebbe lacht. Anekdoten.* Munich: Kindler, 1970.

Hall, G. Stanley and Arthur Allen. "The Psychology of Tickling, Laughing and the Comic," *The American Journal of Psychology* 9, 1 (October 1897), pp. 1-41.

Hancher, Michael. "How to Play Games with Words: Speech-Act Jokes," *Journal of Literary Semantics* 9, 1 (April 1980), pp. 20-29.

Hapgood, Hutchins. *The Spirit of the Ghetto. Studies of the Jewish Quarter of New York.* New York: Schocken, 1966.

Have You Heard This One? Best Scottish, Jewish and Irish Jokes. London: Foulsham, n.d.

Hayman, Joe. *Twenty Different Adventures of Cohen on the Telephone and Other Different Examples of Hebrew Humour.* London: Austin Rogers, 1928.

Hayworth, Donald. "The Social Origin and Function of Laughter," *Psychological Review* 35 (September 1928), pp. 367-384.

Hazlitt, W. Carew. *Shakespeare Jest-Books. Reprints of the Early and Very Rare Jest-Books Supposed to Have Been Used by Shakespeare.* New York: Burt Franklin, 1964. [Hazlitt's reprints of these 16th and 17th Century jest books were first published in 1864.]

Hazlitt, W. Carew. *Jests, New and Old.* London: Jarvis, 1887.

Hebrew Jokes and Dialect Humor. Philadelphia: Royal, 1902.

Herrnfeld, Anton and Donat. *Was tut sich.* Berlin: Baum, 1914.

Hersch, Aaron. *Rare und neue Sammlung schöner Anekdoten, witziger Einfälle, spatziger Schwänke und Schnurren von unsere Leut.* Leipzig: Magasin für Industrie und Literatur, n.d. [1800?].

Hershfield, Harry. *Jewish Jokes.* New York: Simon & Schuster, 1932.

Hershfield, Harry. *Now I'll Tell One.* New York: Greenberg, 1938.

Hershfield, Harry. *Laugh Louder, Live Longer.* New York: Grayson, 1959.

Hetherton, E. Mavis and Nancy P. Wray. "Aggression, Need for Social Approval and Humor Preferences," *Journal of Abnormal and Social Psychology* 68 (1964), pp. 685-689.

Hicks, Seymour. *Chestnuts Reroasted.* London: Hodder & Stroughton, 1924.

Hilarius, Justus [Sebastian Willibald Schiessler]. *Neue Folge frischer Judenkrischen. Eine Sammlung beslustigender Anekdoten, Einfälle, Schwänke und Schnurren von Juden und Judengenossen.* Part One, Meissen: Friedrich Wilh. Goedsche, 1828; Parts Three and Four, Leipzig: Better und Restoskn, 1835.

Hill, Murray. "Humor in Nazi Germany and its Post-War Rehabilitation," *Forum for Modern Language Studies* 20, 1 (January 1984), pp. 1-16.

Hirsch, T. L. *Jüdisches Witzbuch. Amüsante Witzer, Humoresken und Anekdoten.* Berlin: Reform-Verlagshaus, 1913.

Hirsch, Willy. *Neueste jüdische Witze.* Berlin: Berliner, n.d. [c. 1911?].

Hitschmann, Eduard. "Zur Psychologie des jüdischen Witz," *Die psycho-analytische Bewegung* II (1930), pp. 580-586.

Holbek, Bengt. "The Ethnic Joke in Denmark," pp. 327-335 in *Miscellanea. Prof. Em. Dr. K. C. Peeters.* Antwerp: Van Nespen, 1975.

Howe, Irving. "The Nature of Jewish Laughter," *The American Mercury* 72 (1951), pp. 211-219.

Howe, Irving [with Kenneth Libo]. *World of Our Fathers.* New York: Simon & Schuster, 1976.

Hunt, Cecil. *Fun with the Famous.* London: Ernest Benn, n.d. [1929].

Hunter, William C. *Laughing Gas. Sunshine Capsules to Cure the Blues.* Kansas City: Hunter, 1916.

Hupfield, Henry. *Encyclopedia of Wit and Wisdom.* Philadelphia: McKay, 1897.

Isaac, Jacob. *Les joyeuses histoires juives.* Paris: Belles éditions, n.d. [1938].

Isaacs, Abraham Samuel. "Rabbinical Humor," pp. 114-125 in *Stories from the Rabbis.* New York and London: C. L. Webster, 1893.

Isnard, Armand. *Raconte... Popov! Les histoires drôles de derrière le rideau de fer.* Paris: Mengès, 1977.

Itler, H. *Jüdische Witze.* Dresden: Rudoph'sche Verlagsbuchhandlung, [1928].

Jacobsen, Edith. "The Child's Laughter. Theoretical Notes on the Function of the Comic," *Psychoanalytic Study of the Child* 2 (1946), pp. 39-60.

Jaki, Arnold. *Eppis jiddisches.* Stuttgart: Quintus Verlag, 1977.

Janus, Samuel S. "The Great Comedians: Personality and Other Factors," *American Journal of Psychoanalysis* 35 (1975), pp. 169-174.

Jason, Heda. "The Jewish Joke: The Problem of Definition," *Southern Folklore Quarterly* 31, 1 (March 1967), pp. 48-54.

Jean-Charles. *La bataille du rire 1939-1945.* Paris: Presses de la Cité, 1970.

Jeanson, Francis. *La signification du rire.* Paris: Seuil, 1950.

Jekels, Ludwig. "On the Psychology of Comedy," pp. 97-104 in *Selected Papers.* London: Imago, 1952.

Jewish Humor. Program for Workman's Circle Groups. New York: Education Department of the Workman's Circle, 1970.

JokeMeisters. New York: St. Martin's Paperbacks, 1990.

Johnson, John Henry. *The Laughter Library.* Nobbsville, Indiana: Hudler Press, 1936.

Jossel, Chaim. *Schabbes Schmus. Jüdische Witze und Anekdoten.* Berlin: Hermann Seemann, 1907.

Jüdische Schwänke. Vienna: R. Löwit, 1928.

Junior, Allan. *Canny Tales fæ Aberdeen.* Dundee & London: Valentine, 1930; orig. pub. 1925. Illustrated by Gregor McGregor.

Junior, Allan. *The Aberdeen Jew.* Dundee & London: Valentine, 1927.

Katz, Naomi and Eli. "Tradition and Adaptation in American Jewish Humor," *Journal of American Folklore* 84 (1971), pp. 215-220.

Katzir, Benjamin. *Jødiske vitaminer. Humor fra Israel og Adspredelsen.* Almind: Brage, 1990.

Klapp, Michael. *Komische Geschichten aus dem jüdischen Volksleben.* Berlin: Hofmann, 1859.

Klapp, Orrin E. "The Fool as a Social Type," *American Journal of Sociology* 55 (1950), pp. 157-162.

Klein, Oskar. *Humoresken aus dem jüdischen Leben.* Berlin: Carl Dunker, 1898; orig. pub. 1895 under title: *Hechte mit Klössen.*

Klein-Harapash. *Krug und Stein. Jüdische Anekdoten.* Munich: R. Piper, 1961.

Knox, Israel. "The Traditional Roots of Jewish Humor," *Judaism* 12, 3 (Summer 1963), pp. 327-337.

Kohn, P. J. *Rabbinischer Humor aus alter und neuer Zeit. Eine Sammlung von Anekdoten und "guten Wörtschen."* Frankfurt: Kauffmann, 1930; orig. pub. 1915.

Kohn, Pinchas Jakob and Ludwig Davidson. "Jüdische Humor und Witz," *Jüdischer Lexikon.* Berlin: Jüdischer Verlag, 1928; vol. 2, pp. 1686-1694.

Koplev, Kjeld. *Guds udvalgte. Jødisk vid fra Moses til Woody Allen.* Copenhagen: Haase, 1988.

Krag, Helen and Margit Warburg (eds.). *Der var engang... Amol iz geven...* Copenhagen: Gyldendal, 1986.

Kravitz, Seth. "London Jokes and Ethnic Stereotypes," *Western Folklore* 36, 4 (October 1977), pp. 275-301.

Kreppel, J. *Wie der Jude lacht. Anthologie jüdischer Witze, Satiren, Anekdoten, Humoresken, Aphorismen. Ein Beitrag zur Psychologie des jüdischen Witzes und zur jüdischen Volkskunde.* Vienna: Verlag "Das Buch," 1933.

Kris, Ernst. *Psychoanalytic Explorations in Art.* London: George Allen & Unwin, 1952.

Kristol, Irving. "Is Jewish Humor Dead? The Rise and Fall of the Jewish Joke," *Commentary* 12 (November 1951), pp. 431-436.

LaFave, Lawrence and Roger Mannel. "Does Ethnic Humor Serve Prejudice?" *Journal of Communication* 26, 3 (Summer 1976), pp. 116-123.

Landis, Joseph C. *The Dybbuk and Other Great Yiddish Plays.* New York: Bantam, 1966.

Landmann, Salcia. *Der jüdische Witz.* Breisgau: Walter, 1960.

Landmann, Salcia. *Jüdische Witze.* Munich: Deutscher Taschenbuch, 1982; orig. pub. 1962.

Landmann, Salcia. "On Jewish Humor," *Jewish Journal of Sociology* 4, 2 (December 1962), pp. 193-204.

Landmann, Salcia. *Jüdische Anekdoten und Sprichwörter.* Munich: Deutscher Taschenbuch, 1972; orig. pub. 1965.

Landmann, Salcia. *Der klassischen Witze der Juden.* Frankfurt and Berlin: Ullstein, 1989.

Lang, Dov. "On the Biblical Comic," *Judaism* 11 (1962), pp. 249-254.

Lanigan, Suds. *A Minister, a Rabbi, and a Priest.* New York: St. Martin's Press, 1990.

Laytner, Anson. *Arguing with God. A Jewish Tradition.* Northvale, N.J.: Jason Aronson, 1990.

Lazarus, Y. L. *Enzyklopedia fun yidishe witzn.* New York: Pardes, 1928.

Learsi, Rufus [Israel Goldberg]. *The Book of Jewish Humor. Stories of the Wise Men of Chelem and Other Tales.* New York: Bloch, 1941.

Learsi, Rufus [Israel Goldberg] *Filled with Laughter. A Fiesta of Jewish Folk Humor.* New York and London: Thomas Yoseloff, 1961.

Leftwich, Joseph. *An Anthology of Modern Yiddish Literature.* The Hague and Paris: Mouton, 1974.

Legman, G. *Rationale of the Dirty Joke. An Analysis of Sexual Humor.* Vol. 1. London: Jonathan Cape, 1969. Vol. 2. New York: Breaking Point, 1975.

Leonard, Henry. *Open Your Mouth and Say 'Oy'.* New York: Crown, 1960.

Lettslaff, Ike'nsmile. *Jokes, Jokes, Jokes.* London: Universal Publications, 1937.

Levadi, Mosche. *Jüdische Anekdotiade.* Munich: G. Fischer, n.d.

Levensen, Sam. *Meet the Folks. A Session of American-Jewish Humor.* New York: Citadel, 1948; orig. pub. 1946.

Levensen, Sam. "The Dialect Comedian Should Vanish," *Commentary* 14, 2 (August 1952), pp. 168-170.

Levensen, Sam. *You Don't Have to Be in Who's Who to Know What's What.* New York: Simon & Schuster, 1979.

Levine, Jacob (ed.). *Motivation in Humor.* New York: Atherton, 1969.

Levitats, Isaac. *The Jewish Community in Russia 1772-1844.* New York: Octagon, 1970.

Lewin, Kurt. "Self-Hatred Among Jews," *Jewish Record* 4, 3 (June 1941), pp. 219-232.

Lewis, D. B. Wyndham. *I Couldn't Help Laughing! An Anthology of War-Time Humour.* London: Drummond, 1941.

Lewis, E. C. *Ish Ga Bibble (I Should Worry).* Boston: Mutual, 1914.

Liacho, Lazaro. *Anedcotario Judío. Folklore, Humorismo y Chistes.* Buenos Aires: M. Gleizer, 1939.

Lieberman, G. F. *The Greatest Laughs of All Time.* Garden City: Doubleday, 1961.

Lifson, David S. *Epic and Folk Plays of the Yiddish Theatre.* Cranbury and London: Associated University Presses, 1975.

Lipman, Steve. "The laugh's on us. Old chestnuts are warmed over at a Jewish humor conference," *The Brooklyn Jewish Week* (20 June 1986), pp. 3, 30.

Loewe, Heinrich. *Schelme und Narren mit jüdische Kappen.* Berlin: Welt-Verlag, 1920.

Loewe, Heinrich. *Reste von altem jüdischen Volkshumor.* Berlin: Privatdruck, 5682 (1922).

Lunel, Armand. "Humour gaillard des Juifs provençaux," *Revue de la pensée juive* 2,6 (January 1951), pp. 53-60.

Lurie, Charles N. *Make'em Laugh! Humorous Stories for All Occasions.* New York: Putnam's, 1927.

Lurie, Charles N. *Make'em Laugh Again.* New York: Putnam's, 1928.

Marcus, Martin. *Yiddish for Yankees or, Funny You Don't Look Gentile.* Philadelphia: Lippincott, n.d. [c. 1968].

Marks, Alfred. *A Medley of Jewish Humour.* London: Robson Books, 1985.

Marx, Arthur. *Life with Groucho.* New York: Simon & Schuster, 1954.

Marx, Groucho. *Groucho and Me.* New York: Bernard Geis, 1959.

Marx, Groucho. *The Groucho Letters. Letters to and from Groucho Marx.* Introduction by Arthur Sheekman. New York: Simon & Schuster, 1967.

Marx, Groucho. *The Groucho Phile.* Introduction by Hector Arce. London: Wh. H. Allen, 1978.

Marx, Harpo (with Roland Barber). *Harpo Speaks!* London: Victor Gollancz, 1961.

Maslow, A. H. "The Authoritarian Character Structure," *Journal of Social Psychology* 18 (1943), pp. 401-411.

Mauron, Charles. *Psychocritique du genre comique.* Paris: Corti, 1964.

Mazzes. Jüdischer Mutterwitz. Eine Sammlung bilustigender Schwänke und Anekdoten im jüdischer Mundart. Berlin: Siegfried Frankl, 1892; orig. pub. 1889.

McCaffrey, Donald W. *The Golden Age of Sound Comedy. Comic Films and Comedians of the Thirties.* South Brunswick: Barnes, 1973.

McGhee, Paul E. "Cognitive Mastery and Children's Humor," *Psychological Bulletin* 81, 10 (1974), pp. 721-730.

Meerloo, Joost A. M. "The Biology of Laughter," *Psychoanalytic Review* 53 (1966), pp. 189-208.

Meier, Frederick. *The Joke Teller's Joke Book.* Philadelphia: Blakiston, 1944.

Meisses und Schnohkes. Rituelle Scherze und koschere Schmonzes für auserwählte Volk. Budapest: J. Emerich Gerö's Verlag, n.d.

Memmi, Albert. "L'humour du juif" pp. 39-47 in *La libération du juif.* Paris: Payot, 1966.

Mendelsohn, S. Felix. *The Jew Laughs. Humorous Stories and Anecdotes.* Chicago: L. M. Stein, 1935.

Mendelsohn, S. Felix. *Let Laugher Ring.* Philadelphia: Jewish Publication Society, 1941.

Mendelsohn, S. Felix. *Here's a Good One.* New York: Bloch, 1947.

Mendelsohn, S. Felix. *The Merry Heart. Wit and Wisdom from Jewish Folklore.* New York: Bookman, 1951.

Mesnil, Jacqueline. "L'humour juif au pays de Voltaire," *Revue de la pensée juive* 2, 6 (January 1951), pp. 39-52.

Meyerowitz, Jan. *Der echte jüdische Witz.* Berlin: Colloquium Verlag, 1971.

Middleton, R. and J. Moland. "Humor in Negro and White Sub-Cultures: A Study of Jokes Among University Students," *American Sociological Review* 24 (1959), pp. 61-69.

Milburn, George. *The Best Jewish Stories.* Girard: Haldeman-Julius, 1953.

Mindess, Harvey. *The Chosen People. A Testament, both Old and New, to the Therapeutic Power of Jewish Wit and Humor.* Los Angeles: Nash, 1972.

Montgomery, John. *Comedy Films.* London: George Allen & Unwin, 1954.

Moszkowski, Alexander. *Die unsterbliche Kiste. Die 333 besten Witze der Weltliteratur.* Berlin: Verlag der "Lustigen Blätter" Dr. Eisler & Co., 1908.

Moszkowski, Alexander. *Die jüdische Kiste. 399 Juwelen.* Berlin: Lustigen Blätter, 1912.

Moszkowski, Alexander. *Der jüdische Witz und seine Philosophie.* Berlin: Eisler, 1923.

Moszkowski, Alexander. *Goldenes Lachen.* Berlin: Neufeld & Henius, n.d.

Muliar, Fritz. *Das Beste aus meiner jüdischen Witze und Anekdoten-Sammlung.* Munich: Wilhelm Heyne Verlag, 1974.

Mulkay, Michael. *On Humour. Its Nature and its Place in Modern Society.* Cambridge: Polity Press, 1988.

Müller-Iserlohn, Max. *Now Tell It Again! A Collection of Humorous Stories for Students of English.* Leipzig: Emil Rohmerkopf, 1931.

Murray, Henry D. "The Psychology of Humor. Mirth Responses to Disparagement Jokes as a Manifestation of an Aggressive Disposition," *Journal of Abnormal and Social Psychology* 29 (1934-1935), pp. 66-81.

Nador, Georg. *Zur Philosophie des jüdischen Witzes.* Northwood: Bina, 1975.

Nash, Walter. *The Language of Humour. Style and Technique in Comic Discourse.* London and New York: Longman, 1985.

Neches, S. M. *"As 'Twas Told to Me": A Hundred Little Stories of the Old Rabbis.* Los Angeles, 1926.

Neches, Solomon Michael. *Humorous Tales of Later Day Rabbis.* New York: Dobesvage, 1938.

Nègre, Hervé. *Dictionnaire des histoires drôles.* 2 vols. Paris: Fayard, 1973.

Nero [Harry Blacker]. *Some of My Best Jokes are Jewish.* London: W. H. Allen, 1972.

Newman, Louis I. *The Hasidic Anthology. Tales and Teachings of the Hasidim.* New York: Schocken, 1975; orig. pub. 1934.

New Hebrew Joke Book. Baltimore: Ottenheimer, 1907.

New Hebrew Jokes and Monologues. Baltimore: Ottenheimer, 1905.

Nicklas, Hans and Renate. *Schnorrer-Schadchen-Rabbi.* Wiesbaden: Falken-Verlag Erich Sicker, n.d. [1962].

Nikolaus, Paul. *Jüdische Miniaturen. Schnurren und Schwänke.* Hannover and Leipzig: Paul Steegemann Verlag, 1924.

Novak, William and Moshe Waldoks. *The Big Book of Jewish Humor.* New York: Harper & Row, 1981.

Nuél, Manuel [Schnitzer]. *Das Buch der jüdischen Witze.* Berlin: Gustave Riekes Buchhandlung, n.d. [1907].

Nuél, Manuel. *Das Buch der jüdischen Witze.* Neue Folge. Berlin: Gustav Riekes Buchhandlung, n.d. [1907?].

Nuél, Manuel. *Rabbi Lach und seine Geschichten.* Berlin: Hesperus, 1910.

Obrdlik, Antonin. "'Gallows Humor' - A Sociological Phenomenon," *American Journal of Sociology* 47, 5 (March 1942), pp. 709-716.

O'Connell, Walter E. "Resignation, Humor and Wit," *Psychoanalytic Review* 51 (1964), pp. 49-56.

O'Connell, Walter E. "Humor and Death," *Psychological Reports* 22 (1968), pp. 391-402.

Olsvanger, Immanuel. *Contentions with God. A Study in Jewish Folklore.* Capetown: T. Maskew Miller, 1921[?].

Olsvanger, Immanuel. *Rozinkes mit Mandlen. Aus der Volksliteratur des Ostjuden.* Zürich: Die Arche, 1965; orig. pub. 1921.

Olsvanger, Immanuel. *Röyte Pomerantsen, or How to Laugh in Yiddish.* New York: Schocken, 1965; orig. pub. Berlin, 1935.

Olsvanger, Immanuel. *L'Chayim! Jewish Wit and Humor.* New York: Schocken, 1949.

Oring, Elliot. *The Jokes of Sigmund Freud. A Study in Humor and Jewish Identity.* Philadelphia: University of Pennsylvania Press, 1984.

Ostwald, Hans. *Frisch, gesund und meschugge. Schnurren und Anekdoten.* Berlin: Franke, 1928.

Paruit, Alain. *Les barbelés du rire. Humour politique dans les pays de l'est.* Paris: Editions Albatros, 1978.

Peretz, Isaac Loeb. *Bontshe the Silent.* Freeport: Books for Libraries Press, 1971; orig. pub. 1927.

Peretz, Isaac Loeb. *Selected Stories.* New York: Schocken, 1975.

Perez, Jizchock Leib. *Chassidische Geschichten.* Vienna and Berlin: R. Löwit Verlag, 1917.

Petuchowski, Elizabeth. *Das Herz auf der Zunge. Aus der Welt des jüdischen Witzes.* Freiburg: Herder, 1984.

Philipson, David. *Old European Jewries.* Philadelphia: Jewish Publication Society of America, 1896.

Pollio, Howard R. et al. "The Comedian's World: Some Tentative Mappings," *Psychological Reports* 30 (1972), pp. 387-391.

Pollack, Simon R. *Jewish Wit for All Occasions.* New York: A & W Publishers, 1979. [Same as Berman 1975.]

Popeck. *Popeck raconte les meilleures histoires de l'humour juif.* Avec la collaboration de Bernard Stephane. Paris: Mengès, 1978.

Popeck. "Popeck raconte," in *Encyclopédie internationale du rire.* Paris: Mengès, 1981.

Popkin, Henry. "The Vanishing Jew in Our Popular Culture," *Commentary* 14, 1 (July 1951), pp. 46-55.

Prijs, Leo. *Lachen und Überleben. Echte jüdische Witze.* Freiburg: Herder, 1984.

Provenzal, Dino. *Dizionario umoristico.* Milan: Editori Ulrico Hoepli, 1976.

Rabinowitz, Rabbi H. R. *Kosher Humor.* Jerusalem: Rubin Mass, 1977.

Rajower, Ausor. *Masses und Chochmes. Jüdische Humor.* Zürich: Scheffel Verlag, 1959.

Rappaport, Ernest. "From the Keystone of Comedy to the Last of the Clowns,"

Psychoanalytic Review 59 (1972), pp. 333-346.

Raskin, Richard. "En klassisk jødisk vittighed," *Alef. Tidsskrift for jødisk kultur* 4 (December 1989), pp. 8-11.

Raskin, Richard. "Menneske versus Gud i en klassisk jødisk vittighed," *Slagmark. Tidsskrift for idéhistorie* 14 (Autumn 1989), pp. 91-102.

Raskin, Richard. "Jewish Jokes as Reversible Figures: A Major Interpretive Property." Paper delivered at the London Conference of the British Psychological Society in December 1989.

Raskin, Richard. "God versus Man in a Classic Jewish Joke," *Judaism. A Quarterly Journal* 40, 1 (Winter 1991), pp. 39-51.

Raskin, Victor. *Semantic Mechanisms of Humor.* Dordrecht, Boston, Lancaster: Reidel, 1984.

Rawnitzki, J. Ch. *Yidishe Witzn.* 2 vols. New York: Morris S. Sklarsky, 1950; orig. pub. 1923.

Reguer, Sara. "The Jewish Mother and the 'Jewish American Princess': Fact or Fiction?" *USA Today* 108, 2412 (September 1979), pp. 40-42.

Reik, Theodor. "On the Nature of Jewish Wit," pp. 164-173 in *From Thirty Years with Freud.* London: Hogarth, 1940.

Reik, Theodor. "Freud on Jewish Wit," *Psychoanalysis* 2 (1954), pp. 12-20.

Reik, Theodor. *Jewish Wit.* New York: Gamut, 1962.

Reitzer, Avrom. *Gut Jontev. Rituelle Scherze und koschere Schmonzes für unsere Leut.* Pressburg: Adolf Alkalay, n.d.

Reitzer, Avrom. *Gut Schabbes. Eine Sammlung von Lozelech, Schmonzes und Meisses für unsere Leut.* Vienna and Leipzig: J. Deubler's Verlag, n.d.

Reitzer, Avrom. *Mazel Tov.* Pressburg: Adolf Alkalay, n.d. [c. 1900].

Richman, Jacob. *Laughs from Jewish Lore.* New York and London: Funk & Wagnall's, 1926.

Richman, Jacob. *Jewish Wit and Wisdom.* New York: Pardes, 1952.

Roda Roda [Alexander] and Theodor Etzel. "Jiddische Schwänke," in vol. 5,

pp. 148-158 of *Welthumor.* Munich: Simplicissimus Verlag, 1925.

Röhrich, Lutz. *Der Witz. Figuren, Formen, Funktionen.* Stuttgart: Metzler, 1977.

Rokeach, Milton. *The Open and Closed Mind. Investigations into the Nature of Belief Systems and Personality Systems.* New York: Basic Books, 1960.

Rosenbaum, Brenda Z. *How to Avoid the Evil Eye.* New York: St. Martin's Press, 1985.

Rosenberg, Bernard and Gilbert Shapiro. "Marginality and Jewish Humor," *Midstream* 4 (Spring 1958), pp. 70-80.

Rosten, Leo. *The Joys of Yiddish.* London: W. H. Allen, 1970.

Rosten, Leo. *Treasury of Jewish Quotations.* New York: McGraw-Hill, 1972.

Rosten, Leo. *Hooray for Yiddish.* New York: Simon & Schuster, 1982.

Rosten, Leo. *Giant Book of Laughter.* New York: Crown, 1985.

Rothbart, Mary K. "Laughter in Young Children," *Psychological Bulletin* 80, 3 (1973), pp. 247-256.

Rovit, Earl. "Jewish Humor and American Life," *American Scholar* 36 (1967), pp. 237-245.

Rügenwald, Simon Josef. *Humor aus dem jüdischen Leben.* Frankfurt: J. Kauffmann, 1903.

Rund, Moritz. *Perlen jüdischen Humors. Eine Sammlung von Scherzen und kleinen Erzählungen aus dem jüdischen Volksleben.* Berlin: Mar Schildberger, 1914.

Rywell, Martin. *Laughing with Tears.* Harriman: Pioneer Press, 1960.

Samard. *Histoires hitlériennes.* Paris: Eugène Figuière, 1936.

Samuel, Maurice. *Prince of the Ghetto.* New York and Philadelphia: Meridian, 1959; orig. pub. 1948.

Samuel, Maurice. *In Praise of Yiddish.* Chicago: Henry Regnery, 1971.

Sanders, Ronald. *Reflections on a Teapot. The Personal History of a Time.* New York: Harper & Row, 1972.

Sarano, Matilde Cohen. *Storie di Giochà. Racconti popolari giudeo-spagnoli.* Florence: Sansoni, 1990.

Schermerhorn, James. *Schermerhorn's Stories. 1500 Anecdotes from Forty Years* of After Dinner Stories. New York: George Sully, 1928.

Schickel, Richard. "The Basic Woody Allen Joke," New York Times Magazine (January 7, 1973), pp. 10, 33-37.

Schlemiel. Illustrierte jüdisches Witzblatt. Berlin: Verlag Louis Lamm. 1903-1920.

Schlemiel. Jüdische Blätter für Humor und Kunst. Berlin. 1919-1920.

Schilling, Bernard N. "An Essay on Jewish Humor," pp. vii-xxxiii in Israel Zangwill, The King of the Schnorrers! Hamden: Shoe String Press, 1953.

Schlesinger, Kurt. "Jewish Humor as Jewish Identity," International Review of Psychoanalysis 6 (1979), pp. 317-330.

Schmulowitz, Nat. "Jesting Among and About Jews," Jewish Digest 2, 10 (June 1957).

Schnitzer, Manuel. Rabbi Lach. Ein Kulturdokument im Anekdoten. Hamburg: Verlag W. Gente, 1921.

Schnur, Harry. Jewish Humour. London: Allied Book Club, n.d. [1945].

Scholem Aleichem [Sholom Rabinowitz]. Den lille verden. Translated by S. Friedman and Eric Erichsen. Copenhagen: Skandinavisk Bogforlag, 1949.

Scholem-Alejchem [Sholom Rabinowitz]. Mælkemanden Tewje. Preface by Marcus Melchior, postscript by Max Brod. Copenhagen: Wangels Forlag, 1961.

Scholz, Wilhelm. Gewaltsachen. Eine Auswahl der beste jüdischen Anekdoten. Berlin: A. Hofmann, n.d.

Schwartz, David. Hannukkah Latkes and Rothschild's Millions. A Collection of Jewish Wit and Humor. New York: Twayne, 1961.

Searle, J. R. Speech Acts. An Essay in the Philosophy of Language. Cambridge: Cambridge University Press, 1969.

Searle, J. R. "What is a speech act?" pp. 39-53 in The Philosophy of Language, ed. J. R. Searle. Oxford: Oxford University Press, 1971.

Seforim, Mendele Mocher. The Travels and Adventures of Benjamin the Third. New York: Schocken, 1968.

Sholom Aleichem [Sholom Rabinowitz]. Oisgeveilte verk. Moscow: Malocha, 1959.

Sholom Aleichem [Sholom Rabinowitz]. Tevye's Daughters. Translated by Frances Butwin. New York: Crown, 1949.

Sholom Aleichem [Sholom Rabinowitz]. The Great Fair. Scenes from My Childhood. New York: Noonday Press, 1955.

Sholom Aleichem [Sholom Rabinowitz]. Selected Stories. New York: Random House, 1956.

Sholom Aleichem [Sholom Rabinowitz]. Adventures of Motel the Cantor's Son. Translated by Tamara Kahana. New York: Collier, 1961.

Sholom Aleichem [Sholom Rabinowitz]. Inside Kasrilevke. Translated by Isidore Goldstick. New York: Schocken, 1968.

Sholom Aleichem [Sholom Rabinowitz]. Stories and Satires. Translated by Kurt Leviant. London: Collier-Macmillan, 1970.

Simmons, Donald C. "Anti-Italian-American Riddles in New England," Journal of American Folklore 79 (1966), pp. 475-478.

Simon, Ernst. Zum Problem des jüdischen Witzes. Berlin: Soncino, 1929.

Simon, Solomon. The Wise Men of Helm and Their Merry Tales. New York: Behrman, 1945.

Sirecki, Ingetraud (ed.). Des Rebben Pfeifenrohr. Mendele Moicher Sforim, Scholem Alechem, Jizchok Leib Perez. Munoristische Erzälungen aus dem Jiddischen. Berlin: Eulenspiegel Verlag, 1983.

Søeborg, Finn. "Sådan noget man ler af," Politiken (18 Oct. 1990), Sec. 2, pp. 5-6.

Spalding, Henry D. Encyclopedia of Jewish Humor. From Biblical Times to the Modern Age. New York: Jonathan David, 1969.

Spalding, Henry D. A Treasure-Trove of American-Jewish Humor. New York: Jonathan David, 1976.

Starer, Emanuel. "Reactions of Psychiatric Patients to Cartoons and Verbal Jokes," Journal of General Psychiatry 65 (1961), pp. 301-304.

Steiner, Paul. Israel Laughs. A Collection of Humor from the Jewish State. New York: Bloch, 1950.

Stephensen, Richard M. "Conflict and Control Functions of Humor," *American Journal of Sociology* 56, 6 (May 1951), pp. 569-574.

Stora, Judith. "Qu'est-ce que l'humour juif?" *L'Arche* 114-115 (September 1966), p. 324.

Stora-Sandor, Judith. *L'humour juif dans la littérature de Job à Woody Allen*. Paris: PUF, 1984.

Strange Surprising Adventures of the Venerable Gooroo Simple and His Five Disciples, Noodle, Doodle, Wiseacre, Zany and Toozle. London: Trubner, 1861.

Sutton-Smith, Brian (ed.). *The Psychology of Play*. New York: Arno Press, 1976.

Szyk, Arthur. *Le juif qui rit*. Legendes anciennes et nouvelles, arrangées par Curnonsky et J. W. Bienstock. Paris: Albin Michel, 1926.

Szyk, Arthur. *Le juif qui rit. Nouvelles legendes*. Paris: Albin Michel, 1927.

Szyk, Arthur. *The New Order*. New York: Putnam's, 1941.

Tenenbaum, Samuel. *The Wise Men of Chelm*. New York and London: Thomas Yoseloff, 1965.

Todorov, Tzvetan. "Le mot d'esprit," pp. 283-293 in *Les genres du discours*. Paris: Seuil, 1978.

Togeby, Ole. "Jødisk vid," pp. 171-190 in *Der var engang... Amol is geven...*, ed. Helen Krag and Margit Warburg. Copenhagen: Gyldendal, 1986.

Triverton, Sanford. *Complete Book of Ethnic Jokes*. New York: Galahad, 1981.

Untermeyer, Louis. *A Treasury of Laughter*. New York: Simon & Schuster, 1946.

Varvello, Luciana. *Enciclopedia dell' umorismo*. Milan: De Vecchi Editori, 1964.

Weinreich, Uriel. *College Yiddish. An Introduction to the Yiddish Language and to Jewish Life and Culture*. New York: Yivo Institute for Jewish Research, 1981; orig. pub. 1949.

Weisfeld, Israel. *The Pulpit Treasury of Wit and Humor*. New York: Prentice Hall, 1950.

Welch, Joe. *Diamonds. Up to the Minute Hebrew Jokes*. Chicago: Donahue, 1910.

Weller, Leonard et al. "Reactions to Absurd Humor by Jews of Eastern and Western Descent," *Journal of Social Psychology* 98 (1976), pp. 159-163.

Whitfield, Stephen. "Laughter in the Dark: Notes on American-Jewish Humor," *Midstream* 24, 2 (February 1978), pp. 48-58.

Wiesel, Elie. *La nuit*. Paris: Editions de Minuit, 1958.

Wiesel, Elie. *Souls on Fire. Portraits and Legends of Hasidic Masters*. New York: Vintage, 1972.

Wiesel, Elie. *The Trial of God (as it was held on February 25, 1649, in Shamgorod)*. New York: Random House, 1979.

Wilde, Larry. *The Official Jewish Joke Book*. New York: Pinnacle Books, 1964.

Wilde, Larry. *The Great Comedians Talk About Comedy*. New York: Citadel, 1968.

Wilde, Larry. *The Last Official Jewish Joke Book (Maybe Next to Last)*. New York: Bantam, 1980.

Williams, Charletta and David L. Cole. "The Influence of Experimentally Induced Inadequacy Feelings upon the Appreciation of Humor," *Journal of Social Psychology* 64 (1964), pp. 113-117.

Wilson, Christopher. *Jokes. Form, Content, Use and Function*. London: Academic Press, 1978.

Winterstein, Alfred. "Contributions to the Problem of Humor," *Psychoanalytic Quarterly* 3 (1934), pp. 303-316.

Wirth, Louis. *The Ghetto*. Chicago: University of Chicago Press, 1956; orig. pub. 1926.

Wiseman, F. *Cyclopedia of Wit and Wisdom, Being a Selection of Choice Anecdotes*. Manchester: Johnson, 1843.

Wisse, Ruth R. *The Schlemiel as Modern Hero*. Chicago: University of Chicago Press, 1971.

Wit and Humor of the Physician. Philadelphia: Jacobs, 1906.

Wolfenstein, Martha. *Children's Humor. A Psychological Analysis*. Bloomington and London: Indiana University Press, 1978; orig. pub. 1954.

Wolfenstein, Martha. "Two Types of Jewish Mothers," pp. 424-440 in *Childhood in Contemporary Cultures*, ed. Margaret Mead and Martha Wolfenstein. Chicago: University of Chicago Press, 1955.

Woods, Ralph L. *The Joy of Jewish Humor.* New York: Essandess, 1969.

Youngman, Henny. *How Do You Like Me So Far?* New York: Gramercy, 1963.

Zangwill, Israel. *The King of Schnorrers.* Hamden: Shoe String Press, 1953; orig. pub. 1894.

Zborowski, Mark and Elizabeth Herzog. *Life is with People. The Jewish Little-Town of Eastern Europe.* New York: International Universities Press, 1952.

Zenner, Walter P. "Joking and Ethnic Stereotyping," *Anthropological Quarterly* 43 (1970), pp. 93-113.

Zijderveld, Anton C. "Jokes and Their Relation to Social Reality," *Social Research* 35 (1968), pp. 286-311.

Zillmann, Dolf and S. Holly Stocking. "Putdown Humor," *Journal of Communication* 26, 3 (Summer 1976), pp. 154-163.

Zippin, David. "Sex Differences and the Sense of Humor," *Psychoanalytic Review* 53 (1966), pp. 209-219.

Ziv, Avner. *Personality and Sense of Humor.* New York: Springer, 1984.

Ziv, Avner (ed.). *Jewish Humor.* Tel Aviv: Papyrus, 1986.

Zwerling, Israel. "The Favorite Joke in Diagnostic and Therapeutic Interviewing," *Psychoanalytic Quarterly* 24 (1955), pp. 104-114.

Illustriertes jüdisches Witzblatt.

Unter Mitwirkung namhafter jüdischer Künstler und Schriftsteller

herausgegeben von **Dr. Max Jungmann,** Berlin.

Der „Schlemiel" erscheint regelmäßig am 1. eines jeden Monats. Jahresabonnement 2.50 M. (incl. Porto). Einzelnummer 25 (nebst 3 resp. 5 Pf. Porto). Probenummern werden nicht abgegeben. Der Versand geschieht nur nach vorheriger Einsendung Betrages. Abonnements werden von jeder Postanstalt und den Briefträgern entgegen genommen. Inserate 40 Pf. die 4gepaltene Petitze Alle Zuschriften und Anfragen sind zu richten an den

Verlag des „General-Anzeiger für die gesamten Interessen des Judentums". Dr. Moses, Berlin C², Spandauer Brücke 6.

| No. 5 | Sonntag, den 1. Mai 1904. | II. Jahrgang |

The masthead of the Berlin humor magazine in which the
herring riddle (cited on p. 135 above) first appeared.

Additional Chapters to
the Second Edition

Dilemma Resolution in the Hen-and-Rooster Joke

NB. An earlier form of this chapter appeared in Danish as an article in *Udsyn - Tidsskrift om jødisk liv, Israel og Mellemøsten*, Vol. 25, No. 1 (June 2010), pp. 12-14.

The most interesting Jewish jokes are open to two or more radically different interpretations. And this is not just a matter of wordplay or purely verbal ambiguities but rather a question as to how the event enacted in the punchline is understood. In this perspective I would like to discuss a joke Sigmund Freud tells in a letter to Wilhelm Fliess dated 28 May 1899:

A husband and wife who owned one cock and one hen decided to celebrate the holidays by roasting a fowl, but they could not make up their minds which was to be sacrificed and therefore turned to the rabbi. "Rebbe, what are we to do? We have only one cock and one hen. If we kill the cock, the hen will pine; and if we kill the hen, the cock will pine. But we want to eat a fowl on the holiday; rabbi, what are we to do?" The rabbi: "So kill the cock." — "But then the hen will pine." — "Yes, that's true; so kill the hen." — "But rabbi, then the cock will pine." — The rabbi: "So let him pine!"[1]

And here is a somewhat later and further developed version of the joke:

A HEN AND A ROOSTER

Someone came to the rabbi of a small town with a question that baffled him.

"What shall I do?" the man asked. "I have a hen and a rooster and one of them has to go to the pot. But which one? If I take the rooster the hen raises a terrible outcry. She clucks and screams and flaps her wings. If I take the hen, the rooster shrieks so my blood curdles. What shall I do rabbi?"

The old rabbi chewed his beard thoughtfully.

"I must look up the law on this matter," said he. "Come back in three days."

"Nu, rabbi?" said the man three days later.

---

[1] *The Complete Letters of Sigmund Freud to Wilhelm Fliess, 1887-1904*, trans. and edited by Jeffrey Moussaieff Masson, Belknap Press, 2002, p. 353.

"The law is to take the hen," the rabbi replied.
"But the rooster will protest!" the man cried.
"The rooster will protest?" said the rabbi. "Let him protest!" [2]

In Olsvanger's Yiddish versions (1921 and 1935), as can be seen in the joke's publication history at the end of this chapter, even more is made of the rabbi's difficulty in finding an answer during the three days in which he studies the holy texts, sweating profusely with his brow knitted in concentration.

There are clearly two dilemmas in play in this joke. One concerns which of the two animals is to be slaughtered. The other relates to the rabbi's having to pronounce a judgment he is apparently not equipped to provide. And it is of course the rabbi's dilemma and what we are invited to think of his way of managing it, that is the more interesting of the two and the real crux of the joke.

Regarding the attitude we are invited to hold toward the rabbi's solution to his own dilemma as enacted in the punchline, there are essentially two interpretive options.

One is to regard the rabbi's ruling as appropriate, even if his pronouncement as to which animal should be slaughtered appears to be random, arbitrary and unfeeling about the surviving animal's pain. In this perspective the point of the joke would be that the main thing is to go ahead and do something, to overcome the paralysis caused by the dilemma by simply brushing aside whatever prevented action. Or to focus more specifically on the rabbi's dilemma, we could say that in the framework of the joke, the rabbi's pronouncement is validated despite his apparent failings as a judge, since he creates a possibility for action where before there was only paralysis. It is with this understanding of the joke that Freud cites it in connection with his own dilemma regarding marriage versus work or private versus public, scientific life, as Elliot Oring points out.[3] And the same meaning can be found in another joke in which a *shamas* (caretaker of the synagogue) tries to help a widow to overcome her paralyzing dilem-

---

[2] Rufus Learsi, *Filled with Laughter*. New York: Thomas Voseloff, 1961; pp. 246-247.

[3] *The Jokes of Sigmund Freud: A Study in Humor and Jewish Identity*. Philadelphia: University of Pennsylvania Press, 1984; p. 30. After citing the joke, Oring writes: "Perhaps it would not be overextending our interpretation to suggest that the allocation of Freud's libido between wife and work is resolved in this comic parable. In fact, he used the anecdote to illustrate precisely this conflict between his private life and his public, scientific one. In order to make contributions to the understanding of the human psyche, Freud's private life would have to be ignored; that is, his sexual energies must be displaced from females to psychoanalysis. In terms of the anecdote, the hen (the female as object) must die, in which case the cock (das Hahn) will assuredly pine."

ma, and where it simply doesn't matter which of the two courses of action is chosen:

A widow found herself in dire financial straits. She decided to go and bake bagels, but after two months she found that her coffers were still quite empty.

In desperation, she repaired to the cemestry with the idea of consulting her husband who was lying there under the sod.

The shamas (beadle) of the town knew of the woman's proclivity in that direction. He placed himself behind the tombstone of the late departed.

The woman fell upon the grave and sobbed, pouring her heart out to her dead husband. "Oh, Isaac, Isaac, I don't know what to do. I can't get along without you. Oh, Isaac, I baked bagels but from that I cannot make a living."

There emerged a voice from the back of the tombstone, "So don't bake."

The woman called out in desperation, "But Isaac, oh my Isaac, if I don't bake bagels from where will I make a living?"

And the shamas' voice responded, "So bake." [4]

But back to the hen-and-rooster story and to a very different understanding of the point of the joke – this time with the rabbi's judgment seen as scandalous since he resolves his own dilemma by pretending to grasp the problem at hand when in reality he is utterly in the dark and the ruling he pronounces has no basis whatsoever. Seen in this perspective, the rabbi's behavior might be understood as a parody of a Salomonic ruling, as suggested by the title "Salomonische Weisheit" given several versions of the joke (see Moszkowski, Hirsch and Ostwald in the publication history below), and further emphasized by those versions which end with an ironic epilogue of the type "With that ruling our Rabbi made a name for himself"(Olsvanger, Roda and Etzel). And in that respect, the joke would be related to stories making fun of a rabbi by letting him suddenly reveal his total inability to fulfill the role expected of him after an elaborate build-up. For example:

The superstitious believe that the Holy Rabbi of Zhitomir is so powerful that he can even raise the dead.

One day a woman comes and begs him to revive her husband who has just died. The Rabbi accepts the commision and enters the room where the dead man is lying. He reads the Kabbalah, the sacred book of mysticism, from end to end and then commands: "Get up and be alive!"

But the dead man doesn't budge.

Again the Rabbi prays and reads the Kabbalah until he perspires. Again he commands the dead man: "Get up and be alive!" – but the dead man doesn't obey.

---

[4] Henry B. Berman, *Have I Got a Joke for You*. New York: Hart, 1975; pp. 174-175.

The Rabbi prays until all his clothes stick to him; again he recites the Kabbalah; again he commands the dead man to arise. But the corpse continues in its corpse-like passivity. The Rabbi wipes his streaming brow. "Now that's what I call being dead." [5]

SUMMARY

As suggested above, the rabbi's behavior at the end of the hen-and-rooster joke can be understood in two very different ways: a) as an action-enabling model worthy of emulation since despite his apparent failings, the rabbi manages to cut through the dilemma at hand and create an opportunity for moving forward, by simply reframing as acceptable a consequence erroneously presumed to disqualify each of the available options; or b) as an ironically enacted parody of a wise ruling, thoughtlessly improvised at the last moment by a rabbi who pretends to have found the answer in the holy books but is intellectually incapable of resolving the dilemma at hand or even of understanding that he has failed to do so.

---

[5] Harry Schnur, *Jewish Humour*. London: Allied Book Club, n.d. (1945); pp. 18-19. Other versions of this joke can be found in: Raymond Geiger, *Nouvelles histoires juives*. Paris: Gallimard, 1925, pp. 36-37; Fritz Muliar, *Das Beste aus meiner jüdischen Witze- und Anekdoten-Sammlung*. Munich: Wilhelm Heyne Verlag, 1974, pp. 68-69; *Popeck raconte les meilleures histoires de l'humour juif*. Paris: Mengès, 1978, p. 216.

Publication History

Sigmund Freud. *Aus den Anfängen der Psychoanalyse. Brief an Wilhelm Fliess.* London: Imago, 1950; p. 300. Letter dated 28 May 1899.

...Ich habe mich dann in diesem Dilemma benommen wie der Rabbi in der Geschichte vom Hahn und der Henne. Kennst Du sie? „Ein Ehepaar, das einen Hahn und eine Henne besitzt, beschließt, sich zu den Feiertagen einen Hühnerbraten zu gönnen, kann sich aber zur Wahl des Opfers nicht entschließen und wendet sich darum an den Rabbi. ‚Rabbe, was sollen wir tun, wir haben nur einen Hahn und eine Henne. Wenn wir den Hahn schlachten, wird sich die Henne kränken, und wenn wir die Henne schlachten, wird sich der Hahn kränken. Wir wollen aber Huhn essen zum Feiertag; Rabbe, was sollen wir tun?' Der Rabbi: ‚So schlacht's den Hahn.' – ‚Da wird sich doch die Henne kränken.' – ‚Ja, das ist wahr, also schlacht's de Henne.' – ‚Aber Rabbi, dann kränkt sich ja der Hahn.' – Der Rabbi: ‚Loss er sich kränken!!'"

Manuel Nuél, *Das Buch der jüdischen Witze*. Berlin: Gustave Riekes Buchhandlung, n.d. [1907], pp. 29-31. Also included in Schnitzer's Rabbi lach. Verlag W. Gente, 1921; pp. 66-67 under the title "Die Hühnergeschichten."

Zu solch einem kleinen Dorfrabbi kommt eines Tages, kurz vor den hohen Zeiten, ein Weiblein, um sich in folgender Sache Rats zu holen: Sie besitzt einen Hahn und eine Henne und möchte eins davon schlachten lassen, um ihrem Manne ein würdiges Festmahl zu bereiten; sie weiß aber nicht, welches der beiden Tiere, die ihr gleich lieb seien, sie opfern dürfe. Denn, meint sie traurig, „schlacht ich den Hahn, so kränkt sich die Henn', und schlacht ich die Henn', so kränkt sich der Hahn."

Der Fall liegt schwierig, und der Rabbi bestellt das Weiblein für den nächsten Tag; er müsse erst studieren „in die Bücher". Als sie zur bestimmten Stunde wieder erscheint, lätzt er sich die Sache noch einmal vortragen und sagt dann:

„Du kannst schlachten die Henn'... So steht geschrieben in die Bücher."

„Weh!" jammert die Frau, „wird sich doch kränken der Hahn..."

Derauf der Rabbi:

„Nu, wein' nicht... wird ich noch einmal nachsehn in die Bücher. Komm morgen."

Tags darauf empfängt er sie mit den Worten:

„Ich hab wieder nachgesehen in die Bücher... Du kannst schlachten den Hahn und leben lassen die Henn'..."

Die Frau beginnt bitterlich zu weinen.

„O weh... o weh... wird sich doch wieder kränken die Henn'..."

„Nu," sagt der Rabbi, soll sie sich kränken!"

Alexander Moszkowski, *Die unsterbliche Kiste*. Berlin: Verlag der "Lustigen Blätter," 1908, pp. 78-79. Also included in Moszkowski's Die jüdische Kiste. Berlin: Lustigen Blätter, 1911; p. 29.

Salomonische Weisheit

"Weiser Rabbi, ihr müßt mir einen Rat geben, ich bin in großer Verlegenheit. Ich habe einen Hahn und eine Henne und muß eins von den Tieren schlachten. Wenn ich den Hahn schlachte, wird sich die Henne kränken; schlacht' ich die Henne, wird sich der Hahn kränken. Also was soll ich tun?"

„Hört, Aaron," sagte der weise Rabbi, „der Fall liegt sehr schwierig. Laßt mir Zeit bis morgen zur Überlegung."

Am nächsten Tage erneuert der Mann seine frage und erhält den Bescheid: „Ihr müßt die Henne schlachten."

„Aber, Rabbi, da wird sich doch der Hahn kränken?!"

– „Nu, lass er sich kränken!"

Salomonische Weisheit

Willy Hirsch, *Neueste jüdische Witze*. Berlin: Berliner, n.d. [ca 1911?]; p. 56.

Der Kohn trifft den Rabbiner und sagt ihm: „Bin in großer Bedrängnis. Mer hab'n nir ze arbeiten und nir ze essen. Nu hob' ich ä Hahn und ä Henn. Schächt ich den Hahn, so kränkt sich de Henn, schächt ich de Henn, so kränkt sich der Hahn. Was soll ich tun?" Drauf der Rebbe: „Loß' mir drei tag' Bedenkzeit." Nach drei Tagen spricht der Kohn: „No, haft de gefunden en Ausweg?" Sagt der Rebbe: „Jo, schächt' den Hahn." Meint der Kohn: "Da werd' ich aber doch de Henn kränken." Sagt der Rabbiner: "No, laß se sich kränken!"

Der weise Rabbi

T. L. Hirsch. *Jüdisches Witzebuch. Amüsante Witze, Humoresken und Anekdoten*. Berlin: Reform-Verlagshaus, 1913; pp. 54-55.

Zu einem Rabbi kommt eine Fru und erzählt, daß sie einen Hahn und eine Henne besitze und eins von den Tieren schlachten wolle, um ein Festmahl zu bereiten.

Da ihr beide Tiere gleich lieb sind, und sie nicht weiß, welches sie opfern soll, möchte sie vom Rabbi gern Rat haben und sagt traurig zu ihm:

„Schlacht' ich den Hahn, wird sich die Henn' kränken, und schlacht' ich de Henn', kränkt sich der Hahn."

Der Rabbi schickt die Frau wieder nach Hause, sie solle am andern Tage wieder kommen, da der Fall schwierig sei und er erst „in die Bücher" studieren müsse.

Als die Frau am andern Tage wiederkommt, läßt er sich die Sache nochmals erzählen und erklärt dann:

„In die Bücher steht, daß du kannst schlachten die Henn'."

„Aber dann wird sich doch kränken der Hahn," jammert die Frau.

Der Rabbi will sie beruhigen und sagt: „Ich werd' noch mal nachseh'n in die Bücher. Komme morgen wieder."

Am folgenden Tage sagt er ihr: „Ich hab' noch mal nachgeseh'n in die Bücher; du kannst leben lassen die Henn' und schlacten den Hahn."

„Waih geschrieen," ruft die Frau und beginnt zu weinen, „wird sich doch dann kränken die Henn'," worauf der Rabbi erwidert: „Nu, lass' sie sich kränken."

A kluger pssak-din (*Gerichtsentscheidung*)

Immanuel Olsvanger, *Rosinkess mit Mandlen*. Zurich: Verlag der Arche, 1965; pp. 137-138. Orig. pub. 1921.

Unser row is gewen nit fun di gor grêjsse geêjnim (*Genies*), ober er is gewen a id a chochem (*klug*), a pikejach (*weise*). Ot hert sach ajn a majsse, wet ir heren.

Ess is amol gekumen zum row epess ejner a id mit a schajle (*Frage*). Er hot a hon (*Hahn*) mit a hun (*Henne*). Will er kêjlenen (*schlachten*) dem hon, macht di hun gewalten, kêjless (*Lärm*), schrait, as me ken nit derhalten. Wil er kêjlenen di hun, macht der hon gewalten. Woss sol er do ton? Sogt em der row, er sol kumen in a por teg arum, wet er em sogen a t'schuwe (*Bescheid*).

A teg draj is der row gesessen iber di hejlige ssforim (*Bücher*) un hot gekwetscht dem schtern, – ess macht nit auss, er hot gut geschwizt af der schajle.

(cont.)

Olsvanger, *cont.*	In draj teg arum kumt der id un fregt dem row: „Nu, woss is, rebe? Hot ir far mir gefunen an ejze (*Rat*)?" „Awade, wi den?" „Nu, woss sol ich machen?" Sog der row: „Der din (*Gesetz*) is, as du solst kêjlenen di hun". „Woss hejsst, rebe, wet doch der hon schrajen!" „Sol er schrajen!" Mit dem pssak hot sich unser row gemacht a schem (*Name*).

Roda Roda and Theodor Etzel, *Welthumor*. Munich: Simplicissimus Verlag, 1925; vol. V, p. 156.	Unser Row (Rabbi) is gewen nit vun di gor grejse Geejnim (*Genies*), ober er is gewen a Jid a Chochem (*Kluger*), a Pikejach (*Weiser*). Ot hert sach ajn a Meisse, wet ir heren:
	        Es is amol gekummen zum Row epes ejner a Jid mit a Scheile (*Frage*). Er hot a Hohn mit a Huhn. Will er kejlenen (*schlachten*) dem Hohn, macht di Huhn Giwalten, Kejles (*Lärm*), schrejt, az me känn nit derhalten. Will er kejlenen di Huhn, macht der Hohn Giwalten. Wos soll er do ton? – Sogt em der Row, er soll kummen in a por Täg arum, wed er ehm sogen a T'schuwe (*Bescheid*).
	        A Täg drei is der Row gesessen iber di hejligi Sforim (*Bücher*) un hot gequetscht dem Stern (*Stirn*) – es macht nit aus, er hot gut geschwitzt af der Scheile.
	        In drei Täg arum kummt der Jid un frägt dem Row: „Nu, wos is, Rebbe? Hot ihr far mir gefunnen an Ejze (*Rat*)?" – „Awade, wie denn?" – „Nu, wos soll ich machen?" – Sogt der Row: „Der Din (*Gesetz*) is, az du sollst kejlenen die Huhn." – „Wos heisst, Rebbe, wed doch der Hohn schreien!" – „Soll er schreien!"
	        Mit dem Blak hat sich unser Row gemacht a Schem (*Namen*).

Salomonische Weisheit

Hans Ostwald, *Frisch, gesund und meschugge*. Berlin: Franke, 1928; pp. 308-309.	Zum Rabbi kommt eine Frau aus dem Dorf. „Ach, Rabbi, was soll ich tun? Ich hab' einen Hahn und eine Henne, und muß eins davon schlachten. Schlacht' ich nun den Hahn, dann grämt sich die Henne, schlacht' ich die Henne, dann grämt sich der Hahn. Was soll ich nun tun?"
	        Der Rabbi zog seine Stirn in tiefe Falten. „Das ist ein schwerer Fall", sagte er. „Laßt mir bis morgen Zeit zum Überlegen."
	        Am nächsten Tag kam die Frau aufs neue zu ihm und erhielt den Bescheid: „Schlachtet die Henn'!"
	        „Aber, Rabbi, wenn sich nun der Hahn grämt?"
	        „Nu, soll er sich grämen!"

Max Präger and
 	
Siegfried Schmitz,
Jüdische Schwänke.
Vienna: R. Löwit,
1928; pp. 146-147.
	Ein Jude kommt zum Row: „Rabbi, ich habe einen Hahn und eine Henne. Will ich den Hahn schlachten, macht die Henne Lärm und schreit, daß es nicht auszuhalten ist. Will ich die Henne schlachten, macht er Hahn Lärm. Was soll ich tun?"
	        „Komm' in ein paar Tagen, dann werde ich dir Bescheid geben."
	        Der Row macht sich über die heiligen Bücher, studiert drei Tage lang und zerbricht sich den Kopf über die beste Entscheidung. Nach drei Tagen kommt der Jude und fragt: „Nun, Rabbi, habet Ihr einen Rat für mich?"
	        „Natürlich, was denn?"
	        „Nun, was soll ich tun?"
	        „Nach dem Gesetz hast du die Henne zu schlachten."
	        „Aber Rabbi, da wird doch der Hahn schreien."
	        „Soll er schreien!"

A kluger pssak-din (*decision of the court*)

Immanuel Olsvanger, *Röyte Pomerantsen.* New York: Schocken, 1965; pp. 167-168. Orig. publ.1935.

Unzer rov iz geven nit fun di gor gröysse geoynim (*geniuses*), ober er iz geven a id a chochem (*clever*), a pikeach (*wise*). Ot hert zach ayn a maysse, vet ir hern.

Es iz amol gekumen tsum rov epes eyner a id mit a shayle (*question*). Er hot a hon (*rooster*) mit a hun (*hen*). Vil er köylenen (*slaughter*) dem hon, macht di hun gevaltn, köyles (*noise*), shrayt, az me ken nit darhaltn. Vil er köylenen di hun, macht der hon gevaltn. Vos zol er do ton? Zogt em der rov, er zol kumen in a por teg arum, vet er em zogn a t'shuve (*answer*).

A teg dray iz der rov gezessn iber di heylige sforim (*books*) un hot gekvetsht dem shtern, – es macht nit aus, er hot gut geshvitst af der shayle.

In dray teg arum kumt der id un fregt dem rov: „Nu, vos iz, rebe? hot ir far mir gefunen an eytse (*advice*)?" „Avade, vi den?" „Nu, vos zol ich machen?" Zogt der rov: „Der din (*law*) iz, az du zollst köylenen di hun". „Vos heysst, rebe, vet doch der hon shrayen!" „Zol er shrayen!"

Mit dem pssak hot sich unzer rov gemacht a shem (*name, fame*).

Ausor Rajower, *Masses und Chochmes.* Zurich: Scheffelverlag, 1959; pp. 9-10.

Zum Rabbi kommt eines Tages die Witwe Channele, ein altes Mütterlein, um sich von ihm eine Eize zu holen.

„Es sind mir geblieben", beginnt sie, „ein Hahn und eine Henne. Eines davon muß ich schlachten, aber ich weiß nicht, welches."

„So schlachte den Hahn", rät ihr der Rabbi.

„Dann grämt sich aber die Henne."

„So schlachte eben die Henne."

„Dann grämt sich aber der Hahn."

„Dann soll er sich halt grämen."

Salcia Landmann, *Der jüdische Witz.* Breslau: Walter-Verlag, 1960; p. 161. Also appears in Salcia Landmann, *Jüdische Witze.* Munich: Deutscher Taschenbuch Verlag, 1982; p. 91. Orig. pub. 1962.

Eine Jüdin kommt zum Rabbi und fragt:

„Rabbi, ich habe einen Hahn und eine Henne. Eines von beiden muß ich schlachten. Schlachte ich den Hahn, dann kränkt sich das Huhn; schlachte ich das Huhn dann kränkt sich der Hahn. Also was soll ich tun?"

Der Rabbi bittet sich Bedenkzeit aus, und dann entscheidet er: „Du sollst den Hahn schlachten."

„Aber Rabbi", klagt die Jüdin, „dann kränkt sich doch das Huhn!" „Nu", meint der Rabbi, „soll es sich halt kränken!"

A HEN AND A ROOSTER

Rufus Learsi, *Filled with Laughter.* New York: Thomas Yoseloff, 1961; pp. 246-247.

Someone came to the rabbi of a small town with a question that baffled him.

"What shall I do?" the man asked. "I have a hen and a rooster and one of them has to go to the pot. But which one? If I take the rooster the hen raises a terrible outcry. She clucks and screams and flaps her wings. If I take the hen, the rooster shrieks so my blood curdles. What shall I do rabbi?"

The old rabbi chewed his beard thoughtfully.

(cont.)

| Learsi, *cont.* | "I must look up the law on this matter," said he. "Come back in three days."

"Nu, rabbi?" said the man three days later.

"The law is to take the hen," the rabbi replied.

"But the rooster will protest!" the man cried.

"The rooster will protest?" said the rabbi. "Let him protest!" |

| Hermann Hakel, *Oi, bin ich gescheit!* Munich: Südwest Verlag, 1965; pp. 56-57. | Eine brave jüdische Hausfrau kommt zum Rabbiner: „Rabbi, ich hab' einen Hahn und eine Henne. Einen von beiden will ich schlachten. Wenn ich nun den Hahn schlachte, wird doch die Henne sich kränken, und wenn ich die Henne schlachte, wird der Hahn sich kränken. Was soll ich tun?"

„Komm in ein paar Tagen, dann werde ich dir Bescheid geben."

Der Rabbi studiert drei Tage lang den Talmud und zerbricht sich den Kopf über die beste Entscheidung.

Nach drei Tagen kommt die Frau und fragt: „Nun, Rabbi, habt Ihr einen Rat für mich?"

„Natürlich hab' ich einen."

„Nun, was soll ich tun?"

„Nach dem Gesetz hast du die Henne zu schlachten."

„Aber Rabbi, da wird doch der Hahn sich kränken."

"Soll er sich kränken!" |

| Adam, *L'humour juif.* Paris: Denoël, 1966; p. 93. | Quelques jours avant Pessah un paysan vient trouver le rabbin:

– Rabbin, tu sais que je suis un bon juif et je tiens absolument à célébrer Pessah comme il faut et à acheter les matsoth. Mais je suis très pauvre, et j'ai seulement un coq et une poule que je peux vendre pour acheter les matsoth. Alors je viens te demander: qu'est ce que je dois faire? Si je vends la poule, c'est le coq qui va être tout seul et qui va souffrir. Et si je vends le coq, c'est la poule qui sera abandonnée et malheureuse!

– Reviens vendedi, je te dirai, dit le rabbin.
Le vendredi suivant, le paysan revient:

– Alors, tu as réfléchi? Que vais-je faire? Je vends la poule, ou je vends le coq?

– Vends la poule!

– Mais alors, le coq, il va être tout seul, il va souffrir!

– Eh bien, qu'il souffre! |

Jan Meyerowitz, *Der echte jüdische Witz*. Berlin: Colloquium Verlag, 1971; pp. 84-85.

NB. The quote following the joke is from Hegel's *Lectures on the Philosophy of Religion*, which can be accessed in English translation at this link: *https://archive.org/stream/lec turesonphilo03hegegoog#page /n7/mode/2up* If I thought it illuminated the meaningfulness of the joke to any extent whatsoever, I would have commented on this text in the above discussion.

Ein sehr armer Jude hat nur noch einen Hahn und eine Henne. Er gebt zum Rebben und fragt klagend: „Schlacht ich den Hahn werd sich kränken die Henne, schlacht ich die Henne, wird sich kränken der Hahn. Einen miß ich schlachten. Was tu ich?" Der Rabbi verlangt eine Woche Zeit zum Nachdenken. Der nabezu verhungerte Fragesteller kommt zur bestimmten Zeit wieder: „Rebbe, wir haben nichts zu essen! Schlacht ich den Hahn oder schlacht ich die Henne??" „Schlacht die Henne." „Aber Rebbe, werd sich kränken der Hahn!!" „Nu, LASS er sich kränken." (Ein Satz aus Hegels langer Abhandlung über die jüdische Religion mag dem Leser die Bedeutsamkeit dieses Witzes ausloten helfen: "Ein Schwanken tritt im [jüdischen] Geiste nur dann ein, wenn verschiedene Interessen und Gesichtspunkte nebeneinander zu stehen kommen, man kann in solchem Kampfe das Eine oder das Andere ergreifen: in der Concentration des Einzigen Herrn ist der Geist vollkommen festgehalten.")

Ferruccio Fölkel, *Nuove storielle ebraiche*. Milan: Biblioteca Universale Rizzoli, 1990; p. 49.

Micòl si reca dal rabbino e gli chiede: „Rabbi, ho un gallo e une gallina e devo tirare il collo a uno dei due. Però se ammazzo il gallo, sarà molto triste per la gallina; se ammazzo la gallina, sarà triste per il gallo. Cosa devo fare?" Il rabbino medita e decide: „Devi ammazzare il gallo". „Ma, rabbi, pensi al dolore della gallina!" dice Micòl stupefatta. „Insomma" osserva il rabbino „qualcuno deve pur addolorarsi."

Far From Where?
A Classic Jewish Refugee Joke

NB. This chapter originally appeared as an article entitled "Far from Where? On the History and Meanings of a Classic Jewish Refugee Joke," in *American Jewish History*, Vol. 85, No. 2 (June 1997), pp. 143-150.

During and immediately after World War II, a number of Jewish refugee jokes began to appear in anthologies of humor. Three jokes in particular have become familiar landmarks in collections of Jewish humor published from the 1940's to the present. The first two, "Globe" and "Morning or afternoon?", broke into print in 1941 and 1943, respectively, and deal with thwarted efforts to escape from Europe. Both of these jokes end with a question that appears to disregard some basic reality at hand, and which sets in relief the hopelessness of the refugee's situation:

A Viennese Jew entered the office of a travel bureau and said to one of the clerks, "I want a steamship ticket."

"Where to?" asked the clerk.

"Where to? Yes, where to?" repeated the Jew meditatively. "I wish I could answer this question. Let me look at your globe, if you don't mind."

Thereupon the Jew turned the globe around several times, studying carefully countries and continents. After a few minutes, he raised his eyes to the clerk and said, "Pardon me, have you anything else to offer?"[1]

A harassed attache of the American Consulate at Lisbon told the story of a grey-faced little man who leaned over his desk one morning anxiously enquired: "Can you tell me if there is any possibility I could get entrance to your wonderful country?"

The attache pressed by thousands of such requests and haggard from sleepless nights, roughly replied: Impossible now. Come back in another ten years."

The little refugee moved toward the door, stopped, turned and, with a wan smile, asked, "Morning or afternoon?"[2]

[1] S. Felix Mendelsohn, *Let Laughter Ring* (Philadelphia: Jewish Publication Society, 1946; orig. pub. 1941), pp. 135-136..This joke appeared subsequently in Theodor Reik, *Jewish Wit* (New York: Gamut, 1961), p. 48; Hermann Hakel, *Der jüdische Witz* (Munich: Schuler, 1971) p. 63; Harry Golden, *The Golden Book of Jewish Humor* (New York: Putnam, 1972), p. 149; Alexander Drozdzynski, *Jiddische Witze und Schmonzes* (Dusseldorf: Droste Verlag, 1976),

The joke which completes this little triptych first appeared in print in 1948, and deals with the situation of the Jewish refugee in the aftermath of the Second World War. It too ends with a question:

Three weary Jewish refugees stood before the Paris representative of the Jewish Joint Distribution Committee.
    "Where are you all going?" he asked them.
    "I'm on my way to Rome," said the first.
    "London is my destination," said the second.
    "My plan is to go to South Africa," said the third.
    "South Africa? Why so far?"
    "Far? Far from where?" wistfully countered the refugee.[3]

Unlike "Globe" and "Morning or afternoon?", the "Far from where?" joke can be understood in two different ways, and in this respect, is a richer and more interesting joke. In the remainder of this article, I will try to outline the two interpretations to which the joke lends itself.

One interpretation was proposed by Alan Dershowitz in his immensely popular book, *Chutzpah* (1991), in which he wrote:

The concept of the "wandering Jew" gave rise to the old joke about the nineteenth-century Polish Jew from Warsaw, who tells his friend that he is moving to America. The friend exclaims: "But that's so far away." To which the rootless Jew responds: "From what?"[4]

In suggesting that the joke was inspired by the concept of the "wandering Jew," Dershowitz emphasizes the timeless quality of the story as well as its connection to a body of folklore. And in characterizing the joke as expressive of rootlessness ("the rootless Jew

---

p. 31; *Popeck raconte les meilleures histoires de l'humour juif* (Paris: Mengès, 1978), pp. 230-231; William Novak and Moshe Waldoks, *The Big Book of Jewish Humor* (New York: Harper & Row, 1981), p. 61; Leo Rosten, *Hooray for Yiddish* (New York: Simon & Schuster, 1982), p. 354; and Ben Eliezer, *More of the World's Best Jewish Jokes* (London: Angus & Robertson, 1985), p. 22.

[2] Bennet Cerf, *Pocket Book of War Humor* (New York: Pocket Books, 1943), p. 181. Subsequent appearances of this joke are found in S. Felix Mendelsohn, *Here's a Good One* (New York: Bloch, 1947), p. 13; Ausor Rajower, *Masses und Chochmes* (Zurich: Scheffelverlag, 1959), p. 26; Adam, *L'humour juif* (Denoël, 1966), pp. 49-50; Jan Meyerowitz, *Der echte jüdische Witz* (Berlin: Colloquium Verlag, 1971), pp. 87-88; Novak & Waldoks, op. cit., p. 61; Ben Eliezer, op. cit., p. 22; Chaim Bermant, *What's the Joke?* (London: Weidenfeld & Nicolson, 1986), pp. 239-240.

[3] Nathan Ausubel, *A Treasury of Jewish Folklore* (New York: Crown, 1948), p. 25. The publication history of this joke is provided at the end of the present article.

[4] Alan Dershowitz, *Chutzpah* (Boston: Little, Brown & Co., 1991), p. 5.

responds"), Dershowitz further stresses that side of the joke which refers to the properties of the Jewish condition, rather than to anything situated outside of Jewish life. When the joke is interpreted in this way, it would also make sense to view the punchline as spoken with quiet pathos, as is suggested by such expressions as "wistfully" (Ausubel, 1948), "with a catch in his voice" (Spalding, 1969), or a look described as "traurig" (Muliar, 1974).

However, the joke can be understood in another way as well, particularly when it is told in a manner which reflects its original historical context, as is the case when the setting evoked is Paris in 1939 (Rosten, 1970), occupied France (Popeck, 1978), or post-war Paris (Ausubel, 1948); Berlin shortly after Hitler came to power (Landmann 1962/82), Germany in the summer of 1939 (Hakel 1965), or Austria when German troops marched in (Muliar 1974). To whatever degree a national setting at the time of Nazi domination is an essential part of the story, the joke can be seen as in some sense a commentary on that setting. In this perspective, the "Far from where?" question could be understood as a reply to a given nation's indifference to the plight of the Jews, and would imply that the country in question *does not deserve* to be taken as a frame of reference of any kind. Perhaps this is why, in one of the versions (Adam, 1966), the question is spoken "très bas," so that no one else can hear it.

The Dershowitz interpretation focuses on the rootlessness of the Jewish people, and sees the joke as inspired by an ancient legend – in which case the tone of the punchline would be essentially plaintive. According to the alternate reading I have sketched, the joke would be seen as inspired by the Holocaust, and the "Far from where?" punchline as an indictment of a country in which Jews were offered little or no protection from the Nazis. The two interpretations might be represented schematically as seen on the following page.

	interpretation 1 (Dershowitz)	interpretation 2
primary focus	the rootlessness of the Jewish condition	the indifference of a nation to the plight of the Jews
inspiration	the concept of the "wandering Jew"	the Holocaust
spirit of the punchline	plaintive	an indictment

Both interpretations are valid and fully justified by the joke. When both are taken into account, they can be allowed to balance, complete and correct each other. In this respect, the "Far from where?" joke exhibits an interpretive quality found in a number of classic Jewish jokes, which leave us wondering how we are expected to understand the punchline when two or more equally plausible options present themselves.

Publication History

NB. Numerous collections of Jewish jokes, published from about 1820 to the present, and written in English, German, French, Italian, Spanish, Danish and transliterated Yiddish, were consulted. No trace of this joke was found in any anthology published before 1948.

Nathan Ausubel:
A TREASURY OF
JEWISH FOLKLORE.
New York: Crown, 1948;
p. 25.

Three weary Jewish refugees stood before the Paris representative of the Jewish Joint Distribution Committee.
"Where are you all going?" he asked them.
"I'm on my way to Rome," said the first.
"London is my destination," said the second.
"My plan is to go to South Africa," said the third.
"South Africa? Why so far?"
"Far? Far from where?" wistfully countered the refugee.

Ausor Rajower:
MASSES UND
CHOCHMES.
JÜDISCHE HUMOR.
Zurich: Schefferverlag,
1959;
pp. 26-27.

Drei Emigranten, in einem Zürcher Café, unterhalten sich.
"Heute habe ich das Visum nach Amerika bekommen," berichtet Kohn freudestrahlend.
"Und ich reise in einem Montat nach Kanada," sagt Schwarz.
"Und ich nach Chile," erklärt Weiß, der dritte.
"Nach Chile?!" ruft Kohn aus, "ist das nicht ein wenig weit weg?"
"Weit weg?" antwortet Weiß, "von wo?"

Salcia Landmann:
JÜDISCHE WITZE.
Munich: Deutscher
Taschenbuch, 1982;
pp. 235-236.
Orig. pub. 1962.

Beim Auswanderungsbureau in Berlin treffen sich kurz nach Hitlers Machtergreifung zwei Juden.
"Moische," fragt der eine, "wohin willst du auswandern?"
"Nach Schanghai."
"Was! So weit?"
"Weit, von wo?"

Hermann Hakel:
OI, BIN ICH
GESCHEIT!
Munchen: Südwest
Verlag, n.d. [1965]; p.
87.

Zwei Juden treffen einander im Sommer 1939. Sagt der eine:
"Servus, wie geht's dir?"
"Man lebt. Gestern hab' ich endlich meine Ausreise erledigt."
"Du hast aber Glück! Und wohin wirst du auswandern?"
"Nach Australien."
"Geh, Australien – ? Australien ist doch weit –"
"Weit von wo?"

Adam: L'HUMOUR
JUIF.
Paris: Denoël, 1966; p.
19.

Deux amis se rencontrent:
– Je pars demain, Moshé.
– Où ça, Samuel?
– Pour le Brézil.
– Mais c'est loin!
Alors Samuel très bas:
– Loin d'où?

Henry D. Spalding:
ENCYCLOPEDIA OF
JEWISH HUMOR. New
York: Jonathan David,
1969; p. 179.

The following story may well elicit a sigh rather than a chuckle for those Jews who still remember Czarist oppression and the pathos of a people without a home.
Three weary Jews were caught as they attempted to sneak across the Russian boundary.
"Where were you three going?" asked the magistrate sternly.   *(cont.)*

Spalding, *cont.*	"I was hoping to get to Palestine," said the first. "My destination was Rome," said the second. "My plan was to go to Australia," said the third. "Australia!" exclaimed the surprised judge. "Why so far?" "Far?" whispered the Jew with a catch in his voice. "Far from where?"

Leo Rosten:
THE JOYS OF
YIDDISH.
London: W. H. Allen,
1970.
	Paris, 1939.
	    Three weary German refugees stood in line, in the offices of a Relocation Committee.
	    "Where would you like to go?" an official asked the first refugee.
	"London."
	"And you?" the official asked the second.
	"Switzerland."
	"And you?" he asked the third.
	"Australia."
	"Australia?" echoed the official. "Why so far?"
	The refugee said, "Far from where?"

Jan Meyerowitz: DER ECHTE JÜDISCHE WITZ. Berlin: Colloquium Verlag, 1971; p. 88.	Und dieser Emigranten "witz": "Wohin willst du auswandern?" "Nach Chile." "So weit weg?" "Weit weg – wovon?!"

Fritz Muliar: DAS
BESTE AUS MEINER
JÜDISCHEN WITZE-
UND ANEKDONTEN-
SAMMLUNG. Munich:
Wilhelm Heyne Verlag,
1974; p. 91.
	Nach dem Einmarsch der deutschen Truppen in Österreich geht Weichselbaum mit Thugut durch die Pazmanitengasse. Weichselbaum sagt: "Ich geh nach England, dort hab ich Verwandte, und du?"
	    Antwortet Thugut: "Ich hab a Einreise nach Borneo!"
	    "Borneo?" sagt Weichselbaum. "Is aber weit?"
	    Traurig schaut Thugut ihn an: "Weit – von wo?"

POPECK RACONTE
LES MEILLEURES
HISTOIRES DE
L'HUMOUR JUIF. Paris:
Mengès, 1978; p. 133.
	Au début de la guerre, tandis que les troupes allemandes déferlent, deux Juifs se retrouvent sur le quai d'une gare.
	    – Où allez-vous? demande l'un.
	    – A Varsovie... C'est loin...
	    – Ah oui? Loin d'où?

Elizabeth Petuchowski: DAS HERZ AUF DER ZUNGE. AUS DER WELT DES JÜDISCHEN WITZES. Freiburg: Herder, 1984; p. 113.	"Morgen reise ich fort." "Wohin, Samuel?" "Nach Brasilien." "Das ist aber weit weg." "Weit weg von wo?"
Ferruccio Fölkel: STORIELLE EBRAICHE. Milan: Rizzoli, 1988; pp. 176-117.	Avrom e Mendel viaggiano in treno. "Dove vai, Avramole?" "Vado lontano, Mendele." "Ma vai lontano da dove, Avramole?"
Alan Dershowitz: CHUTZPAH. Boston: Little, Brown & Co., 1991; p. 5.	The concept of the "wandering Jew" gave rise to the old joke about the nineteenth-century Polish Jew from Warsaw, who tells his friend that he is moving to America. The friend exclaims: "But that's so far away." To which the rootless Jew responds: "From what?

Name Index

Abraham 54
Acques 176, 213
Adam 47, 64, 73, 95-96,
    145, 160-161, 198,
    208, 267, 270, 271, 273
Adams 17, 38, 130
Adamson 9
Adler, B 49, 65
Adler, H 2
Akiba 52
Alcalay 135
Aleichem 106, 134
Aleksandrowicz 42, 47,
    66, 139, 210
Allen, J 97
Allen, W 123-124, 153-
    154
Altman 220, 239
Andersen, B 225
Andersen, HC 138
Andersen & Clausen 225
Apted 112
Arce 124, 130
Aristotle 8
Asimov 47, 66, 76, 98,
    131, 147, 159, 162,
    181, 187, 209, 214, 231
Astor 85
Atlan 22, 30, 44
Ausubel 16, 31, 37-38,
    47, 62, 81, 142, 151,
    159, 171, 175, 179,
    181, 196, 236, 238,
    270, 271, 273
Ayalti 22, 93
Baron 135
Barrie 143
Beckett 47, 62-63
Belushi 112
Ben-Amos 10, 80, 181
Benny 122
Bergler 10, 78
Bergson 8
Berkowitz 55, 56
Berman /Pollack 16, 17,
    42, 47, 67, 159, 188,
    210, 215, 220-221,
    234, 237, 261
Bietenhard 52
Blumenfeld 159, 208, 236
Bogart 85
Boring 27
Brenner 1

Buber 21, 55, 59, 151,
    184,
Bulakow 219
Bunam 59
Burns 122, 143
Cantor 181
Carlyle 1
Castel 96
Cerf 224, 270
Cohen, MR 21-22
Cohen, SB 57, 91
Coleman 103, 172
Copeland 205
Cowan 130
Cray 89, 181, 186-187,
    230-231
Danero 196
Davies 2, 10, 73, 104-105,
    182
Dershowitz 270-272, 274
Despot 128
Dessauer 14, 33, 166
Dick 12
Diller 123
Dines 73, 96, 118, 172,
    189
Dorinson 130
Dorson 207-208
Drozdzynski 43, 211,
    239, 269
Dundes 10, 76, 100, 181,
    235
Eastman 9
Edel 156
Eliezer 75, 99, 117, 212,
    216, 229, 234, 240, 270
Epstein 53
Etzel 261, 265
Falk 84
Feinsilver 40, 58, 90, 219, 231
Finkelstein 52
Fölkel 69, 181, 200, 203,
    212, 268, 274
Friedman 1
Freud 7, 8, 77, 89, 124,
    132, 135, 136, 156,
    182, 259, 260, 263
Fromm 54
Fuller 186
Galanter 1-3, 5
Gary 82
Geiger 45, 50, 61, 93,
    174, 177, 181, 201,
    217, 235, 262

Gilman 79
Giniewski 52
Ginzberg 74
Golden 208-209, 234, 269
Goldstein 10, 81, 152,
    154, 160, 169, 188
Goodman 236
Gordis 51, 59
Greenberg 110, 233
Grotjahn 79, 110, 214,
    233
Hakel 17, 40, 41, 239,
    267, 269, 271, 273
Hapgood 142
Hayman 204
Hazlitt 103, 170, 172, 223
Heller 90
Hershfield 17, 38, 115,
    116, 174, 194-195,
    204-205, 235
Hicks 168, 186
Hirsh 19, 192, 261, 264
Hitler 171
Hobbes 8
Howe 181
Howe & Greenberg 181
Hunt 204
Itler 19, 175, 194, 238
Jason 181-182
Jessel 125
Jewison 41
Job 50, 51
Jossel 191
Junior 72, 95, 105, 115
Kahn 84
Kant 8
Kasdan 112
Katz & Katz 10, 80, 81,
    181
Klein-Haparash 196-197
Knox 59
Koestler 82
Kohn 134
Koplev 44, 47, 68, 107,
    118, 181, 213
Kreppel 47, 61
Landmann 39-40, 64, 81,
    100, 157, 181, 190,
    197, 240, 266, 273
Lanigan 108, 119, 149,
    164-165
Laurel 133
Lauterbach 74
Lazarus 70

Learsi [Goldberg] *18, 36, 49, 63, 139, 195, 260, 266-267*

Lettslaff *105, 115*

Levi Yitzchok *54*

Lewin *78, 79*

Liacho *170, 223*

Lieberman *157, 197-198*

Loewe *134*

Löwit *36, 81, 181*

Lurie *204*

Manger *56*

Manzoni *14-15, 33*

Marks *47, 68, 75, 99-100*

Marx, A *125, 130*

Marx, G *9, 120-130, 183*

Masson *259*

McCaffrey *124, 130*

Meier *206*

Memmi *10, 71, 75, 76, 79, 83, 84, 97*

Mendelsohn *36-37, 48, 61-62, 81, 87, 140, 158, 171, 174, 181, 195, 205-206, 218, 223, 225-226, 230, 235, 269, 270*

Meyerowitz *268, 270, 274*

Milburn *207*

Mindess *66, 81, 98, 110, 131, 147, 150-152, 162-163, 181, 233*

Montgomery *130*

Moore *84*

Moszkowski *14, 33, 89, 132, 134, 155, 156, 181, 191-192, 261, 263*

Muliar *157-158, 201-202, 262, 271, 274*

Neches *18, 35*

Necker *26, 27*

Nègre *116, 143, 161-162, 209, 228-229*

Newman *54, 94*

Nietzsche *8*

Niklas *39*

Nikolaus *193*

Novak & Waldoks *29, 43, 117-118, 130, 148, 160, 164, 181, 190, 200, 211, 215, 221, 232, 237, 239, 270*

Nuél [Schnitzer] *15, 33-34, 137, 139, 155, 190, 263*

Olsvanger *13, 15, 16, 17, 22, 29, 34, 53, 81, 181*

Oring *1, 89, 260*

Ostwald *156, 189, 261*

Palquera *153, 154*

Penrose *31*

Peretz *54*

Petuchowski *76, 99, 212, 216, 274*

Pirosh & Seaton *9*

Popeck *46, 50, 67, 179, 199, 202, 211, 220, 237, 262, 270, 271, 274*

Präger *265*

Rabinowitz *189, 232*

Radday *1*

Rajower *38-39, 266, 270, 273*

Raskin, V *28*

Rawnitzky *34, 81, 139*

Reik *10, 64, 78, 79, 124, 133, 157, 181, 190, 233, 269*

Renan *1*

Richards *114*

Richman *29, 35, 81, 193-194, 226*

Roda *261, 265*

Rokeach *16, 20, 30, 39*

Rosenberg & Shapiro *176, 213, 227*

Rosten *47, 66, 68, 116, 130, 159, 160, 216, 217, 219, 221, 222, 234, 236, 237, 240, 270, 274*

Rubin *26, 27*

Rufus *52*

Rund *156, 193*

Rywell *16, 29, 39, 81, 238*

Samard *181*

Sarano *44*

Schacht *87*

Schermerhorn *72, 95, 103*

Schlesinger *90, 91, 232*

Schmitz *265*

Schnitzler *263*

Schnur *18, 37, 62, 81, 138, 156-157, 201, 206, 262*

Schopenhauer *8*

Schröder *27*

Schuster *31*

Sheekman *124, 130*

Siddons *102*

Simon, N *84, 85*

Simon, S *139*

Spalding *29, 47, 65, 131, 139, 148, 163, 198-199, 214, 218, 227, 233, 236, 238, 271, 273-274*

Spencer *8*

Spielberg *112*

Stein *41*

Szyk *28, 60, 61, 114, 203*

Taylor *170, 222*

Teitelbaum *206*

Triverton *16, 17, 43, 189, 234, 237*

Untermeyer *177, 207, 218, 235*

Waldoks *270*

Weller et al *180*

Whedbe *1*

White *10*

Whitehead *2*

Wiesel *55, 134*

Wilde *101, 105, 117, 173, 188, 199, 220, 229, 231-232, 239*

Wilson *124, 130, 190*

Winick *2*

Youngman *186, 233*

Zangwill *181*

Zborowski & Herzog *22, 106, 107*

Ziv *10, 81-82*

Zusya *151*

Acknowledgments

The published sources of all cited material were listed as conspicuously as possible throughout this book – particularly in the "publication history" sections in which most of the jokes appear. With the exception of Groucho Marx's resignation telegram, we will never know who actually invented the jokes quoted in this book. Despite the impossibility of identifying and crediting their true inventors, as well as the fact that the jokes have appeared in numerous anthologies (with sources rarely given), I have made every effort to obtain the appropriate authorization for quotations which possibly exceed the "fair use" principle or similar conventions. Despite these efforts, it has proven difficult to locate the rightful copyright owners of some of the material quoted beyond the normal limits not requiring permission. Any such copyright owners are hereby encouraged to contact me c/o the publisher. The same efforts were made with regard to the use of drawings and a photograph.

For graciously authorizing the use of copyright material, I wish to thank the following publishers: Albin Michel, for jokes and drawings from *Le juif qui rit* by Arthur Szyk © 1926 and 1927; Bloch Publishing Company, for jokes from S. Felix Mendelsohn's *Here's a Good One* © 1947; HarperCollins, for jokes from *The Big Book of Jewish Jokes* by William Novak and Moshe Waldoks © 1981; the Jewish Publication Society, for jokes from S. Felix Mendelsohn's *Let Laughter Ring*; © 1941; Jonathan David, for jokes from Henry D. Spalding's *Encyclopedia of Jewish Humor* © 1969; Vallentine Mitchell, for jokes from Isaac Asimov's *Treasury of Humor* © 1972; and Crown for jokes from *A Treasury of Jewish Folklore*, edited by Nathan Ausubel. Copyright 1948, 1976 by Crown Publishers, Inc. Reprinted by permission of Crown Publishers, Inc.

Earlier versions of Chapter 2 appeared as articles in *Slagmark: Tidsskrift for Idéhistorie* 14 (Autumn 1989), pp. 91-102, and *Judaism: A Quarterly Journal* 40, 1 (Winter 1991), pp. 39-51; and an earlier version of Chapter 4 appeared as an article in *Alef: Tidsskrift for jødisk kultur* 4 (December 1989), pp. 8-11.

I would like to express my gratitude to a number of institutions, librarians, colleagues, friends and family members for their help: to the Danish Council for Research in the Humanities and the Aarhus University Research Foundation for grants which made possible the publication of this book; to the staff of the Danish State and University Library, including Bo Mønsted for a chance remark that meant a lot, and Rie Eskerod and Jørn Street-Jensen for extra help with bibliographical questions; to the Hebraica and Judaica Section of the Royal Danish Library, especially to Ulf Haxen; to the librarians at the Jewish Division of the New York Public Library and to Johanna Goldschmid and Susie Taylor at the Special Collections Department of the San Francisco Public Library; to Joshua Lapid at the Elias Sourasky Central Library at Tel Aviv University and to the staff at the Jewish National and University Library in Jerusalem; to the librarians at the Alliance Israélite Universelle in Paris, Jews' College in London and the Yivo Institute for Jewish Research in New York; to Avner Ziv at Tel Aviv University for his interest in this project; to Leo Prijs and his son; to Jacob Schneidman at the Central Yiddish Culture Organization in New York; to Claudio Bogantes, Svend Lindhardtsen, Leonardo Cecchini, Svend Bach and Jørgen Schmitt Jensen for help with translations from Italian and Spanish; to Hélène Wehner Rasmussen for an important article; to Christie Davies for a specimen of a joke that was impossible to find; to Betsy Nolan for having a yiddishe kop; to Tønnes Bekker-Nielsen, for competently managing the publication of this book; to Dieter Britz, for many good discussions at the library cantine and for correcting mistakes I made in translating and transcribing German texts; to the one and only Aage Jørgensen, for taking on a proof-reader's nightmare and for doing a superb job – any typographical errors in the present book resulting from my failure to make all the corrections he proposed; to my brother Neil, for the Triverton book and for telling me the first meaning-of-life joke I ever heard; to Addy, for never saying to me, "What's the matter – the other one you didn't like?" and whose own collection of Jewish jokes was a model I could follow; to my father, for the constant flow of jokes and encouragement, and for the sparkle he gets in his eye when he has thought of something funny; to my daughters, Adina and Melanie, for moral support and practical help when I needed it most – including Adina's mission in New York to bring home a copy of the precious Rawnitzki anthology – and for laughing at the good jokes and groaning at the ones that were pathetic; and above all, to Marilyn as always, for the keenness of her insights and judgment, for putting up with my involvement in a project no one in his right mind would ever have taken on, and for being the real inspiration in my life.

Visit us at *www.quidprobooks.com*.